HEAD to HEAD

ASTON VILLA

Peter Waring

breedon books
PUBLISHING

First published in Great Britain in 2004 by
The Breedon Books Publishing Company Limited
Breedon House, 3 The Parker Centre,
Derby, DE21 4SZ.

The publisher would like to thank
Abdul Rashid, Alan Williams and Janet Tysoe
at Aston Villa FC
for their cooperation and support in the production of this book.
Thanks also to David Bridgewater
for his unrivalled knowledge of the club,
which ensured the accuracy of these pages.

ISBN 1 85983 414 0

Printed and bound by Cromwell Press Ltd,
Trowbridge, Wiltshire.

Introduction

This book contains the results of all matches played by Aston Villa in the following competitions:

- Premiership and Football League
- FA Cup
- League Cup
- Football League play-offs and test matches
- European Cup, Cup-Winners Cup and UEFA Cup

Some clubs have changed their names over the course of their history. Where this has happened, the results are nonetheless included under the club's current name, unless there have been no matches since the name change. Some of the more significant name changes are as follows:

- Arsenal (known as Royal Arsenal until 1893, then Woolwich Arsenal until 1914)
- Birmingham (known as Small Heath until 1905)
- Gateshead (known as South Shields until 1930)
- Leyton Orient (known as Clapton Orient until 1946, and Orient between 1967 and 1987)
- Manchester City (known as Ardwick until 1894)
- Manchester United (known as Newton Heath until 1902)

Furthermore, some clubs have merged, notably in Burton, Rotherham and Walsall, though these are explained under the relevant entries where applicable.

Notes on cups

FA Cup ties have always been straight knockout affairs, except in 1945-46, when all ties up to and including the quarter-finals were played over two legs. Between 1970 and 1974, the losing semi-finalists participated in third place play-offs. Penalty shoot-outs were introduced in 1991 to replace multiple replays.

League cup ties have been decided over one leg, with the following exceptions (played over two legs):

- First round ties (1975-76 to 2000-01)
- Second round ties (1979-80 to 2000-01)
- Semi-finals (every season)

To give you some idea of exactly what stage of the competition each FA Cup tie was played, the following is a list of each season's round of 16 (ie. the round immediately preceding the quarter-finals):

1873-74 to 1875-76	Round 2
1876-77 to 1878-79	Round 3
1879-80 to 1883-84	Round 4
1884-85 to 1887-88	Round 5
1889-90 to 1904-05	Round 2
1905-06 to 1924-25	Round 3
1925-26 to present	Round 5

In the league cup, Round 4 has been the round of 16 every season.

An asterisk after a cup result denotes extra-time was played.

Two final points

The letters appearing after some final league positions denote the following:

- P club was promoted
- R club was relegated
- F club failed to retain league membership for the following season

In the lists entitled 'Played for both clubs', an entry reading, for example, Liverpool 1980-83 would indicate that the player first appeared in a league match for Liverpool in the 1980-81 season, and last appeared in the 1982-83 season. Only league matches are taken into consideration on these lists.

v. Accrington

				Home				Away		Final Positions	
Season	*League*	*Date*	*Result*	Villa	Accrington	*Date*	*Result*	Villa	Accrington	Villa	Accrington
1888-89	Division 1	27 October	Won	**4**	**3**	15 December	Drew	**1**	**1**	2nd	7th
1889-90	Division 1	26 December	Lost	**1**	**2**	30 November	Lost	**2**	**4**	8th	6th
1890-91	Division 1	15 November	Won	**3**	**1**	21 March	Won	**3**	**1**	9th	10th
1891-92	Division 1	12 March	Won	**12**	**2**	4 January	Lost	**2**	**3**	4th	11th
1892-93	Division 1	25 March	Won	**6**	**4**	15 April	Drew	**1**	**1**	4th	15thF

Summary	*P*	*W*	*D*	*L*	*F*	*A*
Villa's home league record:	5	4	0	1	26	12
Villa's away league record:	5	1	2	2	9	10
TOTAL:	**10**	**5**	**2**	**3**	**35**	**22**

FACT FILE

- **The 12-2 win in 1892 is Villa's biggest ever league victory. John Devey and Lewis Campbell scored four goals apiece.**

Villa's top scorers vs Accrington

Jack Devey 8

Albert Brown, Denny Hodgetts 5

Villa hat-tricks vs Accrington

12 Mar 1892 Jack Devey (4)

12 Mar 1892 Lewis Campbell (4)

Tom 'Pongo' Waring. Villa paid £4,700 for his signature and when he made his debut for the Reserves, a crowd of 23,000 turned up to see this goalscoring sensation. He obliged with a hat-trick against Birmingham Reserves and altogether he scored 167 goals in 226 games for Villa's first team. His transfer to Barnsley in 1935 was hugely unpopular with Villa fans. Waring transferred to Accrington Stanley in November 1938.

v. Aldershot

FA Cup		Home				Away				Division	
		Date	Result	Villa	Aldershot	Date	Result	Villa	Aldershot	Villa	Aldershot
1963-64	Round 3	4 January	Drew	**0**	**0**	8 January	Lost	**1**	**2**	Div 1	Div 4

Summary	*P*	*W*	*D*	*L*	*F*	*A*
Villa's cup record:	2	0	1	1	1	2
TOTAL:	**2**	**0**	**1**	**1**	**1**	**2**

FACT FILE

- **Tony Hateley's goal was not enough to prevent an embarrassing defeat.**

Played for both clubs

Jimmy Adam	Aldershot 1950-51	Villa 1959-61

Before signing from Luton Town, winger Jimmy Adam had played for Aldershot. He is seen in the Aston Villa team in 1960-61, the season they reached the first-ever League Cup Final, although the two-legged final itself was held over to the following season when they beat Rotherham 3-2 on aggregate. Standing (left to right): Gerry Hitchens, Stan Lynn, Peter McParland, Nigel Sims, Kevin Keelan, Terry Morrall, John Neal, Jimmy Dugdale. Seated: Ray Shaw (trainer), Jimmy Adam, Jimmy MacEwan, Pat Saward, Vic Crowe, Ron Wylie, Bobby Thomson, Joe Mercer (manager). On ground: Mike Tindall, Alan Deakin.

v. Arsenal

		Home				Away				Final Positions	
Season	League	Date	Result	Villa	Arsenal	Date	Result	Villa	Arsenal	Villa	Arsenal
1904-05	Division 1	26 December	Won	3	1	8 October	Lost	0	1	4th	10th
1905-06	Division 1	27 December	Won	2	1	13 April	Lost	1	2	8th	12th
1906-07	Division 1	29 September	Drew	2	2	1 April	Lost	1	3	5th	7th
1907-08	Division 1	12 October	Lost	0	1	8 February	Won	1	0	2nd	14th=
1908-09	Division 1	13 March	Won	2	1	7 November	Won	1	0	7th	6th
1909-10	Division 1	1 September	Won	5	1	11 April	Lost	0	1	1st	18th
1910-11	Division 1	17 September	Won	3	0	15 March	Drew	1	1	2nd	10th
1911-12	Division 1	9 September	Won	4	1	6 January	Drew	2	2	6th	10th
1912-13	Division 1	24 March	Won	4	1	16 September	Won	3	0	2nd	20thR
1919-20	Division 1	11 February	Won	2	1	24 January	Won	1	0	9th	10th
1920-21	Division 1	28 August	Won	5	0	4 September	Won	1	0	10th	9th
1921-22	Division 1	18 March	Won	2	0	25 March	Lost	0	2	5th	17th
1922-23	Division 1	7 April	Drew	1	1	31 March	Lost	0	2	6th	11th
1923-24	Division 1	12 March	Won	2	1	16 February	Won	1	0	6th	19th
1924-25	Division 1	1 April	Won	4	0	18 October	Drew	1	1	15th	20th
1925-26	Division 1	2 April	Won	3	0	5 April	Lost	0	2	6th	2nd
1926-27	Division 1	18 April	Lost	2	3	15 April	Lost	1	2	10th	11th
1927-28	Division 1	10 September	Drew	2	2	21 January	Won	3	0	8th	10th
1928-29	Division 1	6 April	Won	4	2	24 November	Won	5	2	3rd	9th
1929-30	Division 1	25 September	Won	5	2	3 May	Won	4	2	4th	14th
1930-31	Division 1	14 March	Won	5	1	8 November	Lost	2	5	2nd	1st
1931-32	Division 1	25 April	Drew	1	1	31 October	Drew	1	1	5th	2nd
1932-33	Division 1	19 November	Won	5	3	1 April	Lost	0	5	2nd	1st
1933-34	Division 1	28 October	Lost	2	3	10 March	Lost	2	3	13th	1st
1934-35	Division 1	30 March	Lost	1	3	17 November	Won	2	1	13th	1st
1935-36	Division 1	14 December	Lost	1	7	18 April	Lost	0	1	21stR	6th
1938-39	Division 1	28 January	Lost	1	3	24 September	Drew	0	0	12th	5th
1946-47	Division 1	14 September	Lost	0	2	18 January	Won	2	0	8th	13th
1947-48	Division 1	28 February	Won	4	2	11 October	Lost	0	1	6th	1st
1948-49	Division 1	22 January	Won	1	0	11 September	Lost	1	3	10th	5th
1949-50	Division 1	26 November	Drew	1	1	29 March	Won	3	1	12th	6th
1950-51	Division 1	21 October	Drew	1	1	10 March	Lost	1	2	15th	5th
1951-52	Division 1	8 September	Won	1	0	5 January	Lost	1	2	6th	3rd
1952-53	Division 1	23 August	Lost	1	2	20 December	Lost	1	3	11th	1st
1953-54	Division 1	29 August	Won	2	1	6 April	Drew	1	1	13th	12th
1954-55	Division 1	23 October	Won	2	1	12 March	Lost	0	2	6th	9th
1955-56	Division 1	11 February	Drew	1	1	1 October	Lost	0	1	20th	5th
1956-57	Division 1	16 March	Drew	0	0	3 November	Lost	1	2	10th	5th
1957-58	Division 1	26 December	Won	3	0	2 October	Lost	0	4	14th	12th
1958-59	Division 1	22 October	Lost	1	2	13 December	Won	2	1	21stR	3rd
1960-61	Division 1	4 March	Drew	2	2	15 October	Lost	1	2	9th	11th
1961-62	Division 1	11 November	Won	3	1	31 March	Won	5	4	7th	10th
1962-63	Division 1	10 September	Won	3	1	4 September	Won	2	1	15th	7th
1963-64	Division 1	18 October	Won	2	1	10 September	Lost	0	3	19th	8th

		Home						Away			Final Positions	
Season	*League*	*Date*	*Result*	Villa	Arsenal	*Date*	*Result*	Villa	Arsenal	Villa	Arsenal
1964-65	Division 1	19 December	Won	**3**	**1**	29 August	Lost	**1**	**3**	16th	13th
1965-66	Division 1	30 April	Won	**3**	**0**	4 December	Drew	**3**	**3**	16th	14th
1966-67	Division 1	31 December	Lost	**0**	**1**	27 August	Lost	**0**	**1**	21stR	7th
1975-76	Division 1	13 September	Won	**2**	**0**	10 January	Drew	**0**	**0**	16th	17th
1976-77	Division 1	20 October	Won	**5**	**1**	25 April	Lost	**0**	**3**	4th	8th
1977-78	Division 1	10 September	Won	**1**	**0**	4 February	Won	**1**	**0**	8th	5th
1978-79	Division 1	25 April	Won	**5**	**1**	7 October	Drew	**1**	**1**	8th	7th
1979-80	Division 1	22 September	Drew	**0**	**0**	9 February	Lost	**1**	**3**	7th	4th
1980-81	Division 1	29 November	Drew	**1**	**1**	2 May	Lost	**0**	**2**	1st	3rd
1981-82	Division 1	7 November	Lost	**0**	**2**	27 March	Lost	**3**	**4**	11th	5th
1982-83	Division 1	14 May	Won	**2**	**1**	7 December	Lost	**1**	**2**	6th	10th
1983-84	Division 1	29 October	Lost	**2**	**6**	18 February	Drew	**1**	**1**	10th	6th
1984-85	Division 1	13 March	Drew	**0**	**0**	10 November	Drew	**1**	**1**	10th	7th
1985-86	Division 1	8 March	Lost	**1**	**4**	5 October	Lost	**2**	**3**	16th	7th
1986-87	Division 1	29 November	Lost	**0**	**4**	2 May	Lost	**1**	**2**	22ndR	4th
1988-89	Division 1	31 December	Lost	**0**	**3**	3 September	Won	**3**	**2**	17th	1st
1989-90	Division 1	30 December	Won	**2**	**1**	11 April	Won	**1**	**0**	2nd	4th
1990-91	Division 1	23 December	Drew	**0**	**0**	3 April	Lost	**0**	**5**	17th	1st
1991-92	Division 1	24 August	Won	**3**	**1**	11 January	Drew	**0**	**0**	7th	4th
1992-93	Premiership	28 December	Won	**1**	**0**	12 April	Won	**1**	**0**	2nd	10th
1993-94	Premiership	23 April	Lost	**1**	**2**	6 November	Won	**2**	**1**	10th	4th
1994-95	Premiership	17 April	Lost	**0**	**4**	26 December	Drew	**0**	**0**	18th	12th
1995-96	Premiership	2 December	Drew	**1**	**1**	21 October	Lost	**0**	**2**	4th	5th
1996-97	Premiership	7 September	Drew	**2**	**2**	28 December	Drew	**2**	**2**	5th	3rd
1997-98	Premiership	10 May	Won	**1**	**0**	26 October	Drew	**0**	**0**	7th	1st
1998-99	Premiership	13 December	Won	**3**	**2**	16 May	Lost	**0**	**1**	6th	2nd
1999-00	Premiership	5 March	Drew	**1**	**1**	11 September	Lost	**1**	**3**	6th	2nd
2000-01	Premiership	18 March	Drew	**0**	**0**	14 October	Lost	**0**	**1**	8th	2nd
2001-02	Premiership	17 March	Lost	**1**	**2**	9 December	Lost	**2**	**3**	8th	1st
2002-03	Premiership	5 April	Drew	**1**	**1**	30 November	Lost	**1**	**3**	16th	2nd
2003-04	Premiership	18 January	Lost	**0**	**2**	27 August	Lost	**0**	**2**	6th	1st

FA Cup										*Division*	
1925-26	Round 5	20 February	Drew	**1**	**1**	24 February	Lost	**0**	**2**	Div 1	Div 1
1927-28	Round 5					18 February	Lost	**1**	**4**	Div 1	Div 1
1928-29	Q'ter Final	2 March	Won	**1**	**0**					Div 1	Div 1
1930-31	Round 3	14 January	Lost	**1**	**3**	10 January	Drew	**2**	**2**	Div 1	Div 1
1933-34	Q'ter Final					3 March	Won	**2**	**1**	Div 1	Div 1
1953-54	Round 3					9 January	Lost	**1**	**5**	Div 1	Div 1
1955-56	Round 4					28 January	Lost	**1**	**4**	Div 1	Div 1
1973-74	Round 4	30 January	Won	**2**	**0**	26 January	Drew	**1**	**1**	Div 2	Div 1
1982-83	Q'ter Final					12 March	Lost	**0**	**2**	Div 1	Div 1

League Cup											
1985-86	Q'ter Final	22 January	Drew	**1**	**1**	4 February	Won	**2**	**1**	Div 1	Div 1
1993-94	Round 4					30 November	Won	**1**	**0**	Prem	Prem
1995-96	Semi-Final	21 February	Drew*	**0**	**0**	14 February	Drew	**2**	**2**	Prem	Prem

Summary	P	W	D	L	F	A
Villa's home league record:	75	38	18	19	143	104
Villa's away league record:	75	20	15	40	84	126
Villa's cup record:	17	5	6	6	19	29
TOTAL:	**167**	**63**	**39**	**65**	**246**	**259**

FACT FILE

- **On 2 May 1981, Ron Saunders' Villa travelled to Highbury knowing a victory would earn them their first league championship for 71 years. Their 2-0 defeat, however, was irrelevant as title challengers Ipswich lost 2-1 to Middlesbrough, and the party could begin. An even bigger honour for Villa was just 12 months away, as the club became champions of Europe at the first attempt.**
- **Between 1909 and 1926, Arsenal earned just two draws and no wins in 13 visits to Villa Park.**
- **Villa have not won in their last 11 matches against Arsenal.**
- **Arsenal are unbeaten in their last 11 home matches against Villa, stretching back to 1993.**
- **Villa have won all three league cup ties between the sides.**
- **Villa lost at home to Arsenal 14 December 1935, Ted Drake scoring all seven.**

Villa's top scorers vs Arsenal

Billy Walker, Pongo Waring 15
Eric Houghton 9
Joe Bache 8
Harry Hampton, Johnny Dixon, Peter McParland 7

Villa hat-tricks vs Arsenal

28 Aug 1920 Billy Walker (4)
24 Nov 1928 Pongo Waring
25 Sep 1929 George Brown
25 Apr 1978 Gary Shelton

Played for both clubs

Charlie Hare	Villa 1891-95	Arsenal 1894-96
Robert Gordon	Villa 1894-95	Arsenal 1895-96
Frank Lloyd	Arsenal 1899-1900	Villa 1900-02
Bobby Templeton	Villa 1898-1903	Arsenal 1904-06
Peter Kyle	Arsenal 1906-08	Villa 1907-09
Andy Ducat	Arsenal 1904-12	Villa 1912-21
Dick Roose	Villa 1911-12	Arsenal 1911-12
Chris Buckley	Villa 1906-13	Arsenal 1914-21
Andrew Young	Villa 1919-22	Arsenal 1921-27
George Graham	Villa 1962-64	Arsenal 1966-73
John McLeod	Arsenal 1961-65	Villa 1964-68
Jimmy Rimmer	Arsenal 1973-77	Villa 1977-83
Alex Cropley	Arsenal 1974-77	Villa 1976-80
Martin Keown	Arsenal 1985-86/92-2004	Villa 1986-89
Kevin Richardson	Arsenal 1987-90	Villa 1991-95
David Platt	Villa 1987-91	Arsenal 1995-98
Paul Merson	Arsenal 1986-97	Villa 1998-2002

v. Ashington

FA Cup		Date	Result	Away Villa	Away Ashington	Division Villa	Division Ashington
1923-24	Round 1	12 January	Won	**5**	**1**	Div 1	Div 3N

Summary	*P*	*W*	*D*	*L*	*F*	*A*
Villa's cup record:	1	1	0	0	5	1
TOTAL:	**1**	**1**	**0**	**0**	**5**	**1**

Villa's top scorers vs Ashington

Billy Walker 2

Billy Walker scored 244 goals in 531 League and Cup games for the club and scored twice against Ashington in the First Round FA Cup tie. After his retirement Billy Walker managed both Sheffield Wednesday and Nottingham Forest to FA Cup triumphs.

v. Aston Unity

FA Cup		Date	Result	Home Villa	Home Aston Unity
1882-83	Round 3	6 January	Won	**3**	**1**

Summary	P	W	D	L	F	A
Villa's cup record:	1	1	0	0	3	1
TOTAL:	**1**	**1**	**0**	**0**	**3**	**1**

FACT FILE

- **Davis, Vaughton and Hunter scored the goals for Villa. The two clubs played at grounds very close to each other, and many players appeared for both clubs.**

The goalscorers against Aston Unity were still with Villa when they won the FA Cup in 1887 with this team. Standing (left to right): Coulton, Warner, Dawson, Simmonds, Allen. Seated: Davis, Brown, Hunter, Vaughton, Hodgetts. On ground: Yates, Burton.

v. Barnsley

Season	League	Home Date	Home Result	Home Villa	Home Barnsley	Away Date	Away Result	Away Villa	Away Barnsley	Final Positions Villa	Final Positions Barnsley
1936-37	Division 2	24 October	Won	**4**	**2**	27 February	Won	**4**	**0**	9th	14th
1937-38	Division 2	28 December	Won	**3**	**0**	18 December	Won	**1**	**0**	1stP	21stR
1970-71	Division 3	12 April	Drew	**0**	**0**	12 September	Drew	**1**	**1**	4th	12th
1971-72	Division 3	22 January	Won	**2**	**0**	28 September	Won	**4**	**0**	1stP	22ndR
1987-88	Division 2	12 September	Drew	**0**	**0**	2 January	Won	**3**	**1**	2ndP	14th
1997-98	Premiership	11 March	Lost	**0**	**1**	13 September	Won	**3**	**0**	7th	19thR

FA Cup

										Division	
1902-03	Round 2	21 February	Won	**4**	**1**					Div 1	Div 2
1994-95	Round 3					7 January	Won	**2**	**0**	Prem	Div 1

League Cup

1963-64	Round 2	25 September	Won	**3**	**1**					Div 1	Div 3
1990-91	Round 2	26 September	Won	**1**	**0**	9 October	Won	**1**	**0**	Div 1	Div 2

Summary	*P*	*W*	*D*	*L*	*F*	*A*
Villa's home league record:	6	3	2	1	9	3
Villa's away league record:	6	5	1	0	16	2
Villa's cup record:	5	5	0	0	11	2
TOTAL:	**17**	**13**	**3**	**1**	**36**	**7**

Joining Villa from Barnsley in March 1951, for £15,000, Danny Blanchflower, who went to Oakwell from Glentoran, for £6,500 in 1949, spent three and half years with Villa, making 155 senior appearances, before Tottenham signed him for £30,000 in October 1954.

FACT FILE

- **Barnsley did not win a match against Villa until the 17th attempt.**
- **Villa have kept 11 clean sheets in their 17 matches against Barnsley.**

Villa's top scorers vs Barnsley
Frank Broome 5
Jasper McLuckie, Andy Lochhead 3

Villa hat-tricks vs Barnsley
21 Feb 1903 Jasper McLuckie (cup)

Played for both clubs

Frank Cornan	Barnsley 1902-05/12-13	Villa 1908-09
George Reeves	Barnsley 1906-08	Villa 1907-09
George Travers	Villa 1908-09	Barnsley 1910-14
Frank Barson	Barnsley 1911-20	Villa 1919-22
Ginger Phoenix	Villa 1924-25	Barnsley 1925-26
Pongo Waring	Villa 1927-36	Barnsley 1935-36
Norman Young	Villa 1935-36	Barnsley 1936-37
Danny Blanchflower	Barnsley 1948-51	Villa 1950-55
Jake Findlay	Villa 1973-77	Barnsley 1983-84
Alan Little	Villa 1974-75	Barnsley 1977-80
John Deehan	Villa 1975-80	Barnsley 1990-91
David Geddis	Villa 1979-83	Barnsley 1983-85
Andy Blair	Villa 1981-84/85-88	Barnsley 1987-88
Gareth Williams	Villa 1987-90	Barnsley 1991-94
Stuart Gray	Barnsley 1983-88	Villa 1987-91
Lee Butler	Villa 1988-91	Barnsley 1991-96
Kevin Richardson	Villa 1991-95	Barnsley 1998-2000
Chris Boden	Villa 1993-94	Barnsley 1993-94
Carl Tiler	Barnsley 1987-91	Villa 1995-97

Barnsley's Andy Blair had two spells at Villa after signing from Coventry and left to play for Sheffield Wednesday

v. Birmingham City

		Home				Away				Final Positions	
Season	*League*	*Date*	*Result*	Villa	Birm'ham	*Date*	*Result*	Villa	Birm'ham	Villa	Birm'ham
1894-95	Division 1	1 September	Won	**2**	**1**	20 October	Drew	**2**	**2**	3rd	12th
1895-96	Division 1	7 September	Won	**7**	**3**	26 October	Won	**4**	**1**	1st	15thR
1901-02	Division 1	26 December	Won	**1**	**0**	12 October	Won	**2**	**0**	8th	17thR
1903-04	Division 1	16 January	Drew	**1**	**1**	19 September	Drew	**2**	**2**	5th	11th
1904-05	Division 1	29 October	Won	**2**	**1**	25 February	Won	**3**	**0**	4th	7th
1905-06	Division 1	20 January	Lost	**1**	**3**	16 September	Lost	**0**	**2**	8th	7th
1906-07	Division 1	15 September	Won	**4**	**1**	19 January	Lost	**2**	**3**	5th	9th
1907-08	Division 1	18 January	Lost	**2**	**3**	21 September	Won	**3**	**2**	2nd	20thR
1921-22	Division 1	11 March	Drew	**1**	**1**	15 March	Lost	**0**	**1**	5th	18th
1922-23	Division 1	24 March	Won	**3**	**0**	17 March	Lost	**0**	**1**	6th	17th
1923-24	Division 1	1 September	Drew	**0**	**0**	25 August	Lost	**0**	**3**	6th	14th
1924-25	Division 1	14 February	Won	**1**	**0**	11 October	Lost	**0**	**1**	15th	8th
1925-26	Division 1	17 October	Drew	**3**	**3**	27 February	Lost	**1**	**2**	6th	14th
1926-27	Division 1	19 March	Won	**4**	**2**	30 October	Won	**2**	**1**	10th	17th
1927-28	Division 1	17 March	Drew	**1**	**1**	5 November	Drew	**1**	**1**	8th	11th
1928-29	Division 1	9 March	Lost	**1**	**2**	27 October	Won	**4**	**2**	3rd	15th
1929-30	Division 1	31 August	Won	**2**	**1**	28 December	Drew	**1**	**1**	4th	11th
1930-31	Division 1	18 October	Drew	**1**	**1**	21 February	Won	**4**	**0**	2nd	19th
1931-32	Division 1	21 November	Won	**3**	**2**	2 April	Drew	**1**	**1**	5th	9th
1932-33	Division 1	22 October	Won	**1**	**0**	8 March	Lost	**2**	**3**	2nd	13th
1933-34	Division 1	14 April	Drew	**1**	**1**	2 December	Drew	**0**	**0**	13th	20th
1934-35	Division 1	29 December	Drew	**2**	**2**	25 August	Lost	**1**	**2**	13th	19th
1935-36	Division 1	28 March	Won	**2**	**1**	23 November	Drew	**2**	**2**	21stR	12th
1938-39	Division 1	4 March	Won	**5**	**1**	29 October	Lost	**0**	**3**	12th	21stR
1948-49	Division 1	4 December	Lost	**0**	**3**	30 April	Won	**1**	**0**	10th	17th
1949-50	Division 1	10 December	Drew	**1**	**1**	29 April	Drew	**2**	**2**	12th	22ndR
1955-56	Division 1	5 September	Drew	**0**	**0**	21 September	Drew	**2**	**2**	20th	6th
1956-57	Division 1	27 October	Won	**3**	**1**	10 April	Won	**2**	**1**	10th	12th=
1957-58	Division 1	21 December	Lost	**0**	**2**	24 August	Lost	**1**	**3**	14th	13th
1958-59	Division 1	23 August	Drew	**1**	**1**	20 December	Lost	**1**	**4**	21stR	9th
1960-61	Division 1	22 October	Won	**6**	**2**	11 March	Drew	**1**	**1**	9th	19th
1961-62	Division 1	28 October	Lost	**1**	**3**	17 March	Won	**2**	**0**	7th	17th
1962-63	Division 1	16 March	Won	**4**	**0**	27 October	Lost	**2**	**3**	15th	20th
1963-64	Division 1	30 March	Lost	**0**	**3**	31 March	Drew	**3**	**3**	19th	20th
1964-65	Division 1	12 April	Won	**3**	**0**	13 February	Won	**1**	**0**	16th	22ndR
1967-68	Division 2	7 October	Lost	**2**	**4**	24 February	Lost	**1**	**2**	16th	4th
1968-69	Division 2	12 April	Won	**1**	**0**	21 September	Lost	**0**	**4**	18th	7th
1969-70	Division 2	18 October	Drew	**0**	**0**	30 March	Won	**2**	**0**	21stR	18th
1975-76	Division 1	27 September	Won	**2**	**1**	3 April	Lost	**2**	**3**	16th	19th
1976-77	Division 1	18 September	Lost	**1**	**2**	10 May	Lost	**1**	**2**	4th	13th
1977-78	Division 1	1 October	Lost	**0**	**1**	25 February	Lost	**0**	**1**	8th	11th
1978-79	Division 1	3 March	Won	**1**	**0**	21 October	Won	**1**	**0**	8th	21stR
1980-81	Division 1	13 December	Won	**3**	**0**	11 October	Won	**2**	**1**	1st	13th
1981-82	Division 1	26 September	Drew	**0**	**0**	20 February	Won	**1**	**0**	11th	16th

Season	League	Date	Result	Home Villa	Home Birm'ham	Date	Result	Away Villa	Away Birm'ham	Final Positions Villa	Final Positions Birm'ham
1982-83	Division 1	4 April	Won	**1**	**0**	27 December	Lost	**0**	**3**	6th	17th
1983-84	Division 1	15 October	Won	**1**	**0**	31 March	Lost	**1**	**2**	10th	20thR
1985-86	Division 1	22 March	Lost	**0**	**3**	7 September	Drew	**0**	**0**	16th	21stR
1987-88	Division 2	22 August	Lost	**0**	**2**	12 December	Won	**2**	**1**	2ndP	19th
2002-03	Premiership	3 March	Lost	**0**	**2**	16 September	Lost	**0**	**3**	16th	13th
2003-04	Premiership	22 February	Drew	**2**	**2**	19 October	Drew	**0**	**0**	6th	10th

FA Cup										*Division*	
1887-88	Round 2					5 November	Won	**4**	**0**		
1900-01	Q'ter Final	27 March	Won*	**1**	**0**	23 March	Drew	**0**	**0**	Div 1	Div 2

League Cup											
1962-63	Final	27 May	Drew	**0**	**0**	23 May	Lost	**1**	**3**	Div 1	Div 1
1988-89	Round 2	12 October	Won	**5**	**0**	27 September	Won	**2**	**0**	Div 1	Div 2
1993-94	Round 2	6 October	Won	**1**	**0**	21 September	Won	**1**	**0**	Prem	Div 1

Summary	*P*	*W*	*D*	*L*	*F*	*A*
Villa's home league record:	50	23	14	13	84	64
Villa's away league record:	50	16	13	21	68	77
Villa's cup record:	9	6	2	1	15	3
TOTAL:	**109**	**45**	**29**	**35**	**167**	**144**

Centre-forward Harry Hampton joined Aston Villa in May 1904 and began a career which saw him become the most prolific scorer in Villa's history with 242 goals in 373 League and Cup games. In February 1920, Hampton was transferred to Birmingham, who he helped win the Second Division title in 1921.

FACT FILE

- **Aston Villa's first league meeting with their main local rivals came in September 1903. Pearson (with a penalty) and Garraty scored for Villa in a 2-2 draw at Muntz Street, the home of Small Heath, who changed their name to Birmingham in 1905.**
- **The sides' first FA Cup meeting came in 1887, when two goals from Green, and one each from Allen and Brown, helped Villa to a 4-0 victory.**
- **In terms of league matches, Villa currently lead the series 39-34. Villa have led the series ever since they won the first match between the sides, way back in 1894. The most they have ever led the series by is nine, which occurred between April and August 1957, and again between October 1983 and March 1984.**
- **Villa have done the league double over the Blues eight times, most recently in their title winning season of 1980-81.**
- **Birmingham have done the league double six times, most recently in 2002-03.**
- **Villa have kept eight clean sheets in the sides' nine cup meetings.**
- **Strangely, the sides have not met in the FA Cup for over 100 years.**
- **Villa were undefeated in their first 13 matches against Birmingham.**
- **Villa won their first four home matches against Birmingham.**
- **Birmingham won five in a row at home from 1922 to 1926.**
- **Villa's biggest win was 5-0 in 1988, while Birmingham's biggest was 4-0 in 1968. Villa also won 7-3 in 1895.**
- **Neither side has won more than five matches in a row in the series.**

Villa's top scorers vs Birmingham

Billy Walker 11
Pongo Waring 7
Eric Houghton, Jack Devey, Johnny Campbell 5
Gerry Hitchens 4
(14 players) 3

Villa hat-tricks vs Birmingham

7 Sep 1895 Johnny Campbell (4)
4 Mar 1939 Jackie Martin

Played for both clubs

Will Devey	Villa 1892-94	Birmingham 1898-99
Charlie Hare	Villa 1891-95	Birmingham 1896-98
Denny Hodgetts	Villa 1888-96	Birmingham 1896-97
Fred Wheldon	Birmingham 1892-96	Villa 1896-1900

Charlie Athersmith	Villa 1890-1901	Birmingham 1901-05
Alex Leake	Birmingham 1895-1902	Villa 1902-08
Jimmy Murray	Villa 1900-02	Birmingham 1901-02
Walter Corbett	Villa 1904-07	Birmingham 1907-11
Rowland Harper	Birmingham 1905-07	Villa 1907-08
Frank Cornan	Birmingham 1905-08	Villa 1908-09
Charlie Millington	Villa 1905-08	Birmingham 1909-12
Fred Chapple	Villa 1906-08	Birmingham 1908-10
John Kearns	Birmingham 1905-09	Villa 1908-12
Edmund Eyre	Birmingham 1906-09/13-15	Villa 1908-11
George Travers	Birmingham 1907-09	Villa 1908-09
John Wilcox	Villa 1907-09	Birmingham 1908-11
Billy George	Villa 1897-1911	Birmingham 1911-12
Albert Lindon	Birmingham 1910-11	Villa 1911-12
Harry Hampton	Villa 1904-20	Birmingham 1919-22
Alex McClure	Birmingham 1911-24	Villa 1923-25
Ginger Phoenix	Birmingham 1923-24	Villa 1924-25
Ken Tewkesbury	Birmingham 1929-32	Villa 1932-33
Charlie Phillips	Villa 1935-38	Birmingham 1937-39
Jock Mulraney	Birmingham 1946-47	Villa 1948-49
Stan Lynn	Villa 1950-62	Birmingham 1961-66
Ron Wylie	Villa 1958-65	Birmingham 1965-70
Bobby Thomson	Villa 1959-64	Birmingham 1963-68
John Sleeuwenhoek	Villa 1960-68	Birmingham 1967-71
Cammie Fraser	Villa 1962-64	Birmingham 1964-66
Tony Hateley	Villa 1963-67	Birmingham 1969-71
Colin Withers	Birmingham 1960-65	Villa 1964-69
Bruce Rioch	Villa 1969-74	Birmingham 1978-79
Geoff Vowden	Birmingham 1964-71	Villa 1970-74
Malcolm Beard	Birmingham 1960-71	Villa 1971-73
Trevor Hockey	Birmingham 1965-71	Villa 1973-74
Frank Carrodus	Villa 1974-79	Birmingham 1982-83
Dennis Mortimer	Villa 1975-85	Birmingham 1986-87
Ivor Linton	Villa 1976-82	Birmingham 1983-84
Lee Jenkins	Villa 1978-80	Birmingham 1985-86
Noel Blake	Villa 1979-82	Birmingham 1982-84
David Geddis	Villa 1979-83	Birmingham 1984-87
Robert Hopkins	Villa 1979-83	Birmingham 1982-87/88-91
Tony Morley	Villa 1979-84	Birmingham 1984-85
Des Bremner	Villa 1979-85	Birmingham 1984-89
Peter Withe	Birmingham 1975-77/87-88	Villa 1980-85
Mark Jones	Villa 1981-84	Birmingham 1984-87
Alan Curbishley	Birmingham 1979-83	Villa 1982-85
Kevin Poole	Villa 1984-87	Birmingham 1997-2001
Phil Robinson	Villa 1986-87	Birmingham 1990-91
Les Sealey	Villa 1991-92	Birmingham 1992-93
Bryan Small	Villa 1991-95	Birmingham 1994-95
Gary Charles	Villa 1994-99	Birmingham 2000-01
Carl Tiler	Villa 1995-97	Birmingham 2000-01

v. Blackburn Rovers

		Home					Away			Final Positions	
Season	*League*	*Date*	*Result*	Villa	Blackburn	*Date*	*Result*	Villa	Blackburn	Villa	Blackburn
1888-89	Division 1	13 October	Won	**6**	**1**	17 November	Lost	**1**	**5**	2nd	4th
1889-90	Division 1	31 March	Won	**3**	**0**	19 October	Lost	**0**	**7**	8th	3rd
1890-91	Division 1	13 December	Drew	**2**	**2**	6 December	Lost	**1**	**5**	9th	6th
1891-92	Division 1	5 September	Won	**5**	**1**	5 March	Lost	**3**	**4**	4th	9th
1892-93	Division 1	10 December	Won	**4**	**1**	11 February	Drew	**2**	**2**	4th	9th
1893-94	Division 1	24 March	Won	**2**	**1**	4 November	Lost	**0**	**2**	1st	4th
1894-95	Division 1	8 December	Won	**3**	**0**	1 December	Won	**3**	**1**	3rd	5th
1895-96	Division 1	19 October	Won	**3**	**1**	28 September	Drew	**1**	**1**	1st	8th
1896-97	Division 1	17 April	Won	**3**	**0**	28 November	Won	**5**	**1**	1st	14th
1897-98	Division 1	11 December	Won	**5**	**1**	25 September	Lost	**3**	**4**	6th	15th
1898-99	Division 1	19 November	Won	**3**	**1**	18 March	Drew	**0**	**0**	1st	6th
1899-00	Division 1	23 September	Won	**3**	**1**	20 January	Won	**4**	**0**	1st	14th
1900-01	Division 1	29 October	Drew	**3**	**3**	22 December	Drew	**2**	**2**	15th	9th
1901-02	Division 1	14 September	Drew	**1**	**1**	11 January	Lost	**0**	**4**	8th	4th
1902-03	Division 1	24 January	Won	**5**	**0**	27 September	Won	**2**	**0**	2nd	16th
1903-04	Division 1	12 December	Lost	**2**	**3**	9 April	Won	**3**	**0**	5th	15th
1904-05	Division 1	7 January	Won	**3**	**0**	10 September	Lost	**0**	**4**	4th	13th
1905-06	Division 1	30 December	Lost	**0**	**1**	2 September	Drew	**1**	**1**	8th	9th
1906-07	Division 1	1 September	Won	**4**	**2**	29 December	Lost	**1**	**2**	5th	12th
1907-08	Division 1	4 January	Drew	**1**	**1**	7 September	Lost	**0**	**2**	2nd	14th=
1908-09	Division 1	3 October	Drew	**1**	**1**	15 February	Lost	**1**	**3**	7th	4th
1909-10	Division 1	29 January	Won	**4**	**3**	18 September	Lost	**2**	**3**	1st	3rd
1910-11	Division 1	1 October	Drew	**2**	**2**	24 April	Drew	**0**	**0**	2nd	12th
1911-12	Division 1	17 February	Lost	**0**	**3**	14 October	Lost	**1**	**3**	6th	1st
1912-13	Division 1	15 February	Drew	**1**	**1**	12 October	Drew	**2**	**2**	2nd	5th
1913-14	Division 1	13 September	Lost	**1**	**3**	3 January	Drew	**0**	**0**	2nd	1st
1914-15	Division 1	2 April	Won	**2**	**1**	25 December	Won	**2**	**1**	14th	3rd
1919-20	Division 1	20 March	Lost	**1**	**2**	15 April	Lost	**1**	**5**	9th	20th
1920-21	Division 1	16 April	Won	**3**	**0**	9 April	Won	**1**	**0**	10th	11th
1921-22	Division 1	12 September	Drew	**1**	**1**	1 April	Won	**2**	**1**	5th	15th
1922-23	Division 1	26 August	Won	**2**	**0**	2 September	Lost	**2**	**4**	6th	14th
1923-24	Division 1	2 April	Won	**1**	**0**	1 March	Lost	**1**	**3**	6th	8th
1924-25	Division 1	29 April	Won	**4**	**3**	27 September	Drew	**1**	**1**	15th	16th
1925-26	Division 1	12 December	Lost	**1**	**2**	24 April	Lost	**1**	**3**	6th	12th
1926-27	Division 1	29 January	Won	**4**	**3**	11 December	Won	**2**	**0**	10th	18th
1927-28	Division 1	26 November	Won	**2**	**0**	7 April	Won	**1**	**0**	8th	12th
1928-29	Division 1	17 November	Won	**2**	**1**	30 March	Won	**5**	**2**	3rd	7th
1929-30	Division 1	30 November	Won	**3**	**0**	5 April	Lost	**0**	**2**	4th	6th
1930-31	Division 1	1 November	Won	**5**	**2**	7 March	Won	**2**	**0**	2nd	10th
1931-32	Division 1	19 December	Lost	**1**	**5**	30 April	Lost	**0**	**2**	5th	16th
1932-33	Division 1	17 December	Won	**4**	**0**	29 April	Won	**5**	**0**	2nd	15th
1933-34	Division 1	31 March	Drew	**1**	**1**	18 November	Lost	**1**	**2**	13th	8th
1934-35	Division 1	22 December	Drew	**1**	**1**	4 May	Lost	**0**	**5**	13th	15th
1935-36	Division 1	25 April	Lost	**2**	**4**	21 December	Lost	**1**	**5**	21stR	22ndR

		Home						Away			Final Positions	
Season	*League*	*Date*	*Result*	Villa	Blackburn	*Date*	*Result*	Villa	Blackburn		Villa	Blackburn
1936-37	Division 2	21 November	Drew	**2**	**2**	27 March	Won	**4**	**3**		9th	12th
1937-38	Division 2	11 September	Won	**2**	**1**	27 January	Lost	**0**	**1**		1stP	16th
1946-47	Division 1	10 May	Won	**2**	**1**	5 October	Won	**1**	**0**		8th	17th
1947-48	Division 1	14 April	Won	**3**	**2**	6 September	Drew	**0**	**0**		6th	21stR
1958-59	Division 1	18 February	Won	**1**	**0**	27 September	Won	**3**	**2**		21stR	10th
1960-61	Division 1	21 January	Drew	**2**	**2**	10 September	Lost	**1**	**4**		9th	8th
1961-62	Division 1	3 February	Won	**1**	**0**	16 September	Lost	**2**	**4**		7th	16th
1962-63	Division 1	19 January	Drew	**0**	**0**	8 September	Lost	**1**	**4**		15th	11th
1963-64	Division 1	31 August	Lost	**1**	**2**	21 December	Lost	**0**	**2**		19th	7th
1964-65	Division 1	5 September	Lost	**0**	**4**	2 January	Lost	**1**	**5**		16th	10th
1965-66	Division 1	19 February	Won	**3**	**1**	4 September	Won	**2**	**0**		16th	22ndR
1967-68	Division 2	23 March	Lost	**1**	**2**	13 March	Lost	**1**	**2**		16th	8th
1968-69	Division 2	15 March	Drew	**1**	**1**	24 August	Lost	**0**	**2**		18th	19th
1969-70	Division 2	21 March	Drew	**1**	**1**	6 December	Lost	**0**	**2**		21stR	8th
1971-72	Division 3	30 October	Won	**4**	**1**	19 February	Drew	**1**	**1**		1stP	10th
1987-88	Division 2	30 September	Drew	**1**	**1**	20 February	Lost	**2**	**3**		2ndP	5th
1992-93	Premiership	19 October	Drew	**0**	**0**	21 April	Lost	**0**	**3**		2nd	4th
1993-94	Premiership	1 January	Lost	**0**	**1**	11 April	Lost	**0**	**1**		10th	2nd
1994-95	Premiership	4 March	Lost	**0**	**1**	24 September	Lost	**1**	**3**		18th	1st
1995-96	Premiership	28 February	Won	**2**	**0**	9 September	Drew	**1**	**1**		4th	7th
1996-97	Premiership	20 August	Won	**1**	**0**	22 March	Won	**2**	**0**		5th	13th
1997-98	Premiership	13 August	Lost	**0**	**4**	17 January	Lost	**0**	**5**		7th	6th
1998-99	Premiership	6 February	Lost	**1**	**3**	26 December	Lost	**1**	**2**		6th	19th
2001-02	Premiership	30 September	Won	**2**	**0**	5 March	Lost	**0**	**3**		8th	10th
2002-03	Premiership	2 February	Won	**3**	**0**	3 November	Drew	**0**	**0**		16th	6th
2003-04	Premiership	20 March	Lost	**0**	**2**	20 December	Won	**2**	**0**		6th	15th

FA Cup										*Division*	
1888-89	Q'ter Final					2 March	Lost	**1**	**8**	Div 1	Div 1
1922-23	Round 1	13 January	Lost	**0**	**1**					Div 1	Div 1
1929-30	Round 5	15 February	Won	**4**	**1**					Div 1	Div 1
1979-80	Round 5	20 February	Won	**1**	**0**	16 February	Drew	**1**	**1**	Div 1	Div 3
1989-90	Round 3	10 January	Won	**3**	**1**	6 January	Drew	**2**	**2**	Div 1	Div 2
2002-03	Round 3	4 January	Lost	**1**	**4**					Prem	Prem

Summary	*P*	*W*	*D*	*L*	*F*	*A*
Villa's home league record:	70	37	17	16	144	92
Villa's away league record:	70	19	13	38	92	147
Villa's cup record:	8	3	2	3	13	18
TOTAL:	**148**	**59**	**32**	**57**	**249**	**257**

FACT FILE

- **Villa's biggest ever cup defeat (8-1) came at the hands of Rovers, as did the first of Villa's five seven-goal league defeats. Both of these happened well over a century ago, however...**
- **In 1997-98 the misery returned for Villa. The 5-0 defeat is Villa's heaviest ever Premiership defeat, and the 4-0 defeat is Villa's joint heaviest Premiership home defeat.**
- **Villa Park quickly became one of England's foremost grounds. It has hosted 53 FA Cup semi-final matches (including replays), twenty more than its nearest rival Hillsborough. This includes 39 matches in the last 44 years. It also hosted England's first home international after the closure of Wembley Stadium.**
- **Villa have won only twice in their last 17 away games.**
- **From 1926 to 1929, Villa won seven games in a row against Rovers.**

Villa's top scorers vs Blackburn

Billy Walker 14

Jack Devey, George Brown 10

Joe Bache, Charlie Athersmith, Fred Wheldon 9

Joe Beresford 7

Villa hat-tricks vs Blackburn

5 Mar 1892 Lewis Campbell

1 Dec 1894 Steve Smith

28 Nov 1896 Fred Wheldon

29 Jan 1910 Harry Hampton

15 Feb 1930 George Brown (cup)

29 Apr 1932 George Brown (4)

27 Mar 1937 Frank Broome

Played for both clubs

Tom Wilson	Blackburn 1898-99	Villa 1900-02
George Smith	Villa 1901-02	Blackburn 1903-06
Tom Riley	Blackburn 1902-05	Villa 1905-08
Arthur Cunliffe	Blackburn 1929-33	Villa 1932-36
Ronnie Dix	Blackburn 1932-33	Villa 1932-37
George Hardy	Villa 1936-38	Blackburn 1938-39
John Willis	Blackburn 1955-56	Villa 1958-59
Derek Dougan	Blackburn 1958-61	Villa 1961-63
Mike Ferguson	Blackburn 1962-68	Villa 1968-70
Barry Hole	Blackburn 1966-69	Villa 1968-70
Gordon Cowans	Villa 1975-85/88-92/93-94	Blackburn 1991-93
Bernard Gallacher	Villa 1986-91	Blackburn 1990-91
Chris Price	Blackburn 1986-88/91-93	Villa 1988-92
Dwight Yorke	Villa 1989-99	Blackburn 2002-04
Graham Fenton	Villa 1993-96	Blackburn 1995-97
Alan Wright	Blackburn 1991-95	Villa 1994-2003
Simon Grayson	Villa 1997-99	Blackburn 1999-2000
Peter Enckelman	Villa 1999-2003	Blackburn 2003-04

v. Blackpool

		Home					Away			Final Positions	
Season	League	Date	Result	Villa	Blackpool	Date	Result	Villa	Blackpool	Villa	Blackpool
1930-31	Division 1	28 March	Won	**4**	**1**	22 November	Drew	**2**	**2**	2nd	20th
1931-32	Division 1	7 November	Won	**5**	**1**	19 March	Won	**3**	**1**	5th	20th
1932-33	Division 1	5 November	Won	**6**	**2**	18 March	Lost	**2**	**6**	2nd	22ndR
1936-37	Division 2	20 March	Won	**4**	**0**	14 November	Won	**3**	**2**	9th	2ndP
1938-39	Division 1	14 January	Won	**3**	**1**	10 September	Won	**4**	**2**	12th	15th
1946-47	Division 1	25 January	Drew	**1**	**1**	21 September	Lost	**0**	**1**	8th	5th
1947-48	Division 1	13 September	Lost	**0**	**1**	31 January	Lost	**0**	**1**	6th	9th
1948-49	Division 1	1 January	Lost	**2**	**5**	28 August	Lost	**0**	**1**	10th	16th
1949-50	Division 1	10 September	Drew	**0**	**0**	14 January	Lost	**0**	**1**	12th	7th
1950-51	Division 1	3 February	Lost	**0**	**3**	23 September	Drew	**1**	**1**	15th	3rd
1951-52	Division 1	19 January	Won	**4**	**0**	15 September	Won	**3**	**0**	6th	9th
1952-53	Division 1	6 September	Lost	**1**	**5**	17 January	Drew	**1**	**1**	11th	7th
1953-54	Division 1	12 September	Won	**2**	**1**	23 January	Lost	**2**	**3**	13th	6th
1954-55	Division 1	22 January	Won	**3**	**1**	11 September	Won	**1**	**0**	6th	19th
1955-56	Division 1	10 September	Drew	**1**	**1**	14 January	Lost	**0**	**6**	20th	2nd
1956-57	Division 1	1 September	Won	**3**	**2**	29 December	Drew	**0**	**0**	10th	4th
1957-58	Division 1	1 February	Drew	**1**	**1**	21 September	Drew	**1**	**1**	14th	7th
1958-59	Division 1	20 September	Drew	**1**	**1**	7 February	Lost	**1**	**2**	21stR	8th
1960-61	Division 1	31 December	Drew	**2**	**2**	27 August	Lost	**3**	**5**	9th	20th
1961-62	Division 1	23 September	Won	**5**	**0**	10 February	Won	**2**	**1**	7th	13th
1962-63	Division 1	1 September	Drew	**1**	**1**	29 March	Lost	**0**	**4**	15th	13th
1963-64	Division 1	11 January	Won	**3**	**1**	7 September	Won	**4**	**0**	19th	18th
1964-65	Division 1	16 January	Won	**3**	**2**	12 September	Lost	**1**	**3**	16th	17th
1965-66	Division 1	11 September	Won	**3**	**0**	26 February	Won	**1**	**0**	16th	13th
1966-67	Division 1	14 January	Won	**3**	**2**	10 September	Won	**2**	**0**	21stR	22ndR
1967-68	Division 2	21 October	Won	**3**	**2**	16 March	Lost	**0**	**1**	16th	3rd
1968-69	Division 2	31 August	Lost	**0**	**1**	22 March	Drew	**1**	**1**	18th	8th
1969-70	Division 2	15 November	Drew	**0**	**0**	28 March	Lost	**1**	**2**	21stR	2ndP
1972-73	Division 2	11 November	Drew	**0**	**0**	17 October	Drew	**1**	**1**	3rd	7th
1973-74	Division 2	15 April	Lost	**0**	**1**	16 April	Lost	**1**	**2**	14th	5th
1974-75	Division 2	12 October	Won	**1**	**0**	19 April	Won	**3**	**0**	2ndP	7th

FA Cup

										Division	
1937-38	Round 4	22 January	Won	**4**	**0**					Div 1	Div 1

League Cup

1971-72	Round 4					26 October	Lost	**1**	**4**	Div 3	Div 2

Summary	*P*	*W*	*D*	*L*	*F*	*A*
Villa's home league record:	31	16	9	6	65	39
Villa's away league record:	31	10	7	14	44	51
Villa's cup record:	2	1	0	1	5	4
TOTAL:	**64**	**27**	**16**	**21**	**114**	**94**

FACT FILE

- **From 1953 to 1967, Villa were unbeaten in 14 home games.**
- **Villa won six games in a row from 1965 to 1967.**
- **See also South Shore.**

Villa's top scorers vs Blackpool

Eric Houghton 10
Peter McParland 9
Pongo Waring, Tommy Thompson 8
Harry Burrows 5

Villa hat-tricks vs Blackpool

28 Mar 1931 Pongo Waring
7 Nov 1931 Pongo Waring
20 Mar 1937 Frank Broome
23 Sep 1961 Peter McParland
7 Sep 1963 Harry Burrows

Played for both clubs

Tommy Bowman	Blackpool 1896-98	Villa 1897-1901
Arthur Brown	Villa 1900-01	Blackpool 1905-06
George Reeves	Villa 1907-09	Blackpool 1912-13
Archie Dyke	Villa 1913-15	Blackpool 1921-22
Percy Maggs	Villa 1930-31	Blackpool 1931-32
Fred Butcher	Villa 1934-35	Blackpool 1937-38
Danny Blair	Villa 1931-36	Blackpool 1936-39
Dai Astley	Villa 1931-37	Blackpool 1938-40
Frank O'Donnell	Blackpool 1937-39	Villa 1938-40
John Burridge	Blackpool 1970-76	Villa 1975-77
Colin Gibson	Villa 1978-86	Blackpool 1994-95
Gary Shaw	Villa 1978-88	Blackpool 1987-88
Terry Donovan	Villa 1979-82	Blackpool 1984-85
Les Sealey	Villa 1991-92	Blackpool 1994-95
Kevin Richardson	Villa 1991-95	Blackpool 1999-2000
Graham Fenton	Villa 1993-96	Blackpool 2001-02
Alan Wright	Blackpool 1987-92	Villa 1994-2003
Phil King	Blackpool 1987-92	Villa 1994-95
Richard Walker	Villa 1997-2000	Blackpool 2000-04
Darren Byfield	Villa 1997-98	Blackpool 1999-2000
Simon Grayson	Villa 1997-99	Blackpool 2002-04
Adam Rachel	Villa 1998-99	Blackpool 1999-2000

v. Bolton Wanderers

Season	League	Home Date	Home Result	Villa	Bolton W	Away Date	Away Result	Villa	Bolton W	Final Positions Villa	Final Positions Bolton W
1888-89	Division 1	12 January	Won	6	2	20 October	Won	3	2	2nd	5th
1889-90	Division 1	25 January	Lost	1	2	16 November	Lost	0	2	8th	9th
1890-91	Division 1	22 November	Won	5	0	4 October	Lost	0	4	9th	5th
1891-92	Division 1	10 October	Lost	1	2	2 April	Won	2	1	4th	3rd
1892-93	Division 1	24 December	Drew	1	1	24 September	Lost	0	5	4th	5th
1893-94	Division 1	3 March	Lost	2	3	18 November	Won	1	0	1st	13th
1894-95	Division 1	26 January	Won	2	1	23 March	Lost	3	4	3rd	10th
1895-96	Division 1	14 December	Won	2	0	7 March	Drew	2	2	1st	4th
1896-97	Division 1	22 March	Won	6	2	27 March	Won	2	1	1st	8th
1897-98	Division 1	2 October	Won	3	2	20 November	Lost	0	2	6th	11th
1898-99	Division 1	29 October	Won	2	1	17 April	Drew	0	0	1st	17thR
1900-01	Division 1	26 December	Won	3	0	6 October	Lost	0	1	15th	10th
1901-02	Division 1	9 November	Won	1	0	8 March	Drew	2	2	8th	12th
1902-03	Division 1	15 November	Won	4	2	14 March	Won	1	0	2nd	18thR
1905-06	Division 1	26 December	Drew	1	1	2 January	Lost	1	4	8th	6th
1906-07	Division 1	27 April	Lost	0	2	22 December	Won	2	1	5th	6th
1907-08	Division 1	14 September	Won	2	0	17 April	Lost	1	3	2nd	19thR
1909-10	Division 1	8 January	Won	3	1	4 September	Won	2	1	1st	20thR
1911-12	Division 1	5 April	Lost	0	1	1 January	Lost	0	3	6th	4th
1912-13	Division 1	7 December	Drew	1	1	12 April	Won	3	2	2nd	8th
1913-14	Division 1	25 February	Won	1	0	18 October	Lost	0	3	2nd	6th
1914-15	Division 1	26 December	Lost	1	7	1 January	Drew	2	2	14th	17th
1919-20	Division 1	7 April	Lost	3	6	13 March	Lost	1	2	9th	6th
1920-21	Division 1	7 May	Won	2	0	15 September	Lost	0	5	10th	3rd
1921-22	Division 1	15 April	Won	2	1	22 April	Lost	0	1	5th	6th
1922-23	Division 1	21 October	Won	2	0	28 October	Lost	0	3	6th	13th
1923-24	Division 1	26 January	Won	1	0	19 January	Lost	0	1	6th	4th
1924-25	Division 1	8 November	Drew	2	2	14 March	Lost	0	4	15th	3rd
1925-26	Division 1	26 April	Drew	2	2	19 September	Won	3	1	6th	8th
1926-27	Division 1	25 September	Lost	3	4	12 February	Won	2	0	10th	4th
1927-28	Division 1	28 April	Drew	2	2	17 December	Lost	1	3	8th	7th
1928-29	Division 1	20 October	Lost	3	5	17 April	Lost	1	3	3rd	14th
1929-30	Division 1	8 February	Won	2	0	5 October	Lost	0	3	4th	15th
1930-31	Division 1	17 January	Won	3	1	13 September	Drew	1	1	2nd	14th
1931-32	Division 1	10 October	Won	2	1	20 February	Lost	1	2	5th	17th
1932-33	Division 1	3 September	Won	6	1	7 January	Won	1	0	2nd	21stR
1935-36	Division 1	12 October	Lost	1	2	15 February	Lost	3	4	21stR	13th
1938-39	Division 1	15 April	Lost	1	3	10 December	Won	2	1	12th	8th
1946-47	Division 1	16 November	Drew	1	1	22 March	Lost	1	2	8th	18th
1947-48	Division 1	15 November	Won	3	1	3 April	Lost	0	1	6th	17th
1948-49	Division 1	30 August	Lost	2	4	25 August	Lost	0	3	10th	14th
1949-50	Division 1	22 April	Won	3	0	3 December	Drew	1	1	12th	16th
1950-51	Division 1	16 September	Lost	0	1	20 January	Lost	0	1	15th	8th
1951-52	Division 1	15 December	Drew	1	1	18 August	Lost	2	5	6th	5th

				Home				Away		Final Positions	
Season	League	Date	Result	Villa	Bolton W	Date	Result	Villa	Bolton W	Villa	Bolton W
1952-53	Division 1	4 October	Drew	**1**	**1**	21 February	Drew	**0**	**0**	11th	14th
1953-54	Division 1	31 October	Drew	**2**	**2**	20 March	Lost	**0**	**3**	13th	5th
1954-55	Division 1	12 February	Won	**3**	**0**	25 September	Drew	**3**	**3**	6th	18th
1955-56	Division 1	24 September	Lost	**0**	**2**	18 February	Lost	**0**	**1**	20th	8th
1956-57	Division 1	29 September	Drew	**0**	**0**	9 February	Drew	**0**	**0**	10th	9th
1957-58	Division 1	8 April	Won	**4**	**0**	4 April	Lost	**0**	**4**	14th	15th
1958-59	Division 1	25 October	Won	**2**	**1**	18 March	Won	**3**	**1**	21stR	4th
1960-61	Division 1	4 April	Won	**4**	**0**	3 April	Lost	**0**	**3**	9th	18th
1961-62	Division 1	7 April	Won	**3**	**0**	18 November	Drew	**1**	**1**	7th	11th
1962-63	Division 1	1 December	Won	**5**	**0**	20 April	Lost	**1**	**4**	15th	18th
1963-64	Division 1	2 November	Won	**3**	**0**	28 March	Drew	**1**	**1**	19th	21stR
1967-68	Division 2	20 April	Drew	**1**	**1**	25 November	Won	**3**	**2**	16th	12th
1968-69	Division 2	8 April	Drew	**1**	**1**	18 September	Lost	**1**	**4**	18th	17th
1969-70	Division 2	19 November	Won	**3**	**0**	17 September	Lost	**1**	**2**	21stR	16th
1971-72	Division 3	18 December	Won	**3**	**2**	4 September	Lost	**0**	**2**	1stP	7th
1973-74	Division 2	27 February	Drew	**1**	**1**	13 October	Won	**2**	**1**	14th	11th
1974-75	Division 2	5 March	Drew	**0**	**0**	31 August	Lost	**0**	**1**	2ndR	10th
1978-79	Division 1	7 March	Won	**3**	**0**	5 May	Drew	**0**	**0**	8th	17th
1979-80	Division 1	3 November	Won	**3**	**1**	18 August	Drew	**1**	**1**	7th	22ndR
1995-96	Premiership	30 August	Won	**1**	**0**	10 February	Won	**2**	**0**	4th	20thR
1997-98	Premiership	25 April	Lost	**1**	**3**	4 October	Won	**1**	**0**	7th	18thR
2001-02	Premiership	27 October	Won	**3**	**2**	30 March	Lost	**2**	**3**	8th	16th
2002-03	Premiership	1 January	Won	**2**	**0**	1 September	Lost	**0**	**1**	16th	17th
2003-04	Premiership	5 October	Drew	**1**	**1**	10 April	Drew	**2**	**2**	6th	8th

FA Cup

										Division	
1906-07	Round 2					2 February	Lost	**0**	**2**	Div 1	Div 1
1948-49	Round 3	8 January	Drew*	**1**	**1**	15 January	Drew*	**0**	**0**	Div 1	Div 1
		17 January	Won*	**2**	**1**	(2nd replay)					
1993-94	Round 5					20 February	Lost	**0**	**1**	Prem	Div 1
1999-00	Semi-Final	2 April		Wembley			Drew*	**0**	**0**	Prem	Div 1
							(won 4-1 pens)				

League Cup

2003-04	Semi-Final	27 January	Won	**2**	**0**	21 January	Lost	**2**	**5**	Prem	Prem

Dickie Dorsett, followed by Danny Blanchflower, leads Villa out for their home game against Bolton Wanderers in December 1951. A crowd of 28,257 saw a 1-1 draw.

Summary	P	W	D	L	F	A	
Villa's home league record:	68	37	16	15	145	87	
Villa's away league record:	68	17	14	37	71	132	
Villa's cup record:	8	2	3	3	7	10	
TOTAL:	**144**	**56**	**33**	**55**	**223**	**229**	(+one penalty shoot-out victory)

FACT FILE

- **In March 1897, Villa came from 2-0 down at half-time to produce a stunning second half, and claim a 6-2 win which handed them the league title with over a month of the season to spare. It proved to be the first part of the double, something that would not be achieved again for 64 years.**
- **A tense penalty shoot-out victory at Wembley in 2000 earned Villa their first appearance in an FA Cup final for 43 years. Dion Dublin converted the decisive kick.**
- **Villa have lost just once in their last 21 home games, stretching back to the mid-1950s.**
- **Villa failed to win in 13 away games between 1947 and 1958.**
- **Villa won eight home games in a row from 1895 to 1902.**

Villa's top scorers vs Bolton

Jack Devey, Billy Walker 10
Dicky York 7
Fred Wheldon, Harry Hampton 6
Juan Pablo Angel, Joe Bache, Eric Houghton, George Brown, Johnny Dixon 5

Villa hat-tricks vs Bolton

3 Sep 1932 George Brown (4)
18 Mar 1959 Gerry Hitchens

Played for both clubs

Tom Wilson	Villa 1900-02	Bolton 1904-06
Walter Brown	Bolton 1899-1904	Villa 1904-06
Sam Greenhalgh	Bolton 1902-06/07-14	Villa 1905-08
Tommy Barber	Bolton 1908-13	Villa 1912-15
Tom Griffiths	Bolton 1931-33	Villa 1935-37
John Gregory	Villa 1977-79	Bolton 1989-90
Kevin Poole	Villa 1984-87	Bolton 2001-02
Stuart Gray	Bolton 1982-83	Villa 1987-91
Neil Cox	Villa 1991-94	Bolton 1997-2000
Bryan Small	Villa 1991-95	Bolton 1995-97
Franz Carr	Villa 1994-96	Bolton 1997-98
Gareth Farrelly	Villa 1995-97	Bolton 1999-2003
Sasa Curcic	Bolton 1995-96	Villa 1996-98
Alan Thompson	Bolton 1993-98	Villa 1998-2000

v. AFC Bournemouth

		Home						Away		Final Positions	
Season	League	Date	Result	Villa	B'mouth	Date	Result	Villa	B'mouth	Villa	B'mouth
1971-72	Division 3	12 February	Won	**2**	**1**	23 October	Lost	**0**	**3**	1stP	3rd
1987-88	Division 2	17 October	Drew	**1**	**1**	5 March	Won	**2**	**1**	2ndP	17th

Summary	*P*	*W*	*D*	*L*	*F*	*A*
Villa's home league record:	2	1	1	0	3	2
Villa's away league record:	2	1	0	1	2	4
TOTAL:	**4**	**2**	**1**	**1**	**5**	**6**

Played for both clubs

Andrew Young	Villa 1919-22	Bournemouth 1927-28
Thomas Moore	Villa 1931-32	Bournemouth 1934-35
Joseph Tyrell	Villa 1953-56	Bournemouth 1957-59
Thomas Southren	Villa 1954-59	Bournemouth 1958-60
Alan O'Neill	Villa 1960-63	Bournemouth 1963-66
Tony Scott	Villa 1965-68	Bournemouth 1970-72
Brian Greenhalgh	Villa 1967-69	Bournemouth 1973-75
Tommy Mitchinson	Villa 1967-69	Bournemouth 1971-73
Dave Simmons	Bournemouth 1968-69	Villa 1968-71
Warren Aspinall	Villa 1986-88	Bournemouth 1993-95
Gareth Williams	Villa 1987-90	Bournemouth 1994-95
Shaun Teale	Bournemouth 1988-91	Villa 1991-95
Stephen Cooke	Bournemouth 2001-04	Villa 2002-03
Liam Ridgewell	Bournemouth 2002-03	Villa 2003-04

v. Bradford City

Season	League	Home Date	Result	Villa	Bradford C	Away Date	Result	Villa	Bradford C	Final Positions Villa	Bradford C
1908-09	Division 1	13 February	Lost	**1**	**3**	10 October	Drew	**1**	**1**	7th	18th
1909-10	Division 1	23 October	Won	**3**	**1**	5 March	Won	**2**	**1**	1st	7th
1910-11	Division 1	28 January	Won	**4**	**1**	24 September	Won	**2**	**1**	2nd	5th
1911-12	Division 1	30 December	Drew	**0**	**0**	2 September	Lost	**1**	**2**	6th	11th
1912-13	Division 1	7 September	Won	**3**	**1**	28 December	Drew	**1**	**1**	2nd	13th
1913-14	Division 1	27 December	Lost	**0**	**1**	6 September	Drew	**0**	**0**	2nd	9th
1914-15	Division 1	13 February	Drew	**0**	**0**	10 October	Lost	**0**	**3**	14th	11th
1919-20	Division 1	28 February	Won	**3**	**1**	17 March	Lost	**1**	**3**	9th	15th
1920-21	Division 1	26 February	Lost	**1**	**2**	7 March	Lost	**0**	**3**	10th	15th
1921-22	Division 1	12 November	Won	**7**	**1**	5 November	Lost	**2**	**3**	5th	21stR
1936-37	Division 2	14 September	Won	**5**	**1**	11 November	Drew	**2**	**2**	9th	21stR
1970-71	Division 3	5 December	Won	**1**	**0**	6 February	Lost	**0**	**1**	4th	19th
1971-72	Division 3	4 December	Won	**3**	**0**	22 April	Won	**1**	**0**	1stP	24thR
1987-88	Division 2	2 May	Won	**1**	**0**	28 November	Won	**4**	**2**	2ndP	4th
1999-00	Premiership	18 September	Won	**1**	**0**	26 February	Drew	**1**	**1**	6th	17th
2000-01	Premiership	16 September	Won	**2**	**0**	3 February	Won	**3**	**0**	8th	20thR

FA Cup

Season	Round	Home Date	Result	Villa	Bradford C	Away Date	Result	Villa	Bradford C	Division Villa	Bradford C
1932-33	Round 3	18 January	Won	**2**	**1**	14 January	Drew	**2**	**2**	Div 1	Div 2
1934-35	Round 3	12 January	Lost	**1**	**3**					Div 1	Div 2

League Cup

Season	Round	Home Date	Result	Villa	Bradford C	Away Date	Result	Villa	Bradford C	Division Villa	Bradford C
1961-62	Round 1					13 September	Won	**4**	**3**	Div 1	Div 4
1964-65	Q'ter Final	23 November	Won	**7**	**1**					Div 1	Div 4

Tall centre-forward Ian Ormondroyd was a typical Graham Taylor signing and later re-joined Bradford City a decade later.

FACT FILE

- **Bradford's last win at Villa Park came in 1935. Villa have won all seven meetings there since.**
- **Villa have seven wins and a draw from the sides' last eight matches.**
- **Bradford last finished higher than Villa in the league in 1915.**
- **In May 1988, Villa met Bradford desperately needing a win for a return to the top flight 12 months after a relegation, and David Platt's goal in a very tight game secured that win. Villa duly returned to the top flight, and have stayed there ever since.**

Summary	*P*	*W*	*D*	*L*	*F*	*A*
Villa's home league record:	16	11	2	3	35	12
Villa's away league record:	16	5	5	6	21	24
Villa's cup record:	5	3	1	1	16	10
TOTAL:	**37**	**19**	**8**	**10**	**72**	**46**

Villa's top scorers vs Bradford

Billy Walker 6

Harry Hampton, Tony Hateley 4

Joe Bache, Gordon Hodgson, Ron Wylie 3

Villa hat-tricks vs Bradford

12 Nov 1921 Billy Walker (3 pens)

14 Sep 1936 Gordon Hodgson

23 Nov 1964 Tony Hateley (4) (cup)

Played for both clubs

Willie Clarke	Villa 1901-05	Bradford 1905-09
Ernie Blackburn	Villa 1919-22	Bradford 1922-24
John Graham	Villa 1946-49	Bradford 1953-54
Ivor Powell	Villa 1948-51	Bradford 1952-55
Geoff Crudgington	Bradford 1970-71	Villa 1970-72
Trevor Hockey	Bradford 1959-62/74-76	Villa 1973-74
Bobby Campbell	Villa 1973-75	Bradford 1979-87
Gordon Cowans	Villa 1975-85/88-92/93-94	Bradford 1996-97
Dave Evans	Villa 1978-79	Bradford 1984-90
Gary Williams	Villa 1978-87	Bradford 1991-94
Noel Blake	Villa 1979-82	Bradford 1991-94
Ian Ormondroyd	Bradford 1985-89/95-97	Villa 1988-92
Bryan Small	Villa 1991-95	Bradford 1997-98
Steve Staunton	Bradford 1987-88	Villa 1991-98/2000-03
Dean Saunders	Villa 1992-95	Bradford 1999-2001
Gareth Farrelly	Villa 1995-97	Bradford 2003-04
Stan Collymore	Villa 1997-99	Bradford 2000-01
Simon Grayson	Villa 1997-99	Bradford 2001-02
Benito Carbone	Villa 1999-2000	Bradford 2000-02

v. Bradford Park Avenue

Season	League	Date	Result	Home Villa	Home Bradford PA	Date	Result	Away Villa	Away Bradford PA	Final Positions Villa	Final Positions Bradford PA
1914-15	Division 1	5 December	Lost	**1**	**2**	10 April	Drew	**2**	**2**	14th	9th
1919-20	Division 1	4 October	Won	**1**	**0**	27 September	Lost	**1**	**6**	9th	11th
1920-21	Division 1	20 November	Won	**4**	**1**	27 November	Lost	**0**	**4**	10th	22ndR
1936-37	Division 2	20 February	Won	**4**	**1**	17 October	Drew	**3**	**3**	9th	20th
1937-38	Division 2	27 April	Won	**2**	**0**	27 December	Won	**2**	**1**	1stP	7th

FA Cup

						Division	
1912-13	Round 4	8 March	Won	**5**	**0**	Div 1	Div 2

Summary	*P*	*W*	*D*	*L*	*F*	*A*
Villa's home league record:	5	4	0	1	12	4
Villa's away league record:	5	1	2	2	8	16
Villa's cup record:	1	1	0	0	5	0
TOTAL:	**11**	**6**	**2**	**3**	**25**	**20**

FACT FILE

- **Bradford Park Avenue last won at Villa Park in 1914, and they are somewhat unlikely to change that any time soon.**

Villa's top scorers vs Park Avenue

Clem Stephenson 5

Frank Broome 4

Harry Hampton, Eric Houghton 3

Villa hat-tricks vs Park Avenue

8 Mar 1913 Harry Hampton (cup)

Played for both clubs

George Reeves	Villa 1907-09	Bradford PA 1909-13
Billy Dinsdale	Villa 1924-26	Bradford PA 1928-30
Ken Tewkesbury	Villa 1932-33	Bradford PA 1935-36
Alec Talbot	Villa 1923-35	Bradford PA 1935-36

v. Brentford

Season	League	Date	Result	Home Villa	Home Brentford	Date	Result	Away Villa	Away Brentford	Final Positions Villa	Final Positions Brentford
1935-36	Division 1	25 January	Drew	**2**	**2**	21 September	Won	**2**	**1**	21stR	5th
1938-39	Division 1	17 September	Won	**5**	**0**	8 February	Won	**4**	**2**	12th	18th
1946-47	Division 1	28 September	Won	**5**	**2**	1 February	Won	**2**	**0**	8th	21stR

FA Cup

Season	Round	Date	Result	Home Villa	Home Brentford	Date	Result	Away Villa	Away Brentford	Division Villa	Division Brentford
1952-53	Round 4	31 January	Drew	**0**	**0**	4 February	Won	**2**	**1**	Div 1	Div 2

Summary	*P*	*W*	*D*	*L*	*F*	*A*
Villa's home league record:	3	2	1	0	12	4
Villa's away league record:	3	3	0	0	8	3
Villa's cup record:	2	1	1	0	2	1
TOTAL:	**8**	**6**	**2**	**0**	**22**	**8**

FACT FILE

- **Brentford have played more games without victory against Villa than anyone else.**

Villa's top scorers vs Brentford

Jackie Martin 3

Dai Astley, Frank Broome, Albert Kerr, William Goffin, Trevor Ford 2

Played for both clubs

Reg Boyne	Villa 1913-15	Brentford 1920-21
Edmund Wright	Villa 1920-21	Brentford 1922-23
Billy Cook	Villa 1926-29	Brentford 1931-32
Frank Broome	Villa 1934-47	Brentford 1953-54
Leslie Smith	Brentford 1936-39/52-53	Villa 1946-52
Peter Broadbent	Brentford 1950-51	Villa 1966-69
Dave Simmons	Villa 1968-71	Brentford 1973-76
Terry Bullivant	Villa 1979-82	Brentford 1983-86
David Geddis	Villa 1979-83	Brentford 1986-87
Warren Aspinall	Villa 1986-88	Brentford 1997-99
Paul Mortimer	Villa 1991-92	Brentford 1992-93
Paul Merson	Brentford 1986-87	Villa 1998-2002

v. Brighton & Hove Albion

		Home						Away		Final Positions	
Season	*League*	*Date*	*Result*	Villa	B&HA	*Date*	*Result*	Villa	B&HA	Villa	B&HA
1959-60	Division 2	19 December	Won	**3**	**1**	22 August	Won	**2**	**1**	1stP	14th
1970-71	Division 3	3 October	Drew	**0**	**0**	9 April	Lost	**0**	**1**	4th	14th
1971-72	Division 3	11 September	Won	**2**	**0**	25 March	Lost	**1**	**2**	1stP	2ndP
1972-73	Division 2	2 September	Drew	**1**	**1**	20 January	Won	**3**	**1**	3rd	22ndR
1979-80	Division 1	22 August	Won	**2**	**1**	3 March	Drew	**1**	**1**	7th	16th
1980-81	Division 1	22 October	Won	**4**	**1**	20 December	Lost	**0**	**1**	1st	19th
1981-82	Division 1	12 April	Won	**3**	**0**	28 December	Won	**1**	**0**	11th	13th
1982-83	Division 1	13 November	Won	**1**	**0**	26 March	Drew	**0**	**0**	6th	22ndR

FA Cup										*Division*	
1954-55	Round 3	10 January	Won	**4**	**2**	8 January	Drew	**2**	**2**	Div 1	Div 3S

Summary	*P*	*W*	*D*	*L*	*F*	*A*
Villa's home league record:	8	6	2	0	16	4
Villa's away league record:	8	3	2	3	8	7
Villa's cup record:	2	1	1	0	6	4
TOTAL:	**18**	**10**	**5**	**3**	**30**	**15**

FACT FILE

- **Brighton have played more league games without victory at Villa Park than anyone else.**

Before moving to Brighton, Dennis Mortimer appeared in 404 senior games for the club, scoring 36 goals.

Villa's top scorers vs Brighton

Tommy Thompson, Allan Evans 3

Played for both clubs

Jack Thompson	Villa 1919-21	Brighton 1921-24
Percy Varco	Villa 1923-25	Brighton 1932-33
Ronald Guttridge	Villa 1946-48	Brighton 1948-50
Stanley Crowther	Villa 1956-58	Brighton 1960-61
Geoff Sidebottom	Villa 1960-65	Brighton 1968-71
John Phillips	Villa 1969-70	Brighton 1980-81
Tommy Hughes	Villa 1971-72	Brighton 1972-73
Sammy Morgan	Villa 1973-76	Brighton 1975-77
Graham Moseley	Villa 1974-75	Brighton 1977-86
Dennis Mortimer	Villa 1975-85	Brighton 1985-86
John Gregory	Villa 1977-79	Brighton 1979-81
Mark Jones	Villa 1981-84	Brighton 1983-85
Alan Curbishley	Villa 1982-85	Brighton 1987-90
Steve Foster	Brighton 1979-84/92-96	Villa 1983-85
Warren Aspinall	Villa 1986-88	Brighton 1999-2001
Martin Keown	Brighton 1984-86	Villa 1986-89
Bernard Gallacher	Villa 1986-91	Brighton 1991-93
Dean Saunders	Brighton 1985-87	Villa 1992-95
Phil King	Villa 1994-95	Brighton 1998-99

Future manager John Gregory, a signing from Northampton, featured in 72 games for Villa before transferring to Brighton in 1979. Here are Aston Villa with the Football League Cup which they won in 1977. Back row (left to right): Charlie Young, Jake Findlay, John Burridge, Nigel Spink, Allan Evans, Ivor Linton. Middle row: Roy MacLaren (first-team coach), David Evans, Michael Buttress, John Gregory, Andy Gray, Gordon Smith, David Hughes, Gordon Cowans, Peter Downs (physiotherapist). Front row: John Deehan, Alex Cropley, Leighton Phillips, John Gidman, Ron Saunders (manager), John Robson, Brian Little, Dennis Mortimer, Frank Carrodus.

v. Bristol City

Season	League	Date	Result	Home Villa	Home Bristol C	Date	Result	Away Villa	Away Bristol C	Final Positions Villa	Final Positions Bristol C
1906-07	Division 1	1 December	Won	3	2	6 April	Won	4	2	5th	2nd
1907-08	Division 1	26 October	Drew	4	4	11 March	Drew	2	2	2nd	10th
1908-09	Division 1	28 November	Drew	1	1	3 April	Drew	0	0	7th	8th
1909-10	Division 1	6 November	Won	1	0	19 March	Drew	0	0	1st	16th
1910-11	Division 1	11 March	Won	2	0	5 November	Won	2	1	2nd	19thR
1959-60	Division 2	9 April	Won	2	1	21 November	Won	5	0	1stP	22ndR
1967-68	Division 2	4 May	Lost	2	4	27 February	Drew	0	0	16th	19th
1968-69	Division 2	26 August	Won	1	0	8 October	Lost	0	1	18th	16th
1969-70	Division 2	21 February	Lost	0	2	8 November	Lost	0	1	21stR	14th
1972-73	Division 2	14 April	Won	1	0	27 March	Lost	0	3	3rd	5th
1973-74	Division 2	20 October	Drew	2	2	16 March	Won	1	0	14th	16th
1974-75	Division 2	11 January	Won	2	0	7 December	Lost	0	1	2ndP	5th
1976-77	Division 1	23 October	Won	3	1	2 April	Drew	0	0	4th	18th
1977-78	Division 1	28 January	Won	1	0	3 September	Drew	1	1	8th	17th
1978-79	Division 1	18 November	Won	2	0	26 August	Lost	0	1	8th	13th
1979-80	Division 1	25 August	Lost	0	2	29 December	Won	3	1	7th	20thR

FA Cup										Division	
1899-00	Round 2					10 February	Won	5	1	Div 1	Non L
1920-21	Round 1	8 January	Won	2	0					Div 1	Div 2
1956-57	Round 5	16 February	Won	2	1					Div 1	Div 2
1962-63	Round 3	7 March	Won	3	2	16 January	Drew	1	1	Div 1	Div 3
1981-82	Round 4					23 January	Won	1	0	Div 1	Div 3

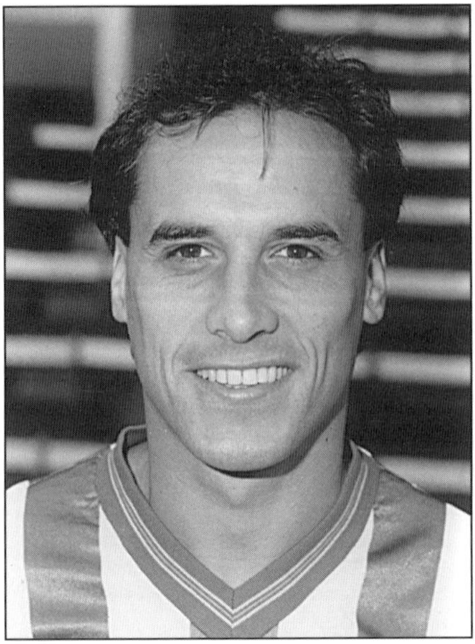

Signed from Walsall, Gary Shelton eventually found his way to Bristol City after he left Aston Villa in 1982 for Sheffield Wednesday.

Summary	P	W	D	L	F	A
Villa's home league record:	16	10	3	3	27	19
Villa's away league record:	16	5	6	5	18	14
Villa's cup record:	6	5	1	0	14	5
TOTAL:	**38**	**10**	**10**	**8**	**59**	**38**

FACT FILE

- **Villa were unbeaten in their first 18 games against Bristol City.**
- **Following that win at Villa Park, things turned round in the series for City, and Villa were only able to score twice in their next nine away games in the series.**

Villa's top scorers vs Bristol City

Harry Hampton 7
Joe Bache 5
Jack Devey, Gary Shaw 4
Gerry Hitchens, Brian Little 3

Villa hat-tricks vs Bristol City

10 Feb 1900 Jack Devey (4) (cup)
6 Apr 1907 Harry Hampton
21 Nov 1959 Gerry Hitchens
29 Dec 1979 Gary Shaw

Played for both clubs

Walter Leigh	Villa 1898-99	Bristol C 1902-03
Alf Gibson	Villa 1900-01	Bristol C 1903-05
Bertie Banks	Villa 1901-02	Bristol C 1901-03
Albert Fisher	Villa 1902-03	Bristol C 1903-05
Fred Chapple	Villa 1906-08	Bristol C 1913-15
Alec Logan	Villa 1906-09	Bristol C 1910-12
John Kearns	Villa 1908-12	Bristol C 1912-15
Arthur Moss	Villa 1909-12	Bristol C 1912-15
Walter Harris	Villa 1924-28	Bristol C 1929-30
Bob Wilson	Villa 1963-64	Bristol C 1969-70
Gary Shelton	Villa 1978-82	Bristol C 1989-94
Paul Mortimer	Villa 1991-92	Bristol C 1999-2000
Scott Murray	Villa 1995-97	Bristol C 1997-2004

v. Bristol Rovers

		Home					Away			Final Positions	
Season	*League*	*Date*	*Result*	Villa	Bristol R	*Date*	*Result*	Villa	Bristol R	Villa	Bristol R
1959-60	Division 2	16 January	Won	**4**	**1**	5 September	Drew	**1**	**1**	1stP	9th
1970-71	Division 3	30 September	Drew	**1**	**1**	9 January	Won	**2**	**1**	4th	6th
1971-72	Division 3	3 April	Won	**2**	**1**	2 October	Won	**1**	**0**	1stP	6th
1974-75	Division 2	26 December	Won	**1**	**0**	14 September	Lost	**0**	**2**	2ndP	19th

FA Cup

										Division	
1960-61	Round 3	9 January	Won	**4**	**0**	7 January	Drew	**1**	**1**	Div 1	Div 2
1979-80	Round 3					4 January	Won	**2**	**1**	Div 1	Div 2
1992-93	Round 3	2 January	Drew	**1**	**1**	20 January	Won	**3**	**0**	Prem	Div 1

League Cup

1970-71	Q'ter Final	25 November	Won	**1**	**0**	17 November	Drew	**1**	**1**	Div 3	Div 3

Summary	*P*	*W*	*D*	*L*	*F*	*A*
Villa's home league record:	4	3	1	0	8	3
Villa's away league record:	4	2	1	1	4	4
Villa's cup record:	7	4	3	0	13	4
TOTAL:	**15**	**9**	**5**	**1**	**25**	**11**

FACT FILE

- **It took Rovers 11 attempts to beat Aston Villa.**

Villa's top scorers vs Bristol Rovers

Bobby Thomson 5

Gerry Hitchens, Andy Lochhead 3

Played for both clubs

Ronnie Dix	Bristol R 1927-32	Villa 1932-37
Oliver Tidman	Villa 1932-33	Bristol R 1936-37
Brian Godfrey	Villa 1967-71	Bristol R 1971-73
Ray Graydon	Bristol R 1965-71	Villa 1971-77
Mark Walters	Villa 1981-88	Bristol R 1999-2002
Gary Penrice	Bristol R 1984-90/97-2000	Villa 1990-92

v. Burnley

		Home					Away			Final Positions	
Season	League	Date	Result	Villa	Burnley	Date	Result	Villa	Burnley	Villa	Burnley
1888-89	Division 1	22 December	Won	**4**	**2**	5 January	Lost	**0**	**4**	2nd	9th
1889-90	Division 1	27 September	Drew	**2**	**2**	5 October	Won	**6**	**2**	8th	11th
1890-91	Division 1	8 November	Drew	**4**	**4**	20 September	Lost	**1**	**2**	9th	8th
1891-92	Division 1	5 December	Won	**6**	**1**	17 October	Lost	**1**	**4**	4th	7th
1892-93	Division 1	4 April	Lost	**1**	**3**	5 September	Won	**2**	**0**	4th	6th
1893-94	Division 1	28 October	Won	**4**	**0**	7 April	Won	**6**	**3**	1st	5th
1894-95	Division 1	6 April	Won	**5**	**0**	23 February	Drew	**3**	**3**	3rd	9th
1895-96	Division 1	2 November	Won	**5**	**1**	23 November	Won	**4**	**3**	1st	10th
1896-97	Division 1	2 January	Lost	**0**	**3**	8 February	Won	**4**	**3**	1st	16thR
1898-99	Division 1	14 January	Won	**4**	**0**	17 September	Won	**4**	**2**	1st	3rd
1899-00	Division 1	25 November	Won	**2**	**0**	31 March	Won	**2**	**1**	1st	17thR
1913-14	Division 1	21 March	Won	**1**	**0**	15 November	Lost	**0**	**4**	2nd	12th
1914-15	Division 1	17 October	Drew	**3**	**3**	22 February	Lost	**1**	**2**	14th	4th
1919-20	Division 1	3 January	Drew	**2**	**2**	17 January	Drew	**0**	**0**	9th	2nd
1920-21	Division 1	9 February	Drew	**0**	**0**	5 February	Lost	**1**	**7**	10th	1st
1921-22	Division 1	14 January	Won	**2**	**0**	31 December	Lost	**1**	**2**	5th	3rd
1922-23	Division 1	26 December	Won	**3**	**1**	25 December	Drew	**1**	**1**	6th	15th
1923-24	Division 1	13 October	Drew	**1**	**1**	6 October	Won	**2**	**1**	6th	17th
1924-25	Division 1	20 December	Won	**3**	**0**	25 April	Drew	**1**	**1**	15th	19th
1925-26	Division 1	29 August	Won	**10**	**0**	2 January	Won	**3**	**2**	6th	20th
1926-27	Division 1	4 September	Drew	**1**	**1**	22 January	Lost	**3**	**6**	10th	5th
1927-28	Division 1	8 February	Won	**3**	**1**	17 September	Lost	**2**	**4**	8th	19th
1928-29	Division 1	2 February	Won	**4**	**2**	22 September	Lost	**1**	**4**	3rd	19th
1929-30	Division 1	5 February	Lost	**1**	**2**	21 September	Won	**4**	**1**	4th	21stR
1936-37	Division 2	9 January	Drew	**0**	**0**	12 September	Won	**2**	**1**	9th	13th
1937-38	Division 2	13 November	Drew	**0**	**0**	5 April	Lost	**0**	**3**	1stP	6th
1947-48	Division 1	29 November	Drew	**2**	**2**	17 April	Lost	**0**	**1**	6th	3rd
1948-49	Division 1	6 November	Won	**3**	**1**	2 April	Drew	**1**	**1**	10th	15th
1949-50	Division 1	25 March	Lost	**0**	**1**	5 November	Lost	**0**	**1**	12th	10th
1950-51	Division 1	17 March	Won	**3**	**2**	28 October	Lost	**0**	**2**	15th	10th
1951-52	Division 1	22 March	Won	**4**	**1**	3 November	Lost	**1**	**2**	6th	14th
1952-53	Division 1	4 April	Won	**2**	**0**	15 November	Lost	**0**	**1**	11th	6th
1953-54	Division 1	10 April	Won	**5**	**1**	21 November	Lost	**2**	**3**	13th	7th
1954-55	Division 1	2 April	Won	**3**	**1**	13 November	Lost	**0**	**2**	6th	10th
1955-56	Division 1	19 March	Won	**2**	**0**	5 November	Lost	**0**	**2**	20th	7th
1956-57	Division 1	10 November	Won	**1**	**0**	15 April	Lost	**1**	**2**	10th	7th
1957-58	Division 1	8 March	Won	**3**	**0**	26 October	Lost	**0**	**3**	14th	6th
1958-59	Division 1	18 April	Drew	**0**	**0**	29 November	Lost	**1**	**3**	21stR	7th
1960-61	Division 1	5 November	Won	**2**	**0**	25 March	Drew	**1**	**1**	9th	4th
1961-62	Division 1	24 March	Lost	**0**	**2**	4 November	Lost	**0**	**3**	7th	2nd
1962-63	Division 1	17 November	Won	**2**	**1**	6 April	Lost	**1**	**3**	15th	3rd
1963-64	Division 1	4 April	Won	**2**	**0**	23 November	Lost	**0**	**2**	19th	9th
1964-65	Division 1	28 November	Won	**1**	**0**	10 April	Drew	**2**	**2**	16th	12th
1965-66	Division 1	16 April	Won	**2**	**1**	20 November	Lost	**1**	**3**	16th	3rd

			Home					Away		Final Positions	
Season	League	Date	Result	Villa	Burnley	Date	Result	Villa	Burnley	Villa	Burnley
1966-67	Division 1	22 April	Lost	**0**	**1**	26 November	Lost	**2**	**4**	21stR	14th
1972-73	Division 2	6 January	Lost	**0**	**3**	26 August	Lost	**1**	**4**	3rd	1stP
1975-76	Division 1	25 October	Drew	**1**	**1**	28 February	Drew	**2**	**2**	16th	21stR

FA Cup										Division	
1906-07	Round 1					12 January	Won	**3**	**1**	Div 1	Div 2
1923-24	Semi-Final	29 March		Bramall Lane			Won	**3**	**0**	Div 1	Div 1
1927-28	Round 3					14 January	Won	**2**	**0**	Div 1	Div 1
1936-37	Round 3	16 January	Lost	**2**	**3**					Div 2	Div 2
1946-47	Round 3					11 January	Lost	**1**	**5**	Div 1	Div 2
1950-51	Round 3	6 January	Won	**2**	**0**					Div 1	Div 1
1956-57	Q'ter Final	6 March	Won	**2**	**0**	2 March	Drew	**1**	**1**	Div 1	Div 1
1958-59	Q'ter Final	28 February	Drew	**0**	**0**	3 March	Won	**2**	**0**	Div 1	Div 1
1973-74	Round 5					16 February	Lost	**0**	**1**	Div 2	Div 1

League Cup											
1960-61	Semi-Final	26 April	Drew*	**2**	**2**	10 April	Drew	**1**	**1**	Div 1	Div 1
		2 May		Old Trafford (replay)			Won	**2**	**1**		
1970-71	Round 2	9 September	Won	**2**	**0**					Div 3	Div 1

Summary	*P*	*W*	*D*	*L*	*F*	*A*
Villa's home league record:	47	28	12	7	109	47
Villa's away league record:	47	11	8	28	71	113
Villa's cup record:	15	8	4	3	25	15
TOTAL:	**109**	**47**	**24**	**38**	**105**	**175**

In 1925 the offside law was changed so that only two, not three, opponents were required to be between a forward and the goal to play the forward onside. The effect saw a landslide of goals as defenders came to terms with the new law, nowhere more so than at Villa Park on the opening day of the season when Aston Villa hit 10 goals past Burnley without reply. Here Billy Walker, who scored a hat-trick, nets Villa's eighth goal. Len Capewell top-scored with five.

FACT FILE

- **Before the start of the 1925-26 season, the powers that be instigated probably the most dramatic change to the rules of football in the last 100 years. They changed the offside rule so that only two, as opposed to three, defenders were needed between an attacker and the goal-line for him to be onside. It was therefore expected that the new season would see more goals being scored, but nowhere was the change better exploited than at Villa Park, where the home side scored 10 times without reply.**
- **In an extraordinary run from 1950 to 1958, 17 successive league games were won by the home side, nine by Burnley and eight by Villa.**
- **Villa have not won a league match at Turf Moor since 1936, since when they have tried and failed 22 times, although they won an FA Cup match there in 1959.**
- **From 1951 to 1956, Villa lost once in 19 home games against Burnley.**

Villa's top scorers vs Burnley

Jack Devey 13
Len Capewell 12
Charlie Athersmith, Dicky York 10
Billy Walker 9
Peter McParland 8
Gerry Hitchens, Denny Hodgetts 7

Villa hat-tricks vs Burnley

5 Oct 1889 Albert Allen
5 Dec 1891 Jack Devey
2 Nov 1895 Charlie Athersmith
8 Feb 1897 Jack Devey
26 Dec 1922 Dicky York
29 Aug 1925 Billy Walker
29 Aug 1925 Len Capewell (5)
2 Feb 1929 Pongo Waring

Played for both clubs

Jimmy Crabtree	Burnley 1889-90/92-95	Villa 1895-1902
Charlie McEleny	Burnley 1895-96	Villa 1899-1900
Alex Leake	Villa 1902-08	Burnley 1907-10
George Brown	Villa 1929-35	Burnley 1934-36
Bob Brocklebank	Villa 1929-36	Burnley 1935-40
Arthur Cunliffe	Villa 1932-36	Burnley 1937-38
Tommy Gardner	Villa 1933-38	Burnley 1938-40
James Clayton	Villa 1937-39	Burnley 1938-40
Doug Winston	Burnley 1951-59	Villa 1958-61
Andy Lochhead	Burnley 1960-69	Villa 1969-73
Gordon Cowans	Villa 1975-85/88-92/93-94	Burnley 1997-98
Terry Donovan	Villa 1979-82	Burnley 1982-84
Tony Morley	Burnley 1975-79/88-89	Villa 1979-84
Adrian Heath	Villa 1989-90	Burnley 1992-97
Gareth Farrelly	Villa 1995-97	Burnley 2003-04

v. Bury

		Home					Away				Final Positions	
Season	League	Date	Result	Villa	Bury	Date	Result	Villa	Bury		Villa	Bury
1895-96	Division 1	28 December	Won	**2**	**0**	21 March	Lost	**3**	**5**		1st	11th
1896-97	Division 1	7 November	Drew	**1**	**1**	6 February	Won	**2**	**0**		1st	9th
1897-98	Division 1	18 September	Won	**3**	**1**	12 March	Won	**2**	**1**		6th	14th
1898-99	Division 1	7 January	Won	**3**	**2**	10 September	Lost	**1**	**2**		1st	10th
1899-00	Division 1	7 October	Won	**2**	**1**	1 January	Lost	**0**	**2**		1st	12th
1900-01	Division 1	10 September	Won	**1**	**0**	8 December	Lost	**1**	**3**		15th	5th
1901-02	Division 1	4 January	Won	**2**	**0**	7 September	Drew	**0**	**0**		8th	7th
1902-03	Division 1	20 September	Drew	**2**	**2**	17 January	Won	**1**	**0**		2nd	8th
1903-04	Division 1	2 April	Lost	**0**	**2**	5 December	Drew	**2**	**2**		5th	12th
1904-05	Division 1	24 December	Won	**2**	**0**	22 April	Won	**3**	**2**		4th	17th
1905-06	Division 1	3 March	Drew	**3**	**3**	28 October	Won	**1**	**0**		8th	17th
1906-07	Division 1	13 October	Won	**3**	**1**	16 February	Won	**3**	**0**		5th	16th
1907-08	Division 1	23 November	Drew	**2**	**2**	21 March	Lost	**1**	**2**		2nd	7th
1908-09	Division 1	26 December	Won	**3**	**0**	1 January	Won	**2**	**1**		7th	17th
1909-10	Division 1	26 March	Won	**4**	**1**	13 November	Won	**2**	**0**		1st	13th
1910-11	Division 1	26 December	Won	**4**	**1**	2 January	Lost	**0**	**1**		2nd	18th
1911-12	Division 1	2 March	Won	**5**	**2**	28 October	Drew	**1**	**1**		6th	20thR

Aston Villa, FA Cup winners 1895. Standing (left to right): J. Grierson (trainer), J. Dunkley (director), Jack Reynolds, C. Johnstone (director), Howard Spencer, John Devey, Tom Wilkes, J.T. Lees (director), Jimmy Welford, unknown, unknown. Front row: G.B. Ramsay (secretary), Charlie Athersmith, Bob Chatt, James Cowan, George Russell, Dennis Hodgetts, Steve Smith.

		Home				Away				Final Positions	
Season	League	Date	Result	Villa	Bury	Date	Result	Villa	Bury	Villa	Bury
1924-25	Division 1	1 September	Drew	**3**	**3**	8 September	Lost	**3**	**4**	15th	5th
1925-26	Division 1	6 March	Drew	**1**	**1**	24 October	Won	**3**	**2**	6th	4th
1926-27	Division 1	18 September	Lost	**1**	**2**	5 February	Won	**1**	**0**	10th	19th
1927-28	Division 1	24 September	Won	**1**	**0**	4 February	Drew	**0**	**0**	8th	5th
1928-29	Division 1	13 October	Won	**7**	**1**	23 February	Drew	**2**	**2**	3rd	21stR
1936-37	Division 2	3 April	Lost	**0**	**4**	28 November	Lost	**1**	**2**	9th	3rd
1937-38	Division 2	19 March	Won	**2**	**1**	6 November	Drew	**1**	**1**	1stP	10th
1968-69	Division 2	15 February	Won	**1**	**0**	30 November	Lost	**2**	**3**	18th	21stR
1970-71	Division 3	11 November	Won	**1**	**0**	20 February	Lost	**1**	**3**	4th	22ndR

FA Cup										Division	
1902-03	Semi-Final	21 March				Goodison Park	Lost	**0**	**3**	Div 1	Div 1
1904-05	Round 2	18 February	Won	**3**	**2**					Div 1	Div 1

Summary	*P*	*W*	*D*	*L*	*F*	*A*
Villa's home league record:	26	17	6	3	59	31
Villa's away league record:	26	10	6	10	39	39
Villa's cup record:	2	1	0	1	3	5
TOTAL:	**54**	**28**	**12**	**14**	**101**	**75**

FACT FILE

- **Villa lost only once in their first 20 home games against Bury.**

Villa's top scorers vs Bury

Harry Hampton 17
Joe Bache 9
Dicky York 8
Jack Devey, Johnny Campbell 5

Villa hat-tricks vs Bury

26 Dec 1908 George Travers
26 Mar 1910 Harry Hampton
2 Mar 1912 Harry Hampton (4)
24 Oct 1925 Dicky York
13 Oct 1928 Dicky York

Played for both clubs

Jasper McLuckie	Bury 1898-1902	Villa 1901-04
Alex Massie	Bury 1926-28	Villa 1935-40
Norman Lockhart	Villa 1952-56	Bury 1956-58
David Hickson	Villa 1955-56	Bury 1961-62
Frank Carrodus	Villa 1974-79	Bury 1983-84
Andy Gray	Villa 1987-89	Bury 1997-98
Bryan Small	Villa 1991-95	Bury 1997-98

v. Cambridge United

FA Cup		Home Date	Result	Villa	Cambridge	Away Date	Result	Villa	Cambridge	Division Villa	Division Cambridge
1979-80	Round 4	30 January	Won	**4**	**1**	26 January	Drew	**1**	**1**	Div 1	Div 2

League Cup		Home Date	Result	Villa	Cambridge	Away Date	Result	Villa	Cambridge	Division Villa	Division Cambridge
1980-81	Round 3					23 September	Lost	**1**	**2**	Div 1	Div 2

Summary	*P*	*W*	*D*	*L*	*F*	*A*
Villa's cup record:	3	1	1	1	6	4
TOTAL:	**3**	**1**	**1**	**1**	**6**	**4**

Villa's top scorers vs Cambridge

Terry Donovan 3

Played for both clubs

Brian Greenhalgh	Villa 1967-69	Cambridge 1971-74
Mike Ferguson	Villa 1968-70	Cambridge 1973-74
Dave Simmons	Villa 1968-71	Cambridge 1972-74/75-76
Sammy Morgan	Villa 1973-76	Cambridge 1977-78
Ray Walker	Villa 1982-86	Cambridge 1994-95
Richard Walker	Villa 1997-2000	Cambridge 1998-99
Darren Byfield	Villa 1997-98	Cambridge 1999-2000
Dion Dublin	Cambridge 1988-92	Villa 1998-2004

v. Cardiff City

Season	League	Date	Result	Home Villa	Home Cardiff	Date	Result	Away Villa	Away Cardiff	Final Positions Villa	Final Positions Cardiff
1921-22	Division 1	29 August	Won	**2**	**1**	5 September	Won	**4**	**0**	5th	4th
1922-23	Division 1	4 September	Lost	**1**	**3**	28 August	Lost	**0**	**3**	6th	9th
1923-24	Division 1	29 December	Won	**2**	**1**	5 January	Won	**2**	**0**	6th	2nd
1924-25	Division 1	6 December	Lost	**1**	**2**	11 April	Lost	**1**	**2**	15th	11th
1925-26	Division 1	31 October	Lost	**0**	**2**	13 March	Lost	**0**	**2**	6th	16th
1926-27	Division 1	31 January	Drew	**0**	**0**	11 September	Won	**3**	**2**	10th	14th
1927-28	Division 1	14 April	Won	**3**	**1**	3 December	Lost	**1**	**2**	8th	6th
1928-29	Division 1	29 September	Won	**1**	**0**	9 February	Won	**2**	**0**	3rd	22ndR
1952-53	Division 1	29 April	Won	**2**	**0**	25 April	Won	**2**	**1**	11th	12th
1953-54	Division 1	19 December	Lost	**1**	**2**	22 August	Lost	**1**	**2**	13th	10th
1954-55	Division 1	4 December	Lost	**0**	**2**	9 April	Won	**1**	**0**	6th	20th
1955-56	Division 1	27 August	Won	**2**	**0**	24 December	Lost	**0**	**1**	20th	17th
1956-57	Division 1	13 March	Won	**4**	**1**	3 April	Lost	**0**	**1**	10th	21stR
1959-60	Division 2	12 December	Won	**2**	**0**	16 April	Lost	**0**	**1**	9th	2ndP
1960-61	Division 1	12 September	Won	**2**	**1**	7 September	Drew	**1**	**1**	7th	15th
1961-62	Division 1	1 May	Drew	**2**	**2**	26 December	Lost	**0**	**1**	15th	21stR
1967-68	Division 2	30 December	Won	**2**	**1**	26 December	Lost	**0**	**3**	16th	13th
1968-69	Division 2	26 December	Won	**2**	**0**	5 October	Drew	**1**	**1**	18th	5th
1969-70	Division 2	7 February	Drew	**1**	**1**	11 October	Lost	**0**	**4**	21stR	7th
1972-73	Division 2	27 January	Won	**2**	**0**	9 September	Won	**2**	**0**	3rd	20th
1973-74	Division 2	6 October	Won	**5**	**0**	23 February	Won	**1**	**0**	14th	17th
1974-75	Division 2	9 April	Won	**2**	**0**	28 December	Lost	**1**	**3**	2ndP	21stR

Willie Anderson joined Villa in January 1967, for £20,000 from Manchester United. After 45 goals in 266 appearances he was transferred to Cardiff City in the 1972 close season.

FA Cup		Home Date	Result	Villa	Cardiff	Away Date	Result	Villa	Cardiff	Final Positions Villa	Cardiff
1926-27	Round 3					8 January	Lost	**1**	**2**	Div 1	Div 1
1928-29	Round 3	12 January	Won	**6**	**1**					Div 1	Div 1
1948-49	Round 4	29 January	Lost	**1**	**2**					Div 1	Div 2

Summary	*P*	*W*	*D*	*L*	*F*	*A*
Villa's home league record:	22	14	3	5	39	20
Villa's away league record:	22	8	2	12	23	30
Villa's cup record:	3	1	0	2	8	5
TOTAL:	**47**	**23**	**5**	**19**	**70**	**55**

FACT FILE

- **Villa are unbeaten in their last 11 home games against Cardiff, since losing in 1954.**
- **The sides have not played a goalless match since 1927, although admittedly they've not played a match since 1975.**

Villa's top scorers vs Cardiff

Bruce Rioch 5

Dicky York, Joe Beresford, Johnny Dixon 4

Played for both clubs

Joe Nicholson	Cardiff 1924-26	Villa 1926-27
Arthur Layton	Villa 1908-11	Cardiff 1920-21
Harry Nash	Villa 1914-20	Cardiff 1920-23
George Blackburn	Villa 1920-26	Cardiff 1926-31
Frank Moss Sr	Villa 1914-29	Cardiff 1928-29
Trevor Ford	Villa 1946-51	Cardiff 1953-57
Gerry Hitchens	Cardiff 1954-58	Villa 1957-61
Bob Wilson	Villa 1963-64	Cardiff 1964-68
Willie Anderson	Villa 1966-73	Cardiff 1972-77
Barry Hole	Cardiff 1959-66	Villa 1968-70
Graham Moseley	Villa 1974-75	Cardiff 1986-88
Leighton Phillips	Cardiff 1967-75	Villa 1974-79
Pat Heard	Villa 1979-83	Cardiff 1990-92
Garry Thompson	Villa 1986-89	Cardiff 1993-95
Dean Saunders	Cardiff 1984-85	Villa 1992-95
David Hughes	Villa 1996-97	Cardiff 2000-02
Mark Delaney	Cardiff 1998-99	Villa 1998-2004

v. Carlisle United

Season	League	Home Date	Home Result	Villa	Carlisle	Away Date	Away Result	Villa	Carlisle	Final Positions Villa	Final Positions Carlisle
1967-68	Division 2	4 November	Won	**1**	**0**	30 March	Won	**2**	**1**	16th	10th
1968-69	Division 2	26 October	Drew	**0**	**0**	28 December	Won	**1**	**0**	18th	12th
1969-70	Division 2	12 November	Won	**1**	**0**	19 August	Drew	**1**	**1**	21stR	12th
1972-73	Division 2	29 August	Won	**1**	**0**	28 April	Drew	**2**	**2**	3rd	18th
1973-74	Division 2	13 March	Won	**2**	**1**	27 April	Lost	**0**	**2**	14th	3rdP

League Cup

Season	Round	Date	Result	Villa	Carlisle	Division Villa	Division Carlisle
1970-71	Round 4	28 October	Won	**1**	**0**	Div 3	Div 2

Summary	*P*	*W*	*D*	*L*	*F*	*A*
Villa's home league record:	5	4	1	0	5	1
Villa's away league record:	5	2	2	1	6	6
Villa's cup record:	1	1	0	0	1	0
TOTAL:	**11**	**7**	**3**	**1**	**12**	**7**

FACT FILE

- **The most recent match between the sides is also the only one Carlisle have won.**

Villa's top scorers vs Carlisle

Ian Hamilton 3

David Rudge 2

Played for both clubs

Brian Tiler	Villa 1968-73	Carlisle 1972-74
Tommy Craig	Villa 1977-79	Carlisle 1981-85
Mervyn Day	Villa 1983-85	Carlisle 1993-94
Warren Aspinall	Villa 1986-88	Carlisle 1994-98
Derek Mountfield	Villa 1988-92	Carlisle 1994-95
Dariusz Kubicki	Villa 1991-94	Carlisle 1998-99
Shaun Teale	Villa 1991-95	Carlisle 1999-2000
David Hughes	Villa 1996-97	Carlisle 1997-98

v. Casuals

FA Cup		Date	Result	Home Villa	Casuals	Division Villa	Casuals
1890-91	Round 1	17 January	Won	**13**	**1**	Div 1	Non L

Summary	P	W	D	L	F	A
Villa's cup record:	1	1	0	0	13	1
TOTAL:	**1**	**1**	**0**	**0**	**13**	**1**

FACT FILE

- **The Casuals were a London-based side who never won a match in the FA Cup proper. They have since merged with the Corinthians.**

Villa's top scorers vs Casuals

Denny Hodgetts 4

Lewis Campbell 3

Villa hat-tricks vs Casuals

17 Jan 1891 Lewis Campbell (cup)

17 Jan 1891 Denny Hodgetts (4) (cup)

Aston Villa, 1891. Standing (left to right): George Campbell, unknown, Billy Dickson, Albert Hinchley, John Baird, Charlie Hare, Bob Oxenbould (trainer), Walter Evans, G.B. Ramsay (secretary). Seated: James Cowan, Charlie Athersmith, James Brown, John Devey, Dennis Hodgetts, Lewis Campbell.

v. Charlton Athletic

Season	League	Home Date	Home Result	Home Villa	Home Charlton	Away Date	Away Result	Away Villa	Away Charlton	Final Positions Villa	Final Positions Charlton
1938-39	Division 1	3 December	Won	**2**	**0**	8 April	Lost	**0**	**1**	12th	3rd
1946-47	Division 1	19 October	Won	**4**	**0**	22 February	Drew	**1**	**1**	8th	19th
1947-48	Division 1	30 March	Won	**2**	**1**	26 March	Drew	**1**	**1**	6th	13th
1948-49	Division 1	23 October	Won	**4**	**3**	16 April	Won	**2**	**0**	10th	9th
1949-50	Division 1	11 April	Drew	**1**	**1**	7 April	Won	**4**	**1**	12th	20th
1950-51	Division 1	26 December	Drew	**0**	**0**	25 December	Drew	**2**	**2**	15th	17th
1951-52	Division 1	10 November	Lost	**0**	**2**	24 April	Won	**1**	**0**	6th	10th
1952-53	Division 1	26 December	Drew	**1**	**1**	18 March	Lost	**1**	**5**	11th	5th
1953-54	Division 1	28 November	Won	**2**	**1**	17 April	Drew	**1**	**1**	13th	9th
1954-55	Division 1	18 September	Lost	**1**	**2**	5 February	Lost	**1**	**6**	6th	15th
1955-56	Division 1	3 March	Drew	**1**	**1**	19 November	Lost	**1**	**3**	20th	14th
1956-57	Division 1	18 August	Won	**3**	**1**	15 December	Won	**2**	**0**	10th	22ndR
1959-60	Division 2	14 November	Won	**11**	**1**	2 April	Lost	**0**	**2**	1stP	7th
1967-68	Division 2	20 January	Won	**4**	**1**	16 September	Lost	**0**	**3**	16th	15th
1968-69	Division 2	7 December	Drew	**0**	**0**	22 February	Drew	**1**	**1**	18th	3rd
1969-70	Division 2	25 February	Won	**1**	**0**	14 March	Lost	**0**	**1**	21stR	20th
1986-87	Division 1	26 December	Won	**2**	**0**	20 April	Lost	**0**	**3**	22ndR	19th
1988-89	Division 1	25 February	Lost	**1**	**2**	15 October	Drew	**2**	**2**	17th	14th
1989-90	Division 1	26 August	Drew	**1**	**1**	13 January	Won	**2**	**0**	2nd	19thR
1998-99	Premiership	8 May	Lost	**3**	**4**	21 December	Won	**1**	**0**	6th	18thR
2000-01	Premiership	28 October	Won	**2**	**1**	17 April	Drew	**3**	**3**	8th	9th
2001-02	Premiership	24 October	Won	**1**	**0**	21 January	Won	**2**	**1**	8th	14th
2002-03	Premiership	11 September	Won	**2**	**0**	22 February	Lost	**0**	**3**	16th	12th
2003-04	Premiership	20 September	Won	**2**	**1**	27 March	Won	**2**	**1**	6th	7th

FA Cup

Season	Round	Home Date	Home Result	Home Villa	Home Charlton	Away Date	Away Result	Away Villa	Away Charlton	Division Villa	Division Charlton
1937-38	Round 5	16 February	Drew	**2**	**2**	12 February	Drew	**1**	**1**	Div 2	Div 1
		21 February		Highbury (2nd replay)			Won	**4**	**1**		
1961-62	Round 5	17 February	Won	**2**	**1**					Div 1	Div 2
1969-70	Round 3	3 January	Drew	**1**	**1**	12 January	Lost	**0**	**1**	Div 2	Div 2

Summary	*P*	*W*	*D*	*L*	*F*	*A*
Villa's home league record:	24	14	6	4	51	24
Villa's away league record:	24	8	7	9	30	41
Villa's cup record:	6	2	3	1	10	7
TOTAL:	**54**	**24**	**16**	**14**	**91**	**72**

FACT FILE

- **The match in November 1959 has proved a landmark in two ways. It was the last time Villa reached double figures in a league match, and the last time a Villa player (namely Gerry Hitchens) scored five goals in a league match.**
- **Villa were unbeaten in nine home games from 1956 to 1986.**

Villa's forward line for their fifth-round FA Cup match at Charlton in February 1938. From left to right are Frank Broome, Freddie Haycock, Frank Shell, Ronnie Starling and Eric Houghton.

Villa's top scorers vs Charlton

Johnny Dixon 6
Gerry Hitchens 5
Frank Broome, Dickie Dorsett 4

Villa hat-tricks vs Charlton

21 Feb 1938 Frank Broome (cup)
14 Nov 1959 Gerry Hitchens (5)

Played for both clubs

Albert Lindon	Villa 1911-12	Charlton 1927-30
Harold Halse	Villa 1912-13	Charlton 1921-23
George T Stephenson	Villa 1921-28	Charlton 1934-37
William Johnson	Villa 1926-28	Charlton 1928-29
Dai Astley	Charlton 1927-31	Villa 1931-37
Charlie Drinkwater	Villa 1935-36	Charlton 1938-39
Sailor Brown	Charlton 1937-39	Villa 1947-49
Mike Kenning	Villa 1960-61	Charlton 1962-67/68-72
John Dunn	Villa 1967-71	Charlton 1971-75
John Phillips	Villa 1969-70	Charlton 1981-82
Harry Gregory	Charlton 1966-71	Villa 1970-72
Leighton Phillips	Villa 1974-79	Charlton 1981-83
Terry Bullivant	Villa 1979-82	Charlton 1982-83
Alan Curbishley	Villa 1982-85	Charlton 1984-87/90-94
Paul Elliott	Charlton 1981-83	Villa 1985-87
Paul Mortimer	Charlton 1987-91/94-99	Villa 1991-92
Carl Tiler	Villa 1995-97	Charlton 1998-2001
Mark Kinsella	Charlton 1996-2002	Villa 2002-04

v. Chelsea

		Home					Away				Final Positions	
Season	League	Date	Result	Villa	Chelsea	Date	Result	Villa	Chelsea	Villa	Chelsea
1907-08	Division 1	28 December	Drew	0	0	25 April	Won	3	1	2nd	13th
1908-09	Division 1	30 January	Drew	0	0	26 September	Won	2	0	7th	11th
1909-10	Division 1	11 September	Won	4	1	22 January	Drew	0	0	1st	19thR
1912-13	Division 1	2 September	Won	1	0	21 March	Won	2	1	2nd	18th
1913-14	Division 1	25 October	Lost	1	2	28 February	Won	3	0	2nd	8th
1914-15	Division 1	3 October	Won	2	1	6 February	Lost	1	3	14th	19th
1919-20	Division 1	25 December	Won	5	2	2 April	Lost	1	2	9th	3rd
1920-21	Division 1	28 March	Won	3	0	29 March	Lost	1	5	10th	18th
1921-22	Division 1	17 April	Lost	1	4	14 April	Lost	0	1	5th	9th
1922-23	Division 1	30 March	Won	1	0	2 April	Drew	1	1	6th	19th
1923-24	Division 1	15 September	Drew	0	0	8 September	Drew	0	0	6th	21stR
1930-31	Division 1	26 December	Drew	3	3	25 December	Won	2	0	2nd	12th
1931-32	Division 1	30 January	Lost	1	3	19 September	Won	6	3	5th	12th
1932-33	Division 1	1 October	Won	3	1	11 February	Won	1	0	2nd	18th
1933-34	Division 1	7 February	Won	2	0	16 September	Lost	0	1	13th	19th
1934-35	Division 1	26 December	Lost	0	3	25 December	Lost	0	2	13th	12th
1935-36	Division 1	16 November	Drew	2	2	21 March	Lost	0	1	21stR	8th
1938-39	Division 1	19 November	Won	6	2	25 March	Lost	1	2	12th	20th
1946-47	Division 1	29 March	Won	2	0	23 November	Won	3	1	8th	15th
1947-48	Division 1	21 February	Won	3	0	4 October	Lost	2	4	6th	18th
1948-49	Division 1	26 March	Drew	1	1	27 November	Lost	1	2	10th	13th
1949-50	Division 1	8 April	Won	4	0	22 October	Won	3	1	12th	13th
1950-51	Division 1	18 November	Won	4	2	7 April	Drew	1	1	15th	20th
1951-52	Division 1	15 April	Won	7	1	14 April	Drew	2	2	6th	19th
1952-53	Division 1	24 January	Drew	1	1	13 September	Lost	0	4	11th	19th
1953-54	Division 1	6 February	Drew	2	2	19 September	Won	2	1	13th	8th
1954-55	Division 1	5 March	Won	3	2	11 December	Lost	0	4	6th	1st
1955-56	Division 1	21 January	Lost	1	4	17 September	Drew	0	0	20th	16th
1956-57	Division 1	24 November	Drew	1	1	6 April	Drew	1	1	10th	12th=
1957-58	Division 1	22 February	Lost	1	3	12 October	Lost	2	4	14th	11th
1958-59	Division 1	31 January	Won	3	1	13 September	Lost	1	2	21stR	14th
1960-61	Division 1	20 August	Won	3	2	17 December	Won	4	2	9th	12th
1961-62	Division 1	26 August	Won	3	1	23 December	Lost	0	1	7th	22ndR
1963-64	Division 1	14 September	Won	2	0	18 January	Lost	0	1	19th	5th
1964-65	Division 1	31 August	Drew	2	2	26 August	Lost	1	2	16th	3rd
1965-66	Division 1	27 November	Lost	2	4	16 May	Won	2	0	16th	5th
1966-67	Division 1	17 September	Lost	2	6	21 January	Lost	1	3	21stR	9th
1977-78	Division 1	15 April	Won	2	0	19 November	Drew	0	0	8th	16th
1978-79	Division 1	28 April	Won	2	1	9 December	Won	1	0	8th	22ndR
1984-85	Division 1	8 September	Won	4	2	16 April	Lost	1	3	10th	6th
1985-86	Division 1	26 April	Won	3	1	23 November	Lost	1	2	16th	6th
1986-87	Division 1	15 November	Drew	0	0	27 December	Lost	1	4	22ndR	14th
1989-90	Division 1	14 April	Won	1	0	1 January	Won	3	0	2nd	5th
1990-91	Division 1	11 May	Drew	2	2	3 November	Lost	0	1	17th	11th

		Home					Away			Final Positions	
Season	League	Date	Result	Villa	Chelsea	Date	Result	Villa	Chelsea	Villa	Chelsea
1991-92	Division 1	20 April	Won	**3**	**1**	18 September	Lost	**0**	**2**	7th	14th
1992-93	Premiership	2 September	Lost	**1**	**3**	13 February	Won	**1**	**0**	2nd	11th
1993-94	Premiership	23 October	Won	**1**	**0**	22 January	Drew	**1**	**1**	10th	14th
1994-95	Premiership	28 December	Won	**3**	**0**	15 April	Lost	**0**	**1**	18th	11th
1995-96	Premiership	14 October	Lost	**0**	**1**	6 April	Won	**2**	**1**	4th	11th
1996-97	Premiership	26 December	Lost	**0**	**2**	15 September	Drew	**1**	**1**	5th	6th
1997-98	Premiership	1 November	Lost	**0**	**2**	8 March	Won	**1**	**0**	7th	4th
1998-99	Premiership	22 March	Lost	**0**	**3**	9 December	Lost	**1**	**2**	6th	3rd
1999-00	Premiership	22 January	Drew	**0**	**0**	21 August	Lost	**0**	**1**	6th	5th
2000-01	Premiership	27 August	Drew	**1**	**1**	1 January	Lost	**0**	**1**	8th	6th
2001-02	Premiership	9 February	Drew	**1**	**1**	11 May	Won	**3**	**1**	8th	6th
2002-03	Premiership	19 April	Won	**2**	**1**	21 December	Lost	**0**	**2**	16th	4th
2003-04	Premiership	12 April	Won	**3**	**2**	27 September	Lost	**0**	**1**	6th	2nd

FA Cup

										Division	
1919-20	Semi-Final	27 March				Bramall Lane	Won	**3**	**1**	Div 1	Div 1
1945-46	Round 5	16 February	Won	**1**	**0**	9 February	Won	**1**	**0**	Div 1	Div 1
1958-59	Round 4					24 January	Won	**2**	**1**	Div 1	Div 1
1959-60	Round 4					30 January	Won	**2**	**1**	Div 1	Div 1
1986-87	Round 3	10 January	Drew	**2**	**2**	21 January	Lost*	**1**	**2**	Div 1	Div 1
1999-00	Final	20 May				Wembley	Lost	**0**	**1**	Prem	Prem

League Cup

1964-65	Semi-Final	20 January	Lost	**2**	**3**	10 February	Drew	**1**	**1**	Div 1	Div 1
1998-99	Round 3					28 October	Lost	**1**	**4**	Prem	Prem
2003-04	Q'ter-Final	17 December	Won	**2**	**1**					Prem	Prem

Summary	*P*	*W*	*D*	*L*	*F*	*A*
Villa's home league record:	57	29	15	13	111	80
Villa's away league record:	57	18	10	29	67	83
Villa's cup record:	12	6	2	4	18	17
TOTAL:	**126**	**53**	**27**	**46**	**196**	**180**

FACT FILE

- **Villa took part in the last-ever FA Cup Final at the old Wembley Stadium, but an uninspiring game ended in agony when Roberto Di Matteo won the cup for Chelsea.**
- **Villa were unbeaten in 12 home games from 1935 to 1955.**
- **Villa failed to score a Premiership goal at home against Chelsea for five seasons in a row (1995 to 2000).**
- **The series between Villa and Chelsea has historically been very close. Neither side has won more than four consecutive home games, and neither side has won a game by more than three goals since 1966.**

Villa's top scorers vs Chelsea

Billy Walker, Tony Hateley 8

Pongo Waring, Johnny Dixon 7

Clem Stephenson, Eric Houghton, Peter McParland 6

Villa hat-tricks vs Chelsea

11 Sep 1909 Billy Gerrish

19 Sep 1931 Pongo Waring (4)

17 Apr 1952 William Goffin

Played for both clubs

Jack Whitley	Villa 1900-02	Chelsea 1907-14
Billy Brawn	Villa 1901-06	Chelsea 1907-11
George Hunter	Villa 1908-12	Chelsea 1912-14
Harold Halse	Villa 1912-13	Chelsea 1913-21
Michael Pinner	Villa 1954-57	Chelsea 1961-62
Stanley Crowther	Villa 1956-58	Chelsea 1958-60
George Graham	Villa 1962-64	Chelsea 1964-67
Tony Hateley	Villa 1963-67	Chelsea 1966-67
John Dunn	Chelsea 1962-66	Villa 1967-71
John Phillips	Villa 1969-70	Chelsea 1970-79
Ian Hamilton	Chelsea 1966-67	Villa 1969-76
Tommy Hughes	Chelsea 1966-70	Villa 1971-72
Kenny Swain	Chelsea 1973-79	Villa 1978-83
Tony Dorigo	Villa 1983-87	Chelsea 1987-91
Paul Elliott	Villa 1985-87	Chelsea 1991-93
Tony Cascarino	Villa 1989-91	Chelsea 1991-94
Mark Bosnich	Villa 1991-99	Chelsea 2001-02
Andy Townsend	Chelsea 1990-93	Villa 1993-98

Villa goalkeeper Sam Hardy punches clear from a Chelsea forward at Stamford Bridge in February 1914. Villa won the game 2-0 and that season finished runners-up to League champions Blackburn Rovers.

v. Chester City

FA Cup		Home Date	Home Result	Home Villa	Home Chester	Away Date	Away Result	Away Villa	Away Chester	Division Villa	Division Chester
1973-74	Round 3	5 January	Won	**3**	**1**					Div 2	Div 4

League Cup		Home Date	Home Result	Home Villa	Home Chester	Away Date	Away Result	Away Villa	Away Chester	Division Villa	Division Chester
1969-70	Round 1					13 August	Won	**2**	**1**	Div 2	Div 4
1974-75	Semi-Final	22 January	Won	**3**	**2**	15 January	Drew	**2**	**2**	Div 2	Div 4
1999-00	Round 2	21 September	Won	**5**	**0**	14 September	Won	**1**	**0**	Prem	Div 3

Summary	*P*	*W*	*D*	*L*	*F*	*A*
Villa's cup record:	6	5	1	0	16	6
TOTAL:	**6**	**5**	**1**	**0**	**16**	**6**

Villa's top scorers vs Chester

Lee Hendrie 3

Keith Leonard, Sammy Morgan 2

Played for both clubs

Roy Chapman	Villa 1953-58	Chester 1969-70
George Ashfield	Villa 1955-58	Chester 1958-59
William Myerscough	Villa 1956-59	Chester 1961-63
Stan Horne	Villa 1963-64	Chester 1973-74
Dave Pountney	Villa 1963-68	Chester 1970-73
Gary Shelton	Villa 1978-82	Chester 1994-99
Cyrille Regis	Villa 1991-93	Chester 1995-96
Earl Barrett	Chester 1985-86	Villa 1991-95
Neil Cutler	Chester 1995-97/98-99	Villa 1999-2000

Bought from Oldham Athletic in 1991, full-back Earl Barrett went on to play for England after starting his League career with Chester before transferring to Manchester City. He left Villa to join Everton.

v. Chesterfield

Season	League	Date	Result	Home Villa	Home Chesterfield	Date	Result	Away Villa	Away Chesterfield	Final Positions Villa	Final Positions Chesterfield
1936-37	Division 2	28 December	Won	**6**	**2**	25 December	Lost	**0**	**1**	9th	15th
1937-38	Division 2	9 October	Lost	**0**	**2**	19 February	Won	**1**	**0**	1stP	11th
1970-71	Division 3	17 October	Drew	**0**	**0**	15 August	Won	**3**	**2**	4th	5th
1971-72	Division 3	5 May	Won	**1**	**0**	19 April	Won	**4**	**0**	1stP	13th

FA Cup

										Division	
1933-34	Round 3	17 January	Won	**2**	**0**	13 January	Drew	**2**	**2**	Div 1	Div 3N

League Cup

1971-72	Round 2					8 September	Won	**3**	**2**	Div 3	Div 3

Summary	*P*	*W*	*D*	*L*	*F*	*A*
Villa's home league record:	4	2	1	1	7	4
Villa's away league record:	4	3	0	1	8	3
Villa's cup record:	3	2	1	0	7	4
TOTAL:	**11**	**7**	**2**	**2**	**22**	**11**

FACT FILE

- **Chesterfield last beat Villa in 1937. Villa have won five and drawn one since then.**

Villa's top scorers vs Chesterfield

Frank Broome, Geoff Vowden 3

Played for both clubs

Sam Hardy	Chesterfield 1902-05	Villa 1912-21
Barney Allen	Villa 1905-06	Chesterfield 1906-07
Albert Wilkes	Villa 1898-1907	Chesterfield 1908-09
Horace Henshall	Villa 1910-12	Chesterfield 1923-24
George Beeson	Chesterfield 1927-29	Villa 1934-37
Phil Robinson	Villa 1986-87	Chesterfield 1994-96
Thomas Hitzlsperger	Villa 2000-04	Chesterfield 2001-03
Stefan Moore	Chesterfield 2001-02	Villa 2002-04

v. Colchester United

League Cup		Home Date	Home Result	Villa	Colchester	Away Date	Away Result	Villa	Colchester	Division Villa	Division Colchester
1974-75	Q'ter Final					3 December	Won	**2**	**1**	Div 2	Div 3
1979-80	Round 2	5 September	Lost* (won 9-8 pens)	**0**	**2**	28 August	Won	**2**	**0**	Div 1	Div 3

Summary	*P*	*W*	*D*	*L*	*F*	*A*	
Villa's cup record:	3	2	0	1	4	3	
TOTAL:	**3**	**2**	**0**	**1**	**4**	**3**	(+one penalty shoot-out victory)

FACT FILE

- **The epic tie in 1979 ended in Villa's first taste of penalty shoot-out drama.**

Villa's top scorers vs Colchester

Gary Shaw 2

Played for both clubs

John Martin	Villa 1964-65	Colchester 1966-69
Dave Simmons	Villa 1968-71	Colchester 1970-73
Robert Hopkins	Villa 1979-83	Colchester 1992-93
Warren Aspinall	Villa 1986-88	Colchester 1998-2000
Mark Kinsella	Colchester 1989-97	Villa 2002-04

v. Coventry City

		Home					Away			Final Positions	
Season	League	Date	Result	Villa	Coventry	Date	Result	Villa	Coventry	Villa	Coventry
1936-37	Division 2	3 October	Drew	**0**	**0**	6 February	Lost	**0**	**1**	9th	8th
1937-38	Division 2	30 October	Drew	**1**	**1**	12 March	Won	**1**	**0**	1stP	4th
1975-76	Division 1	30 August	Won	**1**	**0**	13 April	Drew	**1**	**1**	16th	14th
1976-77	Division 1	20 November	Drew	**2**	**2**	16 April	Won	**3**	**2**	4th	19th
1977-78	Division 1	26 December	Drew	**1**	**1**	21 March	Won	**3**	**2**	8th	7th
1978-79	Division 1	28 March	Drew	**1**	**1**	7 April	Drew	**1**	**1**	8th	10th
1979-80	Division 1	19 December	Won	**3**	**0**	29 April	Won	**2**	**1**	7th	15th
1980-81	Division 1	30 August	Won	**1**	**0**	17 January	Won	**2**	**1**	1st	16th
1981-82	Division 1	27 February	Won	**2**	**1**	10 October	Drew	**1**	**1**	11th	14th
1982-83	Division 1	19 March	Won	**4**	**0**	6 November	Drew	**0**	**0**	6th	19th
1983-84	Division 1	7 April	Won	**2**	**0**	13 March	Drew	**3**	**3**	10th	19th
1984-85	Division 1	25 August	Won	**1**	**0**	19 January	Won	**3**	**0**	10th	18th
1985-86	Division 1	14 September	Drew	**1**	**1**	11 January	Drew	**3**	**3**	16th	17th
1986-87	Division 1	28 March	Won	**1**	**0**	4 October	Won	**1**	**0**	22ndR	10th
1988-89	Division 1	13 May	Drew	**1**	**1**	26 November	Lost	**1**	**2**	17th	7th
1989-90	Division 1	18 November	Won	**4**	**1**	4 March	Lost	**0**	**2**	2nd	12th
1990-91	Division 1	8 September	Won	**2**	**1**	19 January	Lost	**1**	**2**	17th	16th
1991-92	Division 1	2 May	Won	**2**	**0**	28 September	Lost	**0**	**1**	7th	19th
1992-93	Premiership	10 April	Drew	**0**	**0**	26 December	Lost	**0**	**3**	2nd	15th
1993-94	Premiership	11 September	Drew	**0**	**0**	6 March	Won	**1**	**0**	10th	11th
1994-95	Premiership	6 March	Drew	**0**	**0**	29 August	Won	**1**	**0**	18th	16th
1995-96	Premiership	16 December	Won	**4**	**1**	30 September	Won	**3**	**0**	4th	16th
1996-97	Premiership	19 February	Won	**2**	**1**	23 November	Won	**2**	**1**	5th	17th
1997-98	Premiership	6 December	Won	**3**	**0**	11 April	Won	**2**	**1**	7th	11th
1998-99	Premiership	27 February	Lost	**1**	**4**	3 October	Won	**2**	**1**	6th	15th
1999-00	Premiership	11 March	Won	**1**	**0**	22 November	Lost	**1**	**2**	6th	14th
2000-01	Premiership	5 May	Won	**3**	**2**	25 November	Drew	**1**	**1**	8th	19thR

FA Cup										Division	
1945-46	Round 3	8 January	Won	**2**	**0**	5 January	Lost	**1**	**2**	Div 1	Div 2
1964-65	Round 3	9 January	Won	**3**	**0**					Div 1	Div 2
1997-98	Round 5	14 February	Lost	**0**	**1**					Prem	Prem

Summary	P	W	D	L	F	A
Villa's home league record:	27	16	10	1	44	18
Villa's away league record:	27	13	7	7	39	32
Villa's cup record:	4	2	0	2	6	3
TOTAL:	**58**	**31**	**17**	**10**	**89**	**53**

FACT FILE

- **Having failed for 26 matches and over 61 years to win at Villa Park, Coventry then did it twice in a row in 1998 and 1999. Villa have won both home matches since though, the second of which condemned Coventry to relegation.**
- **Between 1937 and 1987, Villa lost only once in 29 matches. That one defeat wasn't too important, though, as it came in the first leg of a tie in the two-legged 1946 FA Cup, and Villa went through on aggregate anyway.**
- **From 1992 to 1998, Villa were unbeaten in 12 Premiership ties against their Midlands rivals, a run which included six successive away wins.**

Villa's top scorers vs Coventry
Dwight Yorke 7
Savo Milosevic 5
Brian Little, Gary Shaw, Peter Withe, David Platt 4

Villa hat-tricks vs Coventry
16 Dec 1995 Savo Milosevic

Played for both clubs

Albert Lindon	Villa 1911-12	Coventry 1919-20
Archie Dyke	Villa 1913-15	Coventry 1920-21
Harry Nash	Villa 1914-20	Coventry 1920-21
George Hadley	Villa 1919-20	Coventry 1920-23
Jimmy Lawrence	Villa 1919-20	Coventry 1920-25
Alex McClure	Villa 1923-25	Coventry 1926-28
Billy Kirton	Villa 1919-27	Coventry 1928-30
James Harrison	Villa 1949-50	Coventry 1951-53
Norman Lockhart	Coventry 1947-53	Villa 1952-56
William Myerscough	Villa 1956-59	Coventry 1960-62
Tony Hateley	Villa 1963-67	Coventry 1968-69
George Curtis	Coventry 1955-70	Villa 1969-72
Ray Graydon	Villa 1971-77	Coventry 1977-78
Bobby McDonald	Villa 1972-76	Coventry 1976-81
Steve Hunt	Villa 1974-77/85-88	Coventry 1978-84
Dennis Mortimer	Coventry 1969-76	Villa 1975-85
Andy Blair	Coventry 1978-81	Villa 1981-84/85-88
Garry Thompson	Coventry 1977-83	Villa 1986-89
Les Sealey	Coventry 1976-83/91-92	Villa 1991-92
Cyrille Regis	Coventry 1984-91	Villa 1991-93
Steve Froggatt	Villa 1991-94	Coventry 1998-2000
Kevin Richardson	Villa 1991-95	Coventry 1994-98
Steve Staunton	Villa 1991-98/2000-03	Coventry 2003-04
Nii Lamptey	Villa 1994-95	Coventry 1995-96
Julian Joachim	Villa 1995-2001	Coventry 2001-04
Dion Dublin	Coventry 1994-99	Villa 1998-2004
George Boateng	Coventry 1997-99	Villa 1999-2002
Mustapha Hadji	Coventry 1999-2001	Villa 2001-04

v. Crewe Alexandra

FA Cup		Home Date	Result	Villa	Crewe	Away Date	Result	Villa	Crewe	Division Villa	Division Crewe
1927-28	Round 4	28 January	Won	**3**	**0**					Div 1	Div 3N
1988-89	Round 3					7 January	Won	**3**	**2**	Div 1	Div 4

League Cup		Home Date	Result	Villa	Crewe	Away Date	Result	Villa	Crewe	Division Villa	Division Crewe
1974-75	Round 3	16 October	Won	**1**	**0**	9 October	Drew	**2**	**2**	Div 2	Div 4

Summary	*P*	*W*	*D*	*L*	*F*	*A*
Villa's cup record:	4	3	1	0	9	4
TOTAL:	4	3	1	0	9	4

Villa's top scorers vs Crewe

Billy Cook 3

Villa hat-tricks vs Crewe

28 Jan 1928 Billy Cook (cup)

Played for both clubs

Joe Walters	Villa 1905-12	Crewe 1923-24
Arthur Moss	Villa 1909-12	Crewe 1921-25
Frank Broome	Villa 1934-47	Crewe 1953-55
Keith Jones	Villa 1947-57	Crewe 1958-60
John Inglis	Villa 1967-68	Crewe 1968-70
John Phillips	Villa 1969-70	Crewe 1979-80
Geoff Crudgington	Villa 1970-72	Crewe 197-78
Kenny Swain	Villa 1978-83	Crewe 1988-92
Stuart Ritchie	Villa 1986-87	Crewe 1987-88
David Platt	Crewe 1984-88	Villa 1987-91

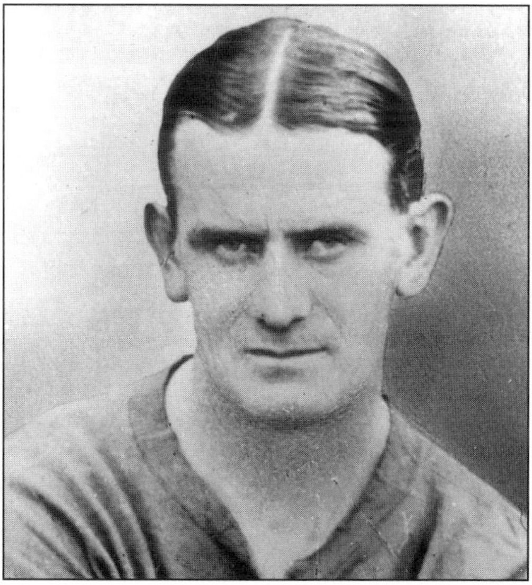

Joey Walters spent over six seasons with Aston Villa. In the 1912 close season, after 41 goals in 120 games for Villa, Walters moved to Oldham and later played for Southend, Millwall, Manchester United, Rochdale and Crewe. It was when he was with the Gresty Road club that Joey Walters died of pneumonia in 1923.

v. Crystal Palace

		Home					Away			Final Positions	
Season	*League*	*Date*	*Result*	Villa	Palace	*Date*	*Result*	Villa	Palace	Villa	Palace
1967-68	Division 2	23 September	Lost	**0**	**1**	3 February	Won	**1**	**0**	16th	11th
1968-69	Division 2	12 October	Drew	**1**	**1**	14 December	Lost	**2**	**4**	18th	2ndP
1973-74	Division 2	23 October	Won	**2**	**1**	11 September	Drew	**0**	**0**	14th	20thR
1979-80	Division 1	2 February	Won	**2**	**0**	15 September	Lost	**0**	**2**	7th	13th
1980-81	Division 1	21 February	Won	**2**	**1**	27 September	Won	**1**	**0**	1st	22ndR
1987-88	Division 2	21 October	Won	**4**	**1**	9 April	Drew	**1**	**1**	2ndP	6th
1989-90	Division 1	28 October	Won	**2**	**1**	24 March	Lost	**0**	**1**	2nd	15th
1990-91	Division 1	1 January	Won	**2**	**0**	13 April	Drew	**0**	**0**	17th	3rd
1991-92	Division 1	4 September	Lost	**0**	**1**	21 March	Drew	**0**	**0**	7th	10th
1992-93	Premiership	5 September	Won	**3**	**0**	10 February	Lost	**0**	**1**	2nd	20thR
1994-95	Premiership	27 August	Drew	**1**	**1**	4 April	Drew	**0**	**0**	18th	19thR
1997-98	Premiership	14 March	Won	**3**	**1**	8 November	Drew	**1**	**1**	7th	20thR

FA Cup

						Division	
1912-13	Round 3	22 February	Won	**5**	**0**	Div 1	Non L
1961-62	Round 3	6 January	Won	**4**	**3**	Div 1	Div 3

League Cup

1971-72	Round 3	13 October	Won	**2**	**0**	5 October	Drew	**2**	**2**	Div 3	Div 1
1978-79	Round 3	4 October	Drew	**1**	**1**	10 October	Drew*	**0**	**0**	Div 1	Div 2
		16 October	Highfield Road, Coventry (2nd replay)				Won	**3**	**0**		
1994-95	Round 4					30 November	Lost	**1**	**4**	Prem	Prem
2003-04	Round 4	3 December	Won	**3**	**0**					Prem	Div 1

Brian Little takes the ball past Crystal Palace defender Jim Cannon in the League Cup third-round game at Villa Park in October 1978. The tie was only decided after three games when Villa won 3-0 at Highfield Road.

Summary	P	W	D	L	F	A
Villa's home league record:	12	8	2	2	22	9
Villa's away league record:	12	2	6	4	6	10
Villa's cup record:	9	5	3	1	21	10
TOTAL:	**33**	**15**	**11**	**7**	**49**	**29**

FACT FILE

- **Villa enjoyed six successive home league wins from 1973 to 1991.**
- **Villa have scored only four goals in their last 12 away matches.**

Villa's top scorers vs Palace
David Platt 5
Mark Walters 3
(10 players) 2

Villa hat-tricks vs Palace
21 Oct 1987 Mark Walters

Played for both clubs

Arthur Davis	Villa 1919-22	Palace 1928-29
George Clarke	Villa 1924-25	Palace 1925-33
Fred Norris	Villa 1925-27	Palace 1933-34
Jackie Palethorpe	Villa 1935-36	Palace 1936-38
Arthur Proudler	Villa 1954-55	Palace 1956-69
George Graham	Villa 1962-64	Palace 1976-78
John Burridge	Villa 1975-77	Palace 1977-80
Garry Thompson	Villa 1986-89	Palace 1989-91
Andy Gray	Palace 1984-88/89-92	Villa 1987-89
Paul Mortimer	Villa 1991-92	Palace 1991-93
Steve Staunton	Villa 1991-98/2000-03	Palace 2000-01
Ray Houghton	Villa 1992-95	Palace 1994-97
John Fashanu	Palace 1983-84	Villa 1994-95
Gareth Southgate	Palace 1990-95	Villa 1995-2001
Sasa Curcic	Villa 1996-98	Palace 1997-99
Stan Collymore	Palace 1990-93	Villa 1997-99
Rob Edwards	Villa 2002-03	Palace 2003-04

John Burridge left Villa to join Crystal Palace in 1977.

v. Darlington

FA Cup		Date	Result	Home Villa	Home Darlington	Division Villa	Division Darlington
1999-00	Round 3	11 December	Won	**2**	**1**	Prem	Div 3

Summary	*P*	*W*	*D*	*L*	*F*	*A*
Villa's cup record:	1	1	0	0	2	1
TOTAL:	**1**	**1**	**0**	**0**	**2**	**1**

FACT FILE

- **Villa became the second team that season to knock Darlington out of the FA Cup. After Manchester United confirmed their withdrawal to play in the World Club Championship in Brazil instead, the FA took the unprecedented decision to award their place in the third-round draw to a team knocked out in the second round. Having lost 3-1 to Gillingham, Darlington posed only minor problems for Villa.**

Played for both clubs

Charlie Slade	Villa 1913-14	Darlington 1925-27
Billy Dinsdale	Darlington 1921-22/31-32	Villa 1924-26
Reg Chester	Villa 1925-35	Darlington 1937-38
George Brown	Villa 1929-35	Darlington 1936-38
John Gidman	Villa 1972-80	Darlington 1988-89
John Burridge	Villa 1975-77	Darlington 1995-97
Allan Evans	Villa 1977-89	Darlington 1990-91
David Geddis	Villa 1979-83	Darlington 1990-91
Mark Burke	Villa 1986-88	Darlington 1990-91
Martin Carruthers	Villa 1991-93	Darlington 1998-2000
Dariusz Kubicki	Villa 1991-94	Darlington 1998-99
Graham Fenton	Villa 1993-96	Darlington 2002-03

v. Darwen

			Home					Away			Final Positions	
Season	League	Date	Result	Villa	Darwen	Date	Result	Villa	Darwen		Villa	Darwen
1891-92	Division 1	26 December	Won	**7**	**0**	28 November	Won	**5**	**1**		4th	14thR
1893-94	Division 1	26 December	Won	**9**	**0**	6 November	Drew	**1**	**1**		1st	15thR

FA Cup										Division	
1886-87	Q'ter Final	12 February	Won	**3**	**2**						
1891-92	Round 2	30 January	Won	**2**	**0**					Div 1	Div 1
1892-93	Round 1					21 January	Lost	**4**	**5**	Div 1	Div 2

Summary	*P*	*W*	*D*	*L*	*F*	*A*
Villa's home league record:	2	2	0	0	16	0
Villa's away league record:	2	1	1	0	6	2
Villa's cup record:	3	2	0	1	9	7
TOTAL:	**7**	**5**	**1**	**1**	**31**	**9**

FACT FILE

- **Maybe Villa would like more Boxing Day fixtures against Darwen, having scored 16 goals without reply in the two games in question.**

Villa's top scorers vs Darwen

Jack Devey 7

Denny Hodgetts 6

Lewis Campbell, Charlie Athersmith 4

Played for both clubs

David Skea	Villa 1892-93	Darwen 1893-94
Jack Whitley	Darwen 1898-99	Villa 1900-02

Aston Villa players and officials in 1894, the year they won their first League championship.

v. Derby County

		Home				Away				Final Positions	
Season	*League*	*Date*	*Result*	Villa	Derby	*Date*	*Result*	Villa	Derby	Villa	Derby
1888-89	Division 1	29 December	Won	**4**	**2**	9 March	Lost	**2**	**5**	2nd	10th
1889-90	Division 1	12 October	Won	**7**	**1**	28 December	Lost	**0**	**5**	8th	7th
1890-91	Division 1	25 October	Won	**4**	**0**	18 October	Lost	**4**	**5**	9th	11th
1891-92	Division 1	9 January	Won	**6**	**0**	3 October	Lost	**2**	**4**	4th	10th
1892-93	Division 1	29 October	Won	**6**	**1**	17 December	Lost	**1**	**2**	4th	13th
1893-94	Division 1	30 September	Drew	**1**	**1**	2 December	Won	**3**	**0**	1st	3rd
1894-95	Division 1	5 January	Won	**4**	**0**	22 September	Won	**2**	**0**	3rd	15th
1895-96	Division 1	21 September	Won	**4**	**1**	8 February	Drew	**2**	**2**	1st	2nd
1896-97	Division 1	24 October	Won	**2**	**1**	17 October	Won	**3**	**1**	1st	3rd
1897-98	Division 1	5 March	Won	**4**	**1**	22 January	Lost	**1**	**3**	6th	10th
1898-99	Division 1	5 November	Won	**7**	**1**	4 March	Drew	**1**	**1**	1st	9th
1899-00	Division 1	3 February	Won	**3**	**2**	30 September	Lost	**0**	**2**	1st	6th
1900-01	Division 1	29 September	Won	**2**	**1**	22 April	Lost	**0**	**3**	15th	12th
1901-02	Division 1	15 February	Won	**3**	**2**	19 October	Lost	**0**	**1**	8th	6th
1902-03	Division 1	6 September	Drew	**0**	**0**	3 January	Lost	**0**	**2**	2nd	9th
1903-04	Division 1	10 October	Won	**3**	**0**	28 December	Drew	**2**	**2**	5th	14th
1904-05	Division 1	15 October	Lost	**0**	**2**	11 February	Won	**2**	**0**	4th	11th
1905-06	Division 1	16 April	Won	**6**	**0**	30 September	Lost	**0**	**1**	8th	15th
1906-07	Division 1	23 March	Won	**2**	**0**	17 November	Won	**1**	**0**	5th	19thR
1912-13	Division 1	19 October	Won	**5**	**1**	12 March	Won	**1**	**0**	2nd	7th
1913-14	Division 1	13 April	Won	**3**	**2**	25 December	Won	**2**	**0**	2nd	20thR
1919-20	Division 1	1 September	Drew	**2**	**2**	8 September	Lost	**0**	**1**	9th	18th
1920-21	Division 1	30 April	Won	**1**	**0**	23 April	Won	**3**	**2**	10th	21stR
1926-27	Division 1	9 October	Won	**3**	**1**	26 February	Won	**3**	**2**	10th	12th
1927-28	Division 1	27 December	Lost	**0**	**1**	26 December	Lost	**0**	**5**	8th	4th
1928-29	Division 1	3 November	Lost	**2**	**3**	16 March	Lost	**0**	**1**	3rd	6th
1929-30	Division 1	9 September	Drew	**2**	**2**	4 September	Lost	**0**	**4**	4th	2nd
1930-31	Division 1	15 November	Lost	**4**	**6**	21 March	Drew	**1**	**1**	2nd	6th
1931-32	Division 1	5 December	Won	**2**	**0**	16 April	Lost	**1**	**3**	5th	15th
1932-33	Division 1	6 May	Won	**2**	**0**	24 December	Drew	**0**	**0**	2nd	7th
1933-34	Division 1	9 December	Lost	**0**	**2**	21 April	Drew	**1**	**1**	13th	4th
1934-35	Division 1	1 September	Won	**3**	**2**	5 January	Drew	**1**	**1**	13th	6th
1935-36	Division 1	28 September	Lost	**0**	**2**	1 February	Won	**3**	**1**	21stR	2nd
1938-39	Division 1	3 September	Lost	**0**	**1**	31 December	Lost	**1**	**2**	12th	6th
1939-40	Division 1					2 September	Lost	**0**	**1**		
1946-47	Division 1	4 January	Won	**2**	**0**	7 September	Won	**2**	**1**	8th	14th
1947-48	Division 1	7 April	Drew	**2**	**2**	20 September	Won	**3**	**1**	6th	4th
1948-49	Division 1	4 September	Drew	**1**	**1**	27 April	Drew	**2**	**2**	10th	3rd
1949-50	Division 1	23 August	Drew	**1**	**1**	31 August	Lost	**2**	**3**	12th	11th
1950-51	Division 1	23 December	Drew	**1**	**1**	26 August	Lost	**2**	**4**	15th	11th
1951-52	Division 1	25 August	Won	**4**	**1**	22 December	Drew	**1**	**1**	6th	17th
1952-53	Division 1	3 January	Won	**3**	**0**	30 August	Won	**1**	**0**	11th	22ndR
1959-60	Division 2	15 March	Won	**3**	**2**	24 October	Drew	**2**	**2**	1stP	18th
1967-68	Division 2	6 January	Won	**2**	**1**	2 September	Lost	**1**	**3**	16th	18th

Season	League	Home Date	Home Result	Villa	Derby	Away Date	Away Result	Villa	Derby	Final Positions Villa	Final Positions Derby
1968-69	Division 2	29 March	Lost	**0**	**1**	7 September	Lost	**1**	**3**	18th	1stP
1975-76	Division 1	19 April	Won	**1**	**0**	27 December	Lost	**0**	**2**	16th	4th
1976-77	Division 1	2 March	Won	**4**	**0**	9 April	Lost	**1**	**2**	4th	15th
1977-78	Division 1	25 March	Drew	**0**	**0**	27 December	Won	**3**	**0**	8th	12th
1978-79	Division 1	11 April	Drew	**3**	**3**	23 December	Drew	**0**	**0**	8th	19th
1979-80	Division 1	1 March	Won	**1**	**0**	20 October	Won	**3**	**1**	7th	21stR
1988-89	Division 1	19 November	Lost	**1**	**2**	6 May	Lost	**1**	**2**	17th	5th
1989-90	Division 1	30 September	Won	**1**	**0**	17 March	Won	**1**	**0**	2nd	16th
1990-91	Division 1	2 February	Won	**3**	**2**	15 September	Won	**2**	**0**	17th	20thR
1996-97	Premiership	24 August	Won	**2**	**0**	12 April	Lost	**1**	**2**	5th	12th
1997-98	Premiership	20 September	Won	**2**	**1**	7 February	Won	**1**	**0**	7th	9th
1998-99	Premiership	27 September	Won	**1**	**0**	10 March	Lost	**1**	**2**	6th	8th
1999-00	Premiership	25 March	Won	**2**	**0**	26 December	Won	**2**	**0**	6th	16th
2000-01	Premiership	30 September	Won	**4**	**1**	24 February	Lost	**0**	**1**	8th	17th
2001-02	Premiership	12 January	Won	**2**	**1**	22 December	Lost	**1**	**3**	8th	19thR

It surprised Derby County supporters when the Rams let left-back John Robson leave the Baseball Ground in December 1972. Villa fans were pleased though, and the £90,000 spent by manager Vic Crowe proved a good investment. For Villa, Robson made 176 senior appearances, winning two League Cup winners' medals and a Second Division promotion. John Robson's career was cut short when he was diagnosed with multiple sclerosis in 1978.

FA Cup		Home Date	Result	Villa	Derby	Away Date	Result	Villa	Derby	Division Villa	Derby
1885-86	Round 2					14 November	Lost	**0**	**2**		
1888-89	Round 2	16 February	Won	**5**	**3**					Div 1	Div 1
1894-95	Round 1	2 February	Won	**2**	**1**					Div 1	Div 1
1895-96	Round 1					1 February	Lost	**2**	**4**	Div 1	Div 1
1897-98	Round 1					29 January	Lost	**0**	**1**	Div 1	Div 1
1909-10	Round 2	5 February	Won	**6**	**1**					Div 1	Div 2
1912-13	Round 1					15 January	Won	**3**	**1**	Div 1	Div 1
1921-22	Round 1	7 January	Won	**6**	**1**					Div 1	Div 2
1945-46	Q'ter Final	2 March	Lost	**3**	**4**	9 March	Drew	**1**	**1**	Div 1	Div 1
1991-92	Round 4					5 February	Won	**4**	**3**	Div 1	Div 2
1996-97	Round 4					25 January	Lost	**1**	**3**	Prem	Prem

League Cup											
1986-87	Round 3	4 November	Won	**2**	**1**	29 October	Drew	**1**	**1**	Div 1	Div 2

Summary	P	W	D	L	F	A
Villa's home league record:	58	39	10	9	143	61
Villa's away league record:	59	19	11	29	77	99
Villa's cup record:	14	7	2	5	36	27
TOTAL:	**131**	**65**	**23**	**43**	**256**	**187**

FACT FILE

- **2 March 1946 saw Villa's biggest ever home attendance as 76,588 people packed in to see a seven-goal thriller in the FA Cup.**
- **Villa have won their last eight home games against Derby.**
- **None of the sides' last 20 league meetings has ended in a draw.**
- **The first 12 meetings between the sides all ended in home wins.**
- **Villa were unbeaten in their first 18 home games.**
- **In 1947, Villa embarked on another unbeaten home run, this time lasting nine games.**

Villa's top scorers vs Derby

Denny Hodgetts, Jack Devey 12
Eric Houghton 8
Harold Halse, Harry Hampton 7
Joe Bache, Dwight Yorke 6

Villa hat-tricks vs Derby

5 Feb 1910 Harry Hampton (cup)
19 Oct 1912 Harold Halse (5)
7 Jan 1922 Billy Walker (cup)
5 Feb 1992 Dwight Yorke (cup)

Played for both clubs

Archie Goodall	Villa 1888-89	Derby 1889-1903
Albert Woolley	Villa 1892-95	Derby 1894-95
George Kinsey	Villa 1894-95	Derby 1895-97

Alf Wood	Villa 1900-05	Derby 1905-07
Billy Matthews	Villa 1903-07	Derby 1912-13
Ben Olney	Derby 1920-28	Villa 1927-30
George T Stephenson	Villa 1921-28	Derby 1927-31
Dai Astley	Villa 1931-37	Derby 1936-39
Ronnie Dix	Villa 1932-37	Derby 1936-39
Frank Broome	Villa 1934-37	Derby 1946-50
Bruce Rioch	Villa 1969-74	Derby 1973-80
John Robson	Derby 1967-73	Villa 1972-78
Bobby Campbell	Villa 1973-75	Derby 1983-84
Jake Findlay	Villa 1973-77	Derby 1983-84
Graham Moseley	Derby 1972-77	Villa 1974-75
John Burridge	Villa 1975-77	Derby 1984-85
Gordon Cowans	Villa 1975-85/88-92/93-94	Derby 1993-95
John Gregory	Villa 1977-79	Derby 1985-88
Eamonn Deacy	Villa 1979-84	Derby 1983-84
Tony Dorigo	Villa 1983-87	Derby 1998-2000
Steve Hodge	Villa 1985-87	Derby 1994-95
David Hunt	Derby 1977-78	Villa 1987-89
Mark Lillis	Derby 1986-88	Villa 1987-89
Nigel Callaghan	Derby 1986-89/90-91	Villa 1988-91
Ian Ormondroyd	Villa 1988-92	Derby 1991-92
Andy Comyn	Villa 1989-91	Derby 1991-93
Paul McGrath	Villa 1989-96	Derby 1996-97
Dean Saunders	Derby 1988-91	Villa 1992-95
Chris Boden	Villa 1993-94	Derby 1994-96
Tommy Johnson	Derby 1991-95	Villa 1994-97
Gary Charles	Derby 1993-95	Villa 1994-99
Ian Taylor	Villa 1994-2003	Derby 2003-04
Benito Carbone	Villa 1999-2000	Derby 2001-02
Rob Edwards	Villa 2002-03	Derby 2003-04

Great things were expected of Watford wingers Nigel Callaghan and John Barnes. Villa signed Callaghan from Derby County in 1988 and he was to rejoin both the Rams and Watford after leaving Villa.

v. Derby Midland

FA Cup		Date	Result	Home Villa	Home Derby Mid
1886-87	Round 2	20 November	Won	**6**	**1**

Summary	P	W	D	L	F	A
Villa's cup record:	1	1	0	0	6	1
TOTAL:	**1**	**1**	**0**	**0**	**6**	**1**

Villa's top scorers vs Derby Midland

Albert Brown, A.A. Loach 2

'Denny' Hodgetts was also on the scoresheet when Villa met Derby Midland. He later became a vice-president of Villa and was still in office when he died, aged 81, in March 1945.

v. Doncaster Rovers

		Home						Away			Final Positions	
Season	League	Date	Result	Villa	Doncaster	Date	Result	Villa	Doncaster		Villa	Doncaster
1936-37	Division 2	30 January	Drew	**1**	**1**	26 September	Lost	**0**	**1**		9th	22ndR
1970-71	Division 3	5 September	Won	**3**	**2**	26 March	Lost	**1**	**2**		4th	23rdR

FA Cup										Division	
1954-55	Round 4	2 February	Drew*	**2**	**2**	29 January	Drew	**0**	**0**	Div 1	Div 2
		7 February				Maine Road (2nd replay)	Drew*	**1**	**1**		
		15 February				The Hawthorns (3rd replay)	Lost	**1**	**3**		

Summary	*P*	*W*	*D*	*L*	*F*	*A*
Villa's home league record:	2	1	1	0	4	3
Villa's away league record:	2	0	0	2	1	3
Villa's cup record:	4	0	3	1	4	6
TOTAL:	**8**	**1**	**4**	**3**	**9**	**12**

FACT FILE

- **The 1955 FA Cup tie took a total of 8½ hours to resolve. The third replay was originally played at Hillsborough, but with the sides about to enter extra-time after a goalless 90 minutes, the match was abandoned due to bad light. In effect, therefore, Villa have only beaten Doncaster once in nine attempts.**

Villa's top scorers vs Doncaster

Tommy Thompson 3
Andy Lochhead 2

Played for both clubs

Alan Wakeman	Villa 1938-50	Doncaster 1950-52
Victor Potts	Doncaster 1938-39	Villa 1946-48
Fred Potter	Villa 1960-61	Doncaster 1962-66
Alfie Hale	Villa 1960-62	Doncaster 1962-65
John Gavan	Villa 1962-66	Doncaster 1967-69
Lew Chatterley	Villa 1962-71	Doncaster 1970-71
Lionel Martin	Villa 1966-72	Doncaster 1970-71
Alan Little	Villa 1974-75	Doncaster 1979-83
Brendan Ormsby	Villa 1978-86	Doncaster 1990-92
Paul Birch	Villa 1983-91	Doncaster 1996-97
Bernard Gallacher	Villa 1986-91	Doncaster 1991-92
John McGrath	Villa 2000-01	Doncaster 2003-04

v. Everton

		Home					Away			Final Positions	
Season	*League*	*Date*	*Result*	Villa	Everton	*Date*	*Result*	Villa	Everton	Villa	Everton
1888-89	Division 1	22 September	Won	**2**	**1**	6 October	Lost	**0**	**2**	2nd	8th
1889-90	Division 1	23 November	Lost	**1**	**2**	4 January	Lost	**0**	**7**	8th	2nd
1890-91	Division 1	11 October	Drew	**2**	**2**	1 January	Lost	**0**	**5**	9th	1st
1891-92	Division 1	28 December	Lost	**3**	**4**	28 November	Lost	**1**	**5**	4th	5th
1892-93	Division 1	10 September	Won	**4**	**1**	1 October	Lost	**0**	**1**	4th	3rd
1893-94	Division 1	23 September	Won	**3**	**1**	16 September	Lost	**2**	**4**	1st	6th
1894-95	Division 1	24 April	Drew	**2**	**2**	17 January	Lost	**2**	**4**	3rd	2nd
1895-96	Division 1	30 September	Won	**4**	**3**	21 December	Lost	**0**	**2**	1st	3rd
1896-97	Division 1	26 September	Lost	**1**	**2**	19 September	Won	**3**	**2**	1st	7th
1897-98	Division 1	13 November	Won	**3**	**0**	25 December	Lost	**1**	**2**	6th	4th
1898-99	Division 1	17 December	Won	**3**	**0**	15 April	Drew	**1**	**1**	1st	4th
1899-00	Division 1	13 January	Drew	**1**	**1**	16 September	Won	**2**	**1**	1st	11th
1900-01	Division 1	15 September	Lost	**1**	**2**	12 January	Lost	**1**	**2**	15th	7th
1901-02	Division 1	28 September	Drew	**1**	**1**	25 December	Won	**3**	**2**	8th	2nd
1902-03	Division 1	18 October	Won	**2**	**1**	14 February	Won	**1**	**0**	2nd	12th
1903-04	Division 1	26 September	Won	**3**	**1**	23 January	Lost	**0**	**1**	5th	3rd
1904-05	Division 1	12 September	Won	**1**	**0**	22 October	Lost	**2**	**3**	4th	2nd
1905-06	Division 1	23 September	Won	**4**	**0**	27 January	Lost	**2**	**4**	8th	11th
1906-07	Division 1	26 January	Won	**2**	**1**	22 September	Won	**2**	**1**	5th	3rd
1907-08	Division 1	28 September	Lost	**0**	**2**	25 January	Lost	**0**	**1**	2nd	11th
1908-09	Division 1	27 February	Won	**3**	**1**	24 October	Lost	**1**	**3**	7th	2nd
1909-10	Division 1	9 October	Won	**3**	**1**	14 March	Drew	**0**	**0**	1st	10th
1910-11	Division 1	27 March	Won	**2**	**1**	22 October	Won	**1**	**0**	2nd	4th
1911-12	Division 1	23 September	Won	**3**	**0**	27 January	Drew	**1**	**1**	6th	2nd
1912-13	Division 1	25 January	Drew	**1**	**1**	28 September	Won	**1**	**0**	2nd	11th
1913-14	Division 1	27 September	Won	**3**	**1**	24 January	Won	**4**	**1**	2nd	15th
1914-15	Division 1	10 February	Lost	**1**	**5**	26 September	Drew	**0**	**0**	14th	1st
1919-20	Division 1	14 February	Drew	**2**	**2**	7 February	Drew	**1**	**1**	9th	16th
1920-21	Division 1	15 January	Lost	**1**	**3**	22 January	Drew	**1**	**1**	10th	7th
1921-22	Division 1	8 February	Won	**2**	**1**	21 January	Lost	**2**	**3**	5th	20th
1922-23	Division 1	21 April	Won	**3**	**0**	14 April	Lost	**1**	**2**	6th	5th
1923-24	Division 1	12 September	Drew	**1**	**1**	19 September	Lost	**0**	**2**	6th	7th
1924-25	Division 1	22 November	Won	**3**	**1**	28 March	Lost	**0**	**2**	15th	17th
1925-26	Division 1	3 April	Won	**3**	**1**	21 November	Drew	**1**	**1**	6th	11th
1926-27	Division 1	4 December	Won	**5**	**3**	23 April	Drew	**2**	**2**	10th	20th
1927-28	Division 1	10 December	Lost	**2**	**3**	21 April	Lost	**2**	**3**	8th	1st
1928-29	Division 1	1 December	Won	**2**	**0**	13 April	Won	**1**	**0**	3rd	18th
1929-30	Division 1	12 October	Won	**5**	**2**	5 March	Won	**4**	**3**	4th	22ndR
1931-32	Division 1	24 October	Lost	**2**	**3**	5 March	Lost	**2**	**4**	5th	1st
1932-33	Division 1	25 March	Won	**2**	**1**	12 November	Drew	**3**	**3**	2nd	11th
1933-34	Division 1	23 December	Won	**2**	**1**	5 May	Drew	**2**	**2**	13th	14th
1934-35	Division 1	13 October	Drew	**2**	**2**	23 February	Drew	**2**	**2**	13th	8th
1935-36	Division 1	8 February	Drew	**1**	**1**	5 October	Drew	**2**	**2**	21stR	16th
1938-39	Division 1	5 September	Lost	**0**	**3**	29 April	Lost	**0**	**3**	12th	1st

		Home				Away				Final Positions	
Season	*League*	*Date*	*Result*	Villa	Everton	*Date*	*Result*	Villa	Everton	Villa	Everton
1939-40	Division 1	28 August	Lost	**1**	**2**						
1946-47	Division 1	2 September	Lost	**0**	**1**	1 January	Lost	**0**	**2**	8th	10th
1947-48	Division 1	8 September	Won	**3**	**0**	17 September	Lost	**0**	**3**	6th	14th
1948-49	Division 1	20 November	Lost	**0**	**1**	19 March	Won	**3**	**1**	10th	18th
1949-50	Division 1	24 September	Drew	**2**	**2**	4 February	Drew	**1**	**1**	12th	18th
1950-51	Division 1	2 December	Drew	**3**	**3**	21 April	Won	**2**	**1**	15th	22ndR
1954-55	Division 1	9 October	Lost	**0**	**2**	4 May	Won	**1**	**0**	6th	11th
1955-56	Division 1	31 March	Won	**2**	**0**	22 October	Lost	**1**	**2**	20th	15th
1956-57	Division 1	12 January	Won	**5**	**1**	8 September	Won	**4**	**0**	10th	15th
1957-58	Division 1	31 August	Lost	**0**	**1**	28 December	Won	**2**	**1**	14th	16th
1958-59	Division 1	8 November	Lost	**2**	**4**	28 March	Lost	**1**	**2**	21stR	16th
1960-61	Division 1	3 September	Won	**3**	**2**	22 March	Won	**2**	**1**	9th	5th
1961-62	Division 1	16 December	Drew	**1**	**1**	19 August	Lost	**0**	**2**	7th	4th
1962-63	Division 1	1 April	Lost	**0**	**2**	13 October	Drew	**1**	**1**	15th	1st
1963-64	Division 1	7 October	Lost	**0**	**1**	28 February	Lost	**2**	**4**	19th	3rd
1964-65	Division 1	5 October	Lost	**1**	**2**	13 March	Lost	**1**	**3**	16th	4th
1965-66	Division 1	11 December	Won	**3**	**2**	8 January	Lost	**0**	**2**	16th	11th
1966-67	Division 1	6 May	Lost	**2**	**4**	1 April	Lost	**1**	**3**	21stR	6th
1975-76	Division 1	22 November	Won	**3**	**1**	18 October	Lost	**1**	**2**	16th	11th
1976-77	Division 1	5 February	Won	**2**	**0**	28 August	Won	**2**	**0**	4th	9th
1977-78	Division 1	27 August	Lost	**1**	**2**	14 January	Lost	**0**	**1**	8th	3rd
1978-79	Division 1	16 September	Drew	**1**	**1**	31 January	Drew	**1**	**1**	8th	4th
1979-80	Division 1	12 January	Won	**2**	**1**	1 September	Drew	**1**	**1**	7th	19th
1980-81	Division 1	13 September	Lost	**0**	**2**	7 February	Won	**3**	**1**	1st	15th
1981-82	Division 1	15 May	Lost	**1**	**2**	19 December	Lost	**0**	**2**	11th	8th
1982-83	Division 1	12 February	Won	**2**	**0**	31 August	Lost	**0**	**5**	6th	7th
1983-84	Division 1	7 May	Lost	**0**	**2**	10 December	Drew	**1**	**1**	10th	7th
1984-85	Division 1	16 March	Drew	**1**	**1**	13 October	Lost	**1**	**2**	10th	1st
1985-86	Division 1	28 September	Drew	**0**	**0**	1 March	Lost	**0**	**2**	16th	2nd
1986-87	Division 1	18 April	Lost	**0**	**1**	1 January	Lost	**0**	**3**	22ndR	1st
1988-89	Division 1	22 October	Won	**2**	**0**	14 February	Drew	**1**	**1**	17th	8th
1989-90	Division 1	5 November	Won	**6**	**2**	5 May	Drew	**3**	**3**	2nd	6th
1990-91	Division 1	30 March	Drew	**2**	**2**	26 December	Lost	**0**	**1**	17th	9th
1991-92	Division 1	2 February	Drew	**0**	**0**	19 October	Won	**2**	**0**	7th	12th
1992-93	Premiership	20 February	Won	**2**	**1**	25 August	Lost	**0**	**1**	2nd	13th
1993-94	Premiership	30 March	Drew	**0**	**0**	31 August	Won	**1**	**0**	10th	17th
1994-95	Premiership	10 December	Drew	**0**	**0**	20 August	Drew	**2**	**2**	18th	15th
1995-96	Premiership	28 October	Won	**1**	**0**	5 May	Lost	**0**	**1**	4th	6th
1996-97	Premiership	5 April	Won	**3**	**1**	3 September	Won	**1**	**0**	5th	15th
1997-98	Premiership	22 November	Won	**2**	**1**	28 March	Won	**4**	**1**	7th	17th
1998-99	Premiership	18 January	Won	**3**	**0**	15 August	Drew	**0**	**0**	6th	14th
1999-00	Premiership	11 August	Won	**3**	**0**	27 November	Drew	**0**	**0**	6th	13th
2000-01	Premiership	14 April	Won	**2**	**1**	5 November	Won	**1**	**0**	8th	16th
2001-02	Premiership	30 January	Drew	**0**	**0**	20 October	Lost	**2**	**3**	8th	15th
2002-03	Premiership	22 September	Won	**3**	**2**	26 April	Lost	**1**	**2**	16th	7th
2003-04	Premiership	25 October	Drew	**0**	**0**	28 February	Lost	**0**	**2**	6th	17th

		Home					Away			Division	
FA Cup		*Date*	*Result*	Villa	Everton	*Date*	*Result*	Villa	Everton	Villa	Everton
1896-97	Final	10 April				Crystal Palace	Won	**3**	**2**	Div 1	Div 1
1904-05	Semi-Final	25 March				Victoria Ground, Stoke	Drew	**1**	**1**	Div 1	Div 1
		29 March				Trent Bridge, Nottingham (replay)	Won	**2**	**1**		
1952-53	Q'ter Final	28 February	Lost	**0**	**1**					Div 1	Div 2
1958-59	Round 5					14 February	Won	**4**	**1**	Div 1	Div 1
1972-73	Round 3					13 January	Lost	**2**	**3**	Div 2	Div 1
1977-78	Round 3					7 January	Lost	**1**	**4**	Div 1	Div 1
1999-00	Q'ter Final					20 February	Won	**2**	**1**	Prem	Prem

League Cup											
1974-75	Round 2	11 September	Drew	**1**	**1**	18 September	Won	**3**	**0**	Div 2	Div 1
1976-77	Final	12 March				Wembley	Drew	**0**	**0**	Div 1	Div 1
		16 March				Hillsborough (replay)	Drew*	**1**	**1**		
		13 April				Old Trafford (2nd replay)	Won*	**3**	**2**		
1979-80	Round 3	25 September	Drew	**0**	**0**	9 October	Lost	**1**	**4**	Div 1	Div 1
1983-84	Semi-Final	22 February	Won	**1**	**0**	15 February	Lost	**0**	**2**	Div 1	Div 1

Summary	*P*	*W*	*D*	*L*	*F*	*A*
Villa's home league record:	90	44	21	25	167	119
Villa's away league record:	89	23	22	44	107	158
Villa's cup record:	17	7	5	5	25	24
TOTAL:	**196**	**74**	**48**	**74**	**299**	**301**

FACT FILE

- **Villa and Everton, who were both founder members of the Football League, have met in the league more often than any other pair of clubs. Only 16 of the 106 league seasons have seen one or other of them outside the top flight. They even met in one of the few games played in the abandoned 1939-40 season as well.**
- **Villa and Everton competed in the only English domestic cup final to go to two replays. After unexciting draws at Wembley and Hillsborough in the 1977 League Cup Final, the second leg proved thrilling. Everton led 1-0 for much of the game, only for Villa to score twice in the last eight minutes. However, there was still time for Lyons to equalise for Everton and force the game into extra time, during which Brian Little won the cup for the men from the Midlands.**
- **Everton have not won at Villa Park since April 1987, and Villa have been unbeaten in 16 games since.**
- **Villa were unbeaten in 11 games from 1996 to 2001.**
- **Everton won their first eight home games in the series, including a 7-0 win which equals Villa's heaviest ever league defeat.**

Villa's top scorers vs Everton

Harry Hampton 15
Billy Walker 11
Dai Astley, Jack Devey, Billy Garraty, Johnny Dixon 8

Villa hat-tricks vs Everton

4 Dec 1926 Len Capewell
12 Oct 1929 George Brown
14 Feb 1959 Ron Wylie (cup)

Played for both clubs

Bertie Banks	Everton 1896-97	Villa 1901-02
Bert Sharp	Villa 1897-99	Everton 1899-1900/01-02
Jack Sharp	Villa 1897-99	Everton 1899-1910
Jack Whitley	Villa 1900-02	Everton 1902-04
Dick Roose	Everton 1904-05	Villa 1911-12
Tom Griffiths	Everton 1926-31	Villa 1935-37
Harry Morton	Villa 1931-37	Everton 1936-39
David Hickson	Everton 1951-56/57-60	Villa 1955-56
Brian Godfrey	Everton 1959-60	Villa 1967-71
Bruce Rioch	Villa 1969-74	Everton 1976-78
John Gidman	Villa 1972-80	Everton 1979-81
Andy Gray	Villa 1975-79/85-87	Everton 1983-85
Ken McNaught	Everton 1974-77	Villa 1977-83
Mike Pejic	Everton 1976-79	Villa 1979-80
Pat Heard	Everton 1978-80	Villa 1979-83
Paul Rideout	Villa 1983-85	Everton 1992-97
Steve McMahon	Everton 1980-83	Villa 1983-86
Warren Aspinall	Everton 1985-87	Villa 1986-88
Martin Keown	Villa 1986-89	Everton 1989-93
Derek Mountfield	Everton 1982-88	Villa 1988-92
Adrian Heath	Everton 1981-89	Villa 1989-90
Earl Barrett	Villa 1991-95	Everton 1994-98
Kevin Richardson	Everton 1981-87	Villa 1991-95
Tommy Johnson	Villa 1994-97	Everton 1999-2000
Gareth Farrelly	Villa 1995-97	Everton 1997-99
Carl Tiler	Villa 1995-97	Everton 1997-99
David Unsworth	Everton 1992-97/98-2004	Villa 1998
Steve Watson	Villa 1998-2000	Everton 2000-04
David Ginola	Villa 2000-02	Everton 2001-02
Gavin McCann	Everton 1997-98	Villa 2003-04

v. Exeter City

FA Cup		Home Date	Home Result	Villa	Exeter	Away Date	Away Result	Villa	Exeter	Division Villa	Division Exeter
1913-14	Round 2					31 January	Won	**2**	**1**	Div 1	Non L
1914-15	Round 1	9 January	Won	**2**	**0**					Div 1	Non L
1993-94	Round 3					8 January	Won	**1**	**0**	Prem	Div 2

League Cup		Home Date	Home Result	Villa	Exeter	Away Date	Away Result	Villa	Exeter	Division Villa	Division Exeter
1977-78	Round 2					31 August	Won	**3**	**1**	Div 1	Div 3
1985-86	Round 2	9 October	Won	**8**	**1**	25 September	Won	**4**	**1**	Div 1	Div 4

Summary	*P*	*W*	*D*	*L*	*F*	*A*
Villa's cup record:	6	6	0	0	20	4
TOTAL:	**6**	**6**	**0**	**0**	**20**	**4**

FACT FILE

- **Exeter are the only team to play this many matches against Villa and lose every time.**
- **Simon Stainrod scored four on his debut.**

Villa's top scorers vs Exeter

Andy Gray 5

Simon Stainrod 5

Villa hat-tricks vs Exeter

31 Aug 1977 Andy Gray (cup)

25 Sep 1985 Simon Stainrod (4) (cup)

Played for both clubs

Percy Varco	Villa 1923-25	Exeter 1929-32
Ginger Phoenix	Villa 1924-25	Exeter 1926-29
Les Dennington	Villa 1924-25	Exeter 1928-31
Billy Armfield	Villa 1923-28	Exeter 1929-32
Bob Wilson	Villa 1963-64	Exeter 1969-76
Graham Parker	Villa 1963-68	Exeter 1968-74
Tony Scott	Villa 1965-68	Exeter 1972-74
Dave Gibson	Villa 1970-72	Exeter 1971-73
Leighton Phillips	Villa 1974-79	Exeter 1982-83
Noel Blake	Villa 1979-82	Exeter 1995-2001
Paul Birch	Villa 1983-91	Exeter 1996-99
Phil King	Exeter 1984-86	Villa 1994-95

v. Fulham

Season	League	Date	Result	Home Villa	Home Fulham	Date	Result	Away Villa	Away Fulham	Final Positions Villa	Final Positions Fulham
1936-37	Division 2	19 September	Lost	**0**	**3**	23 January	Lost	**2**	**3**	9th	11th
1937-38	Division 2	25 September	Won	**2**	**0**	5 February	Drew	**1**	**1**	1stP	8th
1949-50	Division 1	27 August	Won	**3**	**1**	24 December	Lost	**0**	**3**	12th	17th
1950-51	Division 1	13 January	Won	**3**	**0**	9 September	Lost	**1**	**2**	15th	18th
1951-52	Division 1	5 April	Won	**4**	**1**	17 November	Drew	**2**	**2**	6th	22ndR
1960-61	Division 1	19 November	Won	**2**	**1**	8 April	Drew	**1**	**1**	9th	17th
1961-62	Division 1	24 February	Won	**2**	**0**	7 October	Lost	**1**	**3**	7th	20th
1962-63	Division 1	3 November	Lost	**1**	**2**	23 March	Lost	**0**	**1**	15th	16th
1963-64	Division 1	21 March	Drew	**2**	**2**	9 November	Lost	**0**	**2**	19th	15th
1964-65	Division 1	31 October	Won	**2**	**0**	24 April	Drew	**1**	**1**	16th	20th
1965-66	Division 1	12 March	Lost	**2**	**5**	18 September	Won	**6**	**3**	16th	20th
1966-67	Division 1	8 April	Drew	**1**	**1**	12 November	Lost	**1**	**5**	21stR	18th
1968-69	Division 2	17 August	Drew	**1**	**1**	8 March	Drew	**1**	**1**	18th	22ndR
1970-71	Division 3	30 January	Won	**1**	**0**	28 November	Won	**2**	**0**	4th	2ndP
1972-73	Division 2	3 March	Lost	**2**	**3**	7 October	Lost	**0**	**2**	3rd	9th
1973-74	Division 2	19 September	Drew	**1**	**1**	2 October	Lost	**0**	**1**	14th	13th
1974-75	Division 2	8 February	Drew	**1**	**1**	2 November	Lost	**1**	**3**	2ndP	9th
2001-02	Premiership	14 October	Won	**2**	**0**	2 February	Drew	**0**	**0**	8th	13th
2002-03	Premiership	9 November	Won	**3**	**1**	8 February	Lost	**1**	**2**	16th	14th
2003-04	Premiership	28 December	Won	**3**	**0**	11 February	Won	**2**	**1**	6th	9th

FA Cup

Season	Round	Date	Result	Villa	Fulham	Division Villa	Division Fulham
1904-05	Q'ter Final	4 March	Won	**5**	**0**	Div 1	Non L
1998-99	Round 4	23 January	Lost	**0**	**2**	Prem	Div 2

League Cup

Season	Round	Date	Result	Villa	Fulham	Date	Result	Villa	Fulham	Villa	Fulham
1965-66	Round 4	8 November	Won	**2**	**0**	3 November	Drew	**1**	**1**	Div 1	Div 1

Summary	*P*	*W*	*D*	*L*	*F*	*A*
Villa's home league record:	20	11	5	4	38	23
Villa's away league record:	20	3	6	11	23	37
Villa's cup record:	4	2	1	1	8	3
TOTAL:	**44**	**16**	**12**	**16**	**69**	**63**

FACT FILE

- **Fulham were the last lower division side to knock Villa out of the FA Cup. Their 2-0 win in 1999 was a major surprise as Villa were joint top of the Premiership at the time.**
- **Villa won six home games in a row from 1937 to 1962.**
- **Villa failed to win in their first 11 visits to Craven Cottage.**

FA Cup action around the Fulham goal in 1905. The Cottagers won to set up a semi-final against Everton at Stoke, a tie they eventually won after a replay at Nottingham.

Villa's top scorers vs Fulham

Jimmy MacEwan, Tony Hateley, Darius Vassell 4
William Goffin, Johnny Dixon, Harry Burrows,
Mike Tindall, Phil Woosnam, Juan Pablo Angel 3

Played for both clubs

Bobby Templeton	Villa 1898-1903	Fulham 1913-15
Albert Wilkes	Villa 1898-1907	Fulham 1907-09
Charlie Millington	Villa 1905-08	Fulham 1907-09
Andy Ducat	Villa 1912-21	Fulham 1921-24
Edward Lowe	Villa 1946-50	Fulham 1950-63
Stan Horne	Villa 1963-64	Fulham 1968-73
Terry Bullivant	Fulham 1974-80	Villa 1979-82
Des Bremner	Villa 1979-85	Fulham 1989-90
Ray Houghton	Fulham 1982-86	Villa 1992-95
Stan Collymore	Villa 1997-99	Fulham 1999-2000

In March 1905, Villa beat Fulham 5-0 in the quarter-finals of the FA Cup. Here is a small section of the 42,000 crowd.

v. Gillingham

			Home				Away		Final Positions	
Season	League	Date	Result	Villa	Gillingham	Date	Result	Villa	Gillingham	Villa	Gillingham
1970-71	Division 3	23 September	Won	**2**	**1**	10 March	Drew	**0**	**0**	4th	24thR

Summary	P	W	D	L	F	A
Villa's home league record:	1	1	0	0	2	1
Villa's away league record:	1	0	1	0	0	0
TOTAL:	**2**	**1**	**1**	**0**	**2**	**1**

FACT FILE

- **Hamilton and McMahon were Villa's goalscorers against the Gills.**

Played for both clubs

George Travers	Villa 1908-09	Gillingham 1921-22
Billy Armfield	Villa 1923-28	Gillingham 1932-33
William Evans	Villa 1946-49	Gillingham 1953-55
John Overton	Villa 1975-76	Gillingham 1976-81
Charlie Young	Villa 1976-77	Gillingham 1977-82
Mike Buttress	Villa 1976-78	Gillingham 1977-79
Tony Cascarino	Gillingham 1981-87	Villa 1986-91
Tommy Johnson	Villa 1994-97	Gillingham 2002-04
Jlloyd Samuel	Villa 1999-2003	Gillingham 2001-04

Pat McMahon joined Villa on a free transfer from Celtic in June 1969, when Tommy Docherty snapped him up. McMahon had enjoyed an interesting introduction to Parkhead. After writing to Celtic for a trial while playing in junior football, he went to work in London for the GPO and received a telegram asking him to return to play in a junior cup final. Celtic spotted him in that game and signed him but in two seasons he appeared in only three League games, although he did score twice. For Villa he played in the 1971 League Cup Final and gained a Third Division championship medal a year later. After 149 games for Villa, in which he scored 30 goals, McMahon moved to the North American Soccer League.

v. Glossop

				Home				Away		Final Positions	
Season	League	Date	Result	Villa	Glossop	Date	Result	Villa	Glossop	Villa	Glossop
1899-00	Division 1	4 September	Won	**9**	**0**	16 December	Lost	**0**	**1**	1st	18thR

Summary	P	W	D	L	F	A
Villa's home league record:	1	1	0	0	9	0
Villa's away league record:	1	0	0	1	0	1
TOTAL:	**2**	**1**	**0**	**1**	**9**	**1**

Villa's top scorers vs Glossop

Billy Garraty 4

Fred Wheldon 2

Villa hat-tricks vs Glossop

4 Sep 1899 Billy Garraty (4)

Played for both clubs

Archie Goodall	Villa 1888-89	Glossop 1903-05
John Boden	Glossop 1902-05	Villa 1905-07
Stuart Doncaster	Villa 1912-13	Glossop 1913-14
George Hampton	Glossop 1909-14	Villa 1914-15

v. Gravesend & Northfleet

FA Cup		Date	Result	Home Villa	Home Gravesend	Division Villa	Division Gravesend
1995-96	Round 3	6 January	Won	3	0	Prem	Non L

Summary	P	W	D	L	F	A
Villa's cup record:	1	1	0	0	3	0
TOTAL:	**1**	**1**	**0**	**0**	**3**	**0**

FACT FILE

- **Strangely, Gravesend and Northfleet are the only non-league side Villa have faced in the FA Cup since 1920! Draper, Milosevic and Johnson scored in what was officially a home tie for Gravesend, although it was agreed to switch the match to Villa Park.**

Mark Draper, a signing from Notts County, grabbed one of the goals against Gravesend & Northfleet.

v. Grimsby Town

Season	League	Home Date	Home Result	Home Villa	Home Grimsby	Away Date	Away Result	Away Villa	Away Grimsby	Final Positions Villa	Final Positions Grimsby
1901-02	Division 1	14 December	Won	**4**	**1**	12 April	Lost	**1**	**4**	8th	15th
1902-03	Division 1	27 December	Drew	**2**	**2**	25 April	Won	**2**	**0**	2nd	17thR
1929-30	Division 1	2 April	Won	**4**	**1**	26 October	Won	**2**	**0**	4th	18th
1930-31	Division 1	15 September	Won	**2**	**0**	9 September	Won	**2**	**1**	2nd	13th
1931-32	Division 1	12 September	Won	**7**	**0**	2 February	Drew	**2**	**2**	5th	21stR
1934-35	Division 1	16 February	Won	**3**	**2**	6 October	Lost	**1**	**5**	13th	5th
1935-36	Division 1	2 November	Lost	**2**	**6**	4 April	Lost	**1**	**4**	21stR	17th
1938-39	Division 1	24 December	Lost	**0**	**2**	27 August	Won	**2**	**1**	12th	10th
1946-47	Division 1	12 April	Drew	**3**	**3**	7 December	Won	**3**	**0**	8th	16th
1947-48	Division 1	20 December	Drew	**2**	**2**	23 August	Lost	**0**	**3**	6th	22ndR

FA Cup

Season	Round	Home Date	Home Result	Home Villa	Home Grimsby	Away Date	Away Result	Away Villa	Away Grimsby	Division Villa	Division Grimsby
1993-94	Round 4					29 January	Won	**2**	**1**	Prem	Div 1

League Cup

Season	Round	Home Date	Home Result	Home Villa	Home Grimsby	Away Date	Away Result	Away Villa	Away Grimsby	Division Villa	Division Grimsby
1991-92	Round 2	9 October	Drew*	**1**	**1**	25 September	Drew	**0**	**0**	Div 1	Div 2

Summary	*P*	*W*	*D*	*L*	*F*	*A*
Villa's home league record:	10	5	3	2	29	19
Villa's away league record:	10	5	1	4	16	20
Villa's cup record:	3	1	2	0	3	2
TOTAL:	**23**	**11**	**6**	**6**	**48**	**41**

FACT FILE

- **Between 1903 and 1931, Villa won six games in a row.**
- **Villa have not won in their last five home games.**

Villa's top scorers vs Grimsby

Eric Houghton 8

Jasper McLuckie, Pongo Waring 5

Villa hat-tricks vs Grimsby

14 Dec 1901 Jasper McLuckie

Played for both clubs

Jimmy Whitehouse	Grimsby 1892-96/99-1900	Villa 1896-98
Walter Leigh	Villa 1898-99	Grimsby 1900-02
Fred Watkins	Villa 1899-1900	Grimsby 1900-01
Joe Bache	Villa 1900-15	Grimsby 1920-21
Cecil Harris	Villa 1922-26	Grimsby 1926-28
Tommy Gardner	Grimsby 1931-32	Villa 1933-38
Matt Moralee	Grimsby 1931-36	Villa 1936-37
Lew Chatterley	Villa 1962-71	Grimsby 1971-74
Barrie Lynch	Villa 1968-70	Grimsby 1972-73
Chris Nicholl	Villa 1971-77	Grimsby 1983-85
Terry Donovan	Grimsby 1976-79	Villa 1979-82

v. Halifax Town

Season	League	Home Date	Result	Villa	Halifax	Away Date	Result	Villa	Halifax	Final Positions Villa	Halifax
1970-71	Division 3	13 March	Drew	**1**	**1**	14 November	Lost	**1**	**2**	4th	3rd
1971-72	Division 3	1 January	Won	**1**	**0**	18 September	Won	**1**	**0**	1stP	17th

Summary	*P*	*W*	*D*	*L*	*F*	*A*
Villa's home league record:	2	1	1	0	2	1
Villa's away league record:	2	1	0	1	2	2
TOTAL:	**4**	**2**	**1**	**1**	**4**	**3**

FACT FILE

- **Villa have never scored more, or less, than one goal in a game against Halifax.**

Villa's top scorers vs Halifax

Ray Graydon, Fred Turnbull 2

Played for both clubs

Fred Turnbull	Villa 1967-74	Halifax 1969-70
Mike Ferguson	Villa 1968-70	Halifax 1976-77
Chris Nicholl	Halifax 1968-70	Villa 1971-77
Bobby Campbell	Villa 1973-75	Halifax 1974-75/78-79
Alan Little	Villa 1974-75	Halifax 1983-85
John Overton	Villa 1975-76	Halifax 1975-76
Dave Evans	Villa 1978-79	Halifax 1979-84/90-92
Lee Butler	Villa 1988-91	Halifax 1999-2003

Gordon Smith (left) and skipper Chris Nicholl hold aloft the Football League Cup after a memorable Final against Everton which was settled only after three games in 1977. Chris Nicholl scored 20 goals in his 250 games for Villa, but his most memorable was surely the left-footed effort against Everton in the second replay of the League Cup Final. Nicholl signed for Villa from Luton Town in March 1972, for £75,000.

v. Hartlepool United

League Cup		Home Date	Result	Villa	Hartlepool	Away Date	Result	Villa	Hartlepool	Division Villa	Hartlepool
1974-75	Round 4	25 November	Won	**6**	**1**	12 November	Drew	**1**	**1**	Div 2	Div 4

Summary	P	W	D	L	F	A
Villa's cup record:	2	1	1	0	7	2
TOTAL:	**2**	**1**	**1**	**0**	**7**	**2**

Villa's top scorers vs Hartlepool

Ray Graydon, Ian Hamilton, Brian Little 2

Played for both clubs

Frank Barson	Villa 1919-22	Hartlepool 1929-30
Joe Hickman	Hartlepool 1926-29	Villa 1927-28
John Hinchcliffe	Villa 1957-58	Hartlepool 1961-64
Bobby Park	Villa 1964-69	Hartlepool 1974-75
Alan Little	Villa 1974-75	Hartlepool 1985-86
Frank Pimblett	Villa 1974-76	Hartlepool 1979-80
Kevin Poole	Villa 1984-87	Hartlepool 1990-91

Chico Hamilton hammers a penalty past the Hartlepool United goalkeeper in the League Cup fourth-round replay at Villa Park in November 1974. Villa won 6-1 and went on to reach the Final that season, beating Norwich City 1-0.

v. Heanor Town

FA Cup		Date	Result	Home Villa	Home Heanor	Division Villa	Division Heanor
1891-92	Round 1	16 January	Won	**4**	**1**	Div 1	Non L

Summary	P	W	D	L	F	A
Villa's cup record:	1	1	0	0	4	1
TOTAL:	**1**	**1**	**0**	**0**	**4**	**1**

Villa's top scorers vs Heanor

Denny Hodgetts 3

Villa hat-tricks vs Heanor

16 Jan 1892 Denny Hodgetts (cup)

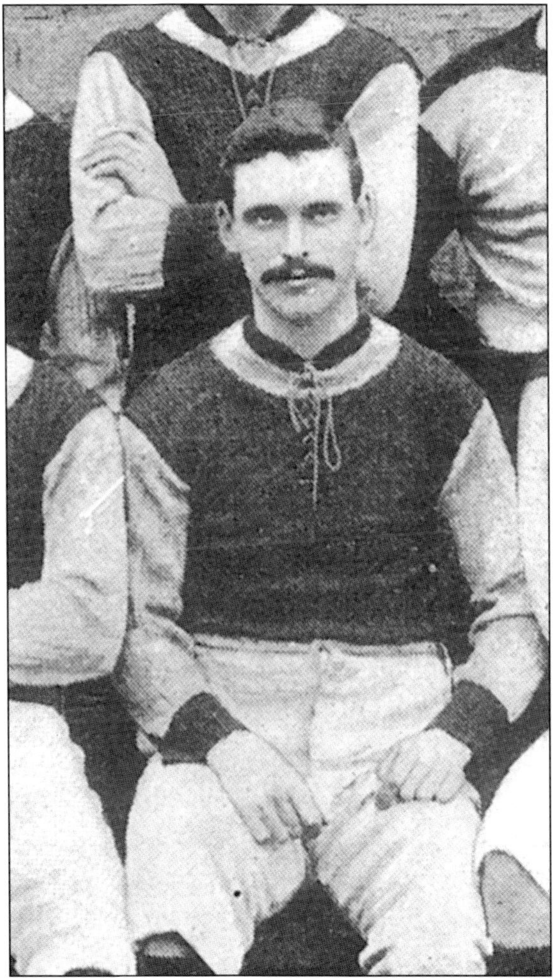

John Devey was the scorer of the other goal against Heanor. He went on to play 306 games and scored 186 goals before joining the Villa board in 1902, serving the club until 1934.

v. Hereford United

League Cup		Date	Result	Home Villa	Home Hereford	Division Villa	Division Hereford
1972-73	Round 1	16 August	Won	4	1	Div 2	Div 4

Summary	P	W	D	L	F	A
Villa's cup record:	1	1	0	0	4	1
TOTAL:	**1**	**1**	**0**	**0**	**4**	**1**

Played for both clubs

Fred Potter	Villa 1960-61	Hereford 1972-74
David Rudge	Villa 1966-70	Hereford 1972-76
Harry Gregory	Villa 1970-72	Hereford 1972-75
Tommy Hughes	Villa 1971-72	Hereford 1973-82
Ian Ross	Villa 1971-76	Hereford 1982-83
Mark Jones	Villa 1981-84	Hereford 1987-91
David Norton	Villa 1984-88	Hereford 1996-97
Chris Price	Hereford 1976-86	Villa 1988-92

Villa goalkeeper Dennis Parsons in action during the 1952-53 season. Parsons was born in Birmingham in 1925 and joined Wolves from the BSA Cycles works team in November 1944. After 23 League games for Wolves he signed for Villa from Hereford United in September 1952 and made 41 League and Cup appearances before being transferred to Kidderminster Harriers in 1955.

v. Horncastle

				Home	
FA Cup		*Date*	*Result*	Villa	Hornchurch
1886-87	Round 5	5 February	Won	**5**	**0**

Summary	*P*	*W*	*D*	*L*	*F*	*A*
Villa's cup record:	1	1	0	0	5	0
TOTAL:	**1**	**1**	**0**	**0**	**5**	**0**

Villa's top scorers vs Horncastle

Albert Brown 3

Villa hat-tricks vs Horncastle

5 Feb 1887 Albert Brown (cup)

Dennis Hodgetts featured in the game against Horncastle in his first season with Villa and went on to net 91 goals in 215 games.

v. Huddersfield Town

Season	League	Date	Result	Home Villa	Home Huddersfield	Date	Result	Away Villa	Away Huddersfield	Final Positions Villa	Final Positions Huddersfield
1920-21	Division 1	12 March	Drew	**0**	**0**	19 March	Lost	**0**	**1**	10th	17th
1921-22	Division 1	25 February	Won	**2**	**0**	5 April	Lost	**0**	**1**	5th	14th
1922-23	Division 1	3 March	Won	**2**	**1**	10 March	Won	**5**	**3**	6th	3rd
1923-24	Division 1	30 April	Won	**3**	**1**	5 April	Lost	**0**	**1**	6th	1st
1924-25	Division 1	4 October	Drew	**1**	**1**	7 February	Lost	**1**	**4**	15th	1st
1925-26	Division 1	14 November	Won	**3**	**0**	27 March	Lost	**1**	**5**	6th	1st
1926-27	Division 1	18 December	Won	**3**	**0**	7 May	Drew	**0**	**0**	10th	2nd
1927-28	Division 1	2 May	Won	**3**	**0**	22 October	Drew	**1**	**1**	8th	2nd
1928-29	Division 1	20 April	Won	**4**	**1**	8 December	Lost	**0**	**3**	3rd	16th
1929-30	Division 1	15 March	Won	**5**	**3**	9 November	Drew	**1**	**1**	4th	10th
1930-31	Division 1	4 October	Won	**6**	**1**	7 February	Won	**6**	**1**	2nd	5th
1931-32	Division 1	7 May	Lost	**2**	**3**	31 August	Drew	**1**	**1**	5th	4th
1932-33	Division 1	18 February	Lost	**0**	**3**	8 October	Drew	**0**	**0**	2nd	6th
1933-34	Division 1	7 October	Won	**4**	**3**	21 February	Lost	**1**	**2**	13th	2nd
1934-35	Division 1	19 April	Drew	**1**	**1**	24 April	Drew	**1**	**1**	13th	16th
1935-36	Division 1	25 December	Won	**4**	**1**	4 April	Lost	**1**	**4**	21stR	3rd
1938-39	Division 1	15 February	Won	**4**	**0**	8 October	Drew	**1**	**1**	12th	19th
1946-47	Division 1	25 December	Drew	**2**	**2**	26 December	Lost	**0**	**1**	8th	20th
1947-48	Division 1	27 September	Won	**2**	**1**	14 February	Won	**1**	**0**	6th	19th
1948-49	Division 1	18 September	Drew	**3**	**3**	12 February	Won	**1**	**0**	10th	20th
1949-50	Division 1	18 February	Won	**2**	**1**	1 October	Lost	**0**	**1**	12th	15th
1950-51	Division 1	3 March	Lost	**0**	**1**	14 October	Lost	**2**	**4**	15th	19th
1951-52	Division 1	10 September	Won	**1**	**0**	19 September	Lost	**1**	**3**	6th	21stR
1953-54	Division 1	20 February	Drew	**2**	**2**	3 October	Lost	**0**	**4**	13th	3rd
1954-55	Division 1	2 October	Drew	**0**	**0**	23 February	Won	**2**	**1**	6th	12th
1955-56	Division 1	31 December	Won	**3**	**0**	3 September	Drew	**1**	**1**	20th	21stR
1959-60	Division 2	6 February	Won	**4**	**0**	19 September	Won	**1**	**0**	1stP	6th
1967-68	Division 2	2 December	Drew	**0**	**0**	27 April	Drew	**0**	**0**	16th	14th
1968-69	Division 2	11 January	Won	**1**	**0**	2 November	Lost	**1**	**3**	18th	6th
1969-70	Division 2	8 October	Won	**4**	**1**	16 August	Lost	**0**	**2**	21stR	1stP
1972-73	Division 2	19 August	Won	**2**	**0**	30 December	Drew	**1**	**1**	3rd	21stR
1987-88	Division 2	28 December	Drew	**1**	**1**	19 September	Won	**1**	**0**	2ndP	23rdR

FA Cup

Season	Round	Date	Result	Villa	Huddersfield	Venue	Result	Villa	Huddersfield	Division Villa	Division Huddersfield
1919-20	Final	24 April				Stamford Bridge	Won*	**1**	**0**	Div 1	Div 2
1920-21	Round 3	19 February	Won	**2**	**0**					Div 1	Div 1
1929-30	Q'ter Final	1 March	Lost	**1**	**2**					Div 1	Div 1
1935-36	Round 3	11 January	Lost	**0**	**1**					Div 1	Div 1
1961-62	Round 4	27 January	Won	**2**	**1**					Div 1	Div 2

League Cup

Season	Round	Date	Result	Villa	Huddersfield	Division Villa	Division Huddersfield
1960-61	Round 2	12 October	Won	**4**	**1**	Div 1	Div 2

Summary	*P*	*W*	*D*	*L*	*F*	*A*
Villa's home league record:	32	20	9	3	74	31
Villa's away league record:	32	7	10	15	32	51
Villa's cup record:	6	4	0	2	10	5
TOTAL:	**70**	**31**	**19**	**20**	**116**	**87**

FACT FILE

- **Huddersfield were the opponents in Villa's first ever League Cup match. Villa went on to become the first winners of the competition, and have won it five times overall, a record matched only by Liverpool.**
- **Villa were unbeaten in their first 10 home games against Huddersfield.**
- **Villa are unbeaten in their last 12 home games against Huddersfield. Huddersfield's last win there was in 1951.**

Villa's top scorers vs Huddersfield

Billy Walker 15
Pongo Waring 9
Eric Houghton 8
Trevor Ford 6
Len Capewell 5
Dai Astley, Arthur Dorrell 4

Villa hat-tricks vs Huddersfield

10 Mar 1923 Billy Walker
14 Nov 1925 Len Capewell
20 Apr 1929 Reg Chester
4 Oct 1930 Billy Walker
25 Dec 1935 Dai Astley
6 Feb 1960 Bobby Thomson

Played for both clubs

Dick Roose	Huddersfield 1910-11	Villa 1911-12
Frank Mann	Villa 1911-12	Huddersfield 1912-23
Charlie Slade	Villa 1913-14	Huddersfield 1913-23
Clem Stephenson	Villa 1910-21	Huddersfield 1920-29
Billy Cook	Huddersfield 1923-27	Villa 1926-29
George Brown	Huddersfield 1921-29	Villa 1929-35
Reg Chester	Villa 1925-35	Huddersfield 1935-37
Jackie Williams	Huddersfield 1932-36	Villa 1935-36
Jeff Barker	Villa 1937-38	Huddersfield 1945-48
David Hickson	Villa 1955-56	Huddersfield 1955-57
Pat Saward	Villa 1955-61	Huddersfield 1960-63
Brian Greenhalgh	Villa 1967-69	Huddersfield 1969-71
Bobby Campbell	Villa 1973-75	Huddersfield 1975-77/78-79
Peter Withe	Villa 1980-85	Huddersfield 1988-90
Phil Robinson	Villa 1986-87	Huddersfield 1992-94
Mark Lillis	Huddersfield 1978-85	Villa 1987-89
Nigel Callaghan	Villa 1988-91	Huddersfield 1991-92

v. Hull City

Season	League	Date	Result	Home Villa	Home Hull	Date	Result	Away Villa	Away Hull	Final Positions Villa	Final Positions Hull
1959-60	Division 2	28 December	Drew	**1**	**1**	26 December	Won	**1**	**0**	1stP	21stR
1967-68	Division 2	18 November	Lost	**2**	**3**	13 April	Lost	**0**	**3**	16th	17th
1968-69	Division 2	14 September	Drew	**1**	**1**	19 April	Lost	**0**	**1**	18th	11th
1969-70	Division 2	20 September	Won	**3**	**2**	10 March	Lost	**1**	**3**	21stR	13th
1972-73	Division 2	2 December	Won	**2**	**0**	7 April	Won	**2**	**1**	3rd	13th
1973-74	Division 2	17 November	Drew	**1**	**1**	13 April	Drew	**1**	**1**	14th	9th
1974-75	Division 2	28 August	Won	**6**	**0**	20 August	Drew	**1**	**1**	2ndP	8th
1987-88	Division 2	1 January	Won	**5**	**0**	29 August	Lost	**1**	**2**	2ndP	15th

FA Cup										Division	
1907-08	Round 2	1 February	Won	**3**	**0**					Div 1	Div 2
1925-26	Round 3					9 January	Won	**3**	**0**	Div 1	Div 2
1955-56	Round 3	7 January	Drew	**1**	**1**	12 January	Won	**2**	**1**	Div 1	Div 2
1998-99	Round 3	2 January	Won	**3**	**0**					Prem	Div 3

Summary	*P*	*W*	*D*	*L*	*F*	*A*
Villa's home league record:	8	4	3	1	21	8
Villa's away league record:	8	2	2	4	7	12
Villa's cup record:	5	4	1	0	12	2
TOTAL:	**21**	**10**	**6**	**5**	**40**	**22**

FACT FILE

- **Villa are unbeaten in their last seven home games. They have won the last three of these with a combined score of 14-0.**

Villa's top scorers vs Hull

Warren Aspinall, Ian Hamilton, Brian Little, Sammy Morgan 3

Villa hat-tricks vs Hull

28 Aug 1974 Sammy Morgan

Played for both clubs

Bert Goode	Villa 1911-12	Hull 1912-13
Ronnie Starling	Hull 1927-30 Villa	1936-47
Tommy Gardner	Hull 1932-34 Villa	1933-38
Arthur Cunliffe	Villa 1932-36	Hull 1938-40
Jackie Sewell	Villa 1955-60	Hull 1959-61
John Neal	Hull 1949-56 Villa	1959-63
Pat Heard	Villa 1979-83	Hull 1985-88/92-93
David Norton	Villa 1984-88	Hull 1990-94
Gareth Williams	Villa 1987-90	Hull 1992-94/98-2000
Kevin Gage	Villa 1987-91	Hull 1997-99
Lee Butler	Villa 1988-91	Hull 1990-91
Ian Ormondroyd	Villa 1988-92	Hull 1994-95
Martin Carruthers	Villa 1991-93	Hull 1992-93
Garry Parker	Hull 1985-88	Villa 1991-95

v. Ipswich Town

Season	League	Date	Result	Home Villa	Home Ipswich	Date	Result	Away Villa	Away Ipswich	Final Positions Villa	Final Positions Ipswich
1959-60	Division 2	12 September	Won	3	1	23 January	Lost	1	2	1stP	11th
1961-62	Division 1	9 December	Won	3	0	28 April	Lost	0	2	7th	1st
1962-63	Division 1	29 September	Won	4	2	21 May	Drew	1	1	15th	17th
1963-64	Division 1	30 November	Drew	0	0	11 April	Lost	3	4	19th	22ndR
1967-68	Division 2	6 April	Drew	2	2	11 November	Lost	1	2	16th	1stP
1975-76	Division 1	6 March	Drew	0	0	1 November	Lost	0	3	16th	6th
1976-77	Division 1	4 September	Won	5	2	12 February	Lost	0	1	4th	3rd
1977-78	Division 1	29 April	Won	6	1	3 December	Lost	0	2	8th	18th
1978-79	Division 1	2 May	Drew	2	2	9 September	Won	2	0	8th	6th
1979-80	Division 1	22 March	Drew	1	1	10 November	Drew	0	0	7th	3rd
1980-81	Division 1	14 April	Lost	1	2	6 September	Lost	0	1	1st	2nd
1981-82	Division 1	31 October	Lost	0	1	20 March	Lost	1	3	11th	2nd
1982-83	Division 1	29 December	Drew	1	1	2 April	Won	2	1	6th	9th
1983-84	Division 1	17 December	Won	4	0	12 May	Lost	1	2	10th	12th
1984-85	Division 1	2 February	Won	2	1	29 September	Lost	0	3	10th	17th
1985-86	Division 1	16 April	Won	1	0	21 September	Won	3	0	16th	20thR
1987-88	Division 2	16 January	Won	1	0	15 August	Drew	1	1	2ndP	8th
1992-93	Premiership	6 February	Won	2	0	15 August	Drew	1	1	2nd	16th
1993-94	Premiership	12 March	Lost	0	1	18 September	Won	2	1	10th	19th
1994-95	Premiership	10 September	Won	2	0	1 April	Won	1	0	18th	22ndR
2000-01	Premiership	10 March	Won	2	1	9 September	Won	2	1	8th	5th
2001-02	Premiership	17 December	Won	2	1	23 March	Drew	0	0	8th	18thR

FA Cup

										Division	
1938-39	Round 3	7 January	Drew	1	1	11 January	Won	2	1	Div 1	Div 3S
1974-75	Round 5					15 February	Lost	2	3	Div 2	Div 1
1980-81	Round 3	3 January	Lost	0	1					Div 1	Div 1
1995-96	Round 5					17 February	Won	3	1	Prem	Div 1

League Cup

1961-62	Round 3	21 November	Lost	2	3					Div 1	Div 1
1988-89	Round 4	30 November	Won	6	2					Div 1	Div 2
1992-93	Round 4	2 December	Drew	2	2	15 December	Lost	0	1	Prem	Prem

Summary	*P*	*W*	*D*	*L*	*F*	*A*
Villa's home league record:	22	13	6	3	44	19
Villa's away league record:	22	6	5	11	22	31
Villa's cup record:	9	3	2	4	18	15
TOTAL:	**53**	**22**	**13**	**18**	**84**	**65**

FACT FILE

- **Villa have won six and drawn one of their last seven games with Ipswich.**
- **Villa were unbeaten in their first 10 home league games agsinst Ipswich. Their first defeat there came at the worst time; in April 1981 as both teams were challenging for the league championship. Happily though, Villa won the war despite losing the battle. Ipswich had already won at Villa Park in the FA Cup earlier that season.**
- **From 1960 to 1977, Villa lost eight and drew one on their nine trips to Suffolk.**

Villa's top scorers vs Ipswich

Andy Gray 5

Peter McParland, David Platt, Dean Saunders, Bobby Thomson, Peter Withe 4

Villa hat-tricks vs Ipswich

4 Sep 1976 Andy Gray

30 Nov 1988 David Platt (4) (cup)

Played for both clubs

Jimmy McLuckie	Villa 1934-36	Ipswich 1938-46
Jackie Williams	Villa 1935-36	Ipswich 1938-39
Jock Mulraney	Ipswich 1938-39	Villa 1948-49
John Deehan	Villa 1975-80	Ipswich 1986-88
David Geddis	Ipswich 1976-79	Villa 1979-83
Dalian Atkinson	Ipswich 1985-89	Villa 1991-95

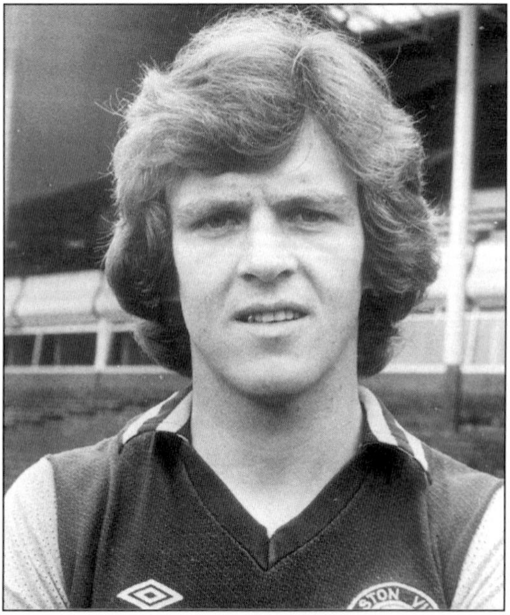

John Deehan signed professional forms for Villa in April 1975 and scored 50 goals in 139 senior appearances before moving to West Brom for £424,000 in September 1979. He was the first player to move from Villa to Albion since George Harris in 1909 but the transfer was not successful and Deehan soon went on to Norwich and later Ipswich. He achieved plenty with both East Anglian clubs to add to the League Cup medal he gained with Villa in 1977.

v. King's Lynn

FA Cup		Date	Result	Home Villa	Home King's Lynn	Division Villa	Division King's Lynn
1905-06	Round 1	13 January	Won	**11**	**0**	Div 1	Non L

Summary	P	W	D	L	F	A
Villa's cup record:	1	1	0	0	11	0
TOTAL:	**1**	**1**	**0**	**0**	**11**	**0**

FACT FILE

- **This was the last time Villa reached double figures in an FA Cup match.**

Villa's top scorers vs King's Lynn

Charlie Millington 4

Albert Hall 3

Billy Garraty 2

Villa hat-tricks vs King's Lynn

13 Jan 1906 Charlie Millington (4) (cup)

13 Jan 1906 Albert Hall (cup)

Aston Villa after they won the FA Cup in 1905 and started their defence against King's Lynn. Standing (left to right): G.B. Ramsay (secretary), Freddie Miles, H. Toney (director), Howard Spencer (captain), F.W. Rinder (chairman), Billy George, John Devey (director), J. Grierson (trainer). Seated: D.V.A. Jones (director), Billy Brawn, Billy Garraty, Harry Hampton, Joe Bache, Albert Hall, J.T. Lees (director). On ground: Joe Pearson. Alex Leake, Jack Windmill.

v. Leeds United

Season	League	Home Date	Home Result	Home Villa	Home Leeds	Away Date	Away Result	Away Villa	Away Leeds	Final Positions Villa	Final Positions Leeds
1924-25	Division 1	26 December	Won	2	1	25 December	Lost	0	6	15th	18th
1925-26	Division 1	3 February	Won	3	1	5 September	Drew	2	2	6th	19th
1926-27	Division 1	28 December	Won	5	1	15 September	Lost	1	3	10th	21stR
1928-29	Division 1	29 December	Won	1	0	25 August	Lost	1	4	3rd	13th
1929-30	Division 1	4 January	Lost	3	4	7 September	Lost	1	4	4th	5th
1930-31	Division 1	13 December	Won	4	3	18 April	Won	2	0	2nd	21stR
1932-33	Division 1	22 April	Drew	0	0	10 December	Drew	1	1	2nd	8th
1933-34	Division 1	30 April	Won	3	0	4 November	Won	4	2	13th	9th
1934-35	Division 1	8 December	Drew	1	1	20 April	Drew	1	1	13th	18th
1935-36	Division 1	14 March	Drew	3	3	26 October	Lost	2	4	21stR	11th
1938-39	Division 1	17 December	Won	2	1	22 April	Lost	0	2	12th	13th
1946-47	Division 1	14 December	Won	2	1	19 April	Drew	1	1	8th	22ndR
1956-57	Division 1	2 February	Drew	1	1	22 September	Lost	0	1	10th	8th
1957-58	Division 1	26 August	Won	2	0	4 September	Lost	0	4	14th	17th
1958-59	Division 1	7 March	Won	2	1	18 October	Drew	0	0	21stR	15th
1964-65	Division 1	22 August	Lost	1	2	12 December	Lost	0	1	16th	2nd
1965-66	Division 1	23 August	Lost	0	2	1 September	Lost	0	2	16th	2nd
1966-67	Division 1	8 October	Won	3	0	25 February	Won	2	0	21stR	4th
1975-76	Division 1	16 August	Lost	1	2	20 December	Lost	0	1	16th	5th
1976-77	Division 1	7 May	Won	2	1	11 December	Won	3	1	4th	10th
1977-78	Division 1	26 April	Won	3	1	5 October	Drew	1	1	8th	9th
1978-79	Division 1	26 December	Drew	2	2	14 April	Lost	0	1	8th	5th
1979-80	Division 1	24 November	Drew	0	0	19 April	Drew	0	0	7th	11th
1980-81	Division 1	15 November	Drew	1	1	16 August	Won	2	1	1st	9th
1981-82	Division 1	28 April	Lost	1	4	3 October	Drew	1	1	11th	20thR
1987-88	Division 2	12 March	Lost	1	2	10 October	Won	3	1	2ndP	7th
1990-91	Division 1	27 October	Drew	0	0	4 May	Lost	2	5	17th	4th
1991-92	Division 1	24 November	Lost	1	4	3 March	Drew	0	0	7th	1st
1992-93	Premiership	19 August	Drew	1	1	13 September	Drew	1	1	2nd	17th
1993-94	Premiership	6 February	Won	1	0	16 March	Lost	0	2	10th	5th
1994-95	Premiership	2 January	Drew	0	0	29 April	Lost	0	1	18th	5th
1995-96	Premiership	3 February	Won	3	0	26 August	Lost	0	2	4th	13th
1996-97	Premiership	19 October	Won	2	0	22 April	Drew	0	0	5th	11th
1997-98	Premiership	30 August	Won	1	0	28 December	Drew	1	1	7th	5th
1998-99	Premiership	17 February	Lost	1	2	19 September	Drew	0	0	6th	4th
1999-00	Premiership	9 April	Won	1	0	3 January	Won	2	1	6th	3rd
2000-01	Premiership	24 January	Lost	1	2	23 December	Won	2	1	8th	4th
2001-02	Premiership	13 April	Lost	0	1	25 November	Drew	1	1	8th	5th
2002-03	Premiership	6 October	Drew	0	0	11 May	Lost	1	3	16th	15th
2003-04	Premiership	7 February	Won	2	0	26 December	Drew	0	0	6th	19thR

FA Cup

Season	Round	Date	Result	Villa	Leeds	Division Villa	Division Leeds
1923-24	Round 3	23 February	Won	3	0	Div 1	Div 2
1959-60	Round 3	9 January	Won	2	1	Div 2	Div 1

FA Cup		Home Date	Result	Villa	Leeds	Away Date	Result	Villa	Leeds	Division Villa	Leeds
1987-88	Round 3					9 January	Won	**2**	**1**	Div 2	Div 2
1999-00	Round 5	30 January	Won	**3**	**2**					Prem	Prem

League Cup		Home Date	Result	Villa	Leeds	Away Date	Result	Villa	Leeds	Division Villa	Leeds
1964-65	Round 3					14 October	Won	**3**	**2**	Div 1	Div 1
1972-73	Round 3	4 October	Drew	**1**	**1**	11 October	Lost	**0**	**2**	Div 2	Div 1
1980-81	Round 2	27 August	Won	**1**	**0**	3 September	Won	**3**	**1**	Div 1	Div 1
1985-86	Round 3					30 October	Won	**3**	**0**	Div 1	Div 2
1990-91	Q'ter Final					16 January	Lost	**1**	**4**	Div 1	Div 1
1995-96	Final	24 March		Wembley			Won	**3**	**0**	Prem	Prem
1996-97	Round 3					23 October	Won	**2**	**1**	Prem	Prem

Summary	*P*	*W*	*D*	*L*	*F*	*A*
Villa's home league record:	40	19	11	10	63	45
Villa's away league record:	40	8	15	17	38	63
Villa's cup record:	13	10	1	2	27	15
TOTAL:	**93**	**37**	**27**	**29**	**128**	**123**

FACT FILE

- **In 1996, Villa swept Leeds aside with ease to win their fifth League Cup, which equalled the record at the time. This trophy, won under the managership of Brian Little, was to be the last major trophy won by an English manager for eight years.**
- **Villa failed to win at Elland Road in nine league games from 1991 to 1998.**
- **Villa were unbeaten in 11 home games from 1930 to 1960.**

Villa's top scorers vs Leeds

Dwight Yorke 7
Dai Astley 6
Len Capewell, Gary Shaw, Pongo Waring 5
Eric Houghton, Billy Walker 4

Villa hat-tricks vs Leeds

30 Apr 1933 Dai Astley
30 Jan 2000 Benito Carbone (cup)

Played for both clubs

George Brown	Villa 1929-35	Leeds 1935-37
Gordon Hodgson	Villa 1935-37	Leeds 1936-40
Con Martin	Leeds 1946-49	Villa 1948-56
Bobby McDonald	Villa 1972-76	Leeds 1986-88
Brendan Ormsby	Villa 1978-86	Leeds 1985-89
Gary Williams	Villa 1978-87	Leeds 1987-89
Noel Blake	Villa 1979-82	Leeds 1988-90
Mervyn Day	Villa 1983-85	Leeds 1984-93
Tony Dorigo	Villa 1983-87	Leeds 1991-97
Steve Hodge	Villa 1985-87	Leeds 1991-94
Simon Grayson	Leeds 1987-88	Villa 1997-99

v. Leicester City

		Home					Away				Final Positions	
Season	League	Date	Result	Villa	Leicester	Date	Result	Villa	Leicester	Villa	Leicester
1908-09	Division 1	31 October	Drew	1	1	27 March	Lost	2	4	7th	20thR
1925-26	Division 1	10 March	Drew	2	2	10 October	Won	2	1	6th	17th
1926-27	Division 1	16 April	Won	2	0	27 November	Lost	1	5	10th	7th
1927-28	Division 1	27 August	Lost	0	3	31 December	Lost	0	3	8th	3rd
1928-29	Division 1	2 April	Won	4	2	1 April	Lost	1	4	3rd	2nd
1929-30	Division 1	19 October	Won	3	0	22 February	Lost	3	4	4th	8th
1930-31	Division 1	28 February	Won	4	2	25 October	Lost	1	4	2nd	16th
1931-32	Division 1	29 August	Won	3	2	2 January	Won	8	3	5th	19th
1932-33	Division 1	17 September	Won	4	2	9 February	Lost	0	3	2nd	19th
1933-34	Division 1	26 August	Lost	2	3	30 December	Drew	1	1	13th	17th
1934-35	Division 1	19 January	Won	5	0	8 September	Lost	0	5	13th	21stR
1936-37	Division 2	5 December	Lost	1	3	10 April	Lost	0	1	9th	1stP
1938-39	Division 1	22 October	Lost	1	2	25 February	Drew	1	1	12th	22ndR
1954-55	Division 1	6 November	Lost	2	5	26 March	Lost	2	4	6th	21stR
1957-58	Division 1	28 September	Won	5	1	8 February	Lost	1	6	14th	18th
1958-59	Division 1	4 April	Lost	1	2	15 November	Lost	3	6	21stR	19th
1960-61	Division 1	1 October	Lost	1	3	19 April	Lost	1	3	9th	6th
1961-62	Division 1	21 April	Won	8	3	2 December	Won	2	0	7th	14th
1962-63	Division 1	15 May	Won	3	1	8 December	Drew	3	3	15th	4th
1963-64	Division 1	18 April	Lost	1	3	7 December	Drew	0	0	19th	11th
1964-65	Division 1	20 April	Won	1	0	19 April	Drew	1	1	16th	18th
1965-66	Division 1	28 August	Drew	2	2	5 February	Lost	1	2	16th	7th
1966-67	Division 1	4 February	Lost	0	1	24 September	Lost	0	5	21stR	8th
1969-70	Division 2	27 August	Lost	0	1	4 April	Lost	0	1	21stR	3rd

Andy Lochhead came under the label of 'much-travelled striker' and his stay at Villa Park saw him score 44 goals in 153 senior appearances and win a Third Division championship medal as well as play in the 1971 League Cup Final against Spurs. Born near Glasgow in 1941, his first senior club was Burnley, for whom he scored over 100 goals. Then Leicester took him and he played for them in the 1969 FA Cup Final. Villa signed Lochhead in February 1970 and in August 1973 he was on his way once more, this time to Oldham Athletic. He later played in the North American Soccer League and coached at several clubs.

Season	League	Home Date	Result	Villa	Leicester	Away Date	Result	Villa	Leicester	Final Positions Villa	Leicester
1975-76	Division 1	29 November	Drew	**1**	**1**	20 March	Drew	**2**	**2**	16th	7th
1976-77	Division 1	25 September	Won	**2**	**0**	5 March	Drew	**1**	**1**	4th	11th
1977-78	Division 1	4 March	Drew	**0**	**0**	8 October	Won	**2**	**0**	8th	22ndR
1980-81	Division 1	1 November	Won	**2**	**0**	4 April	Won	**4**	**2**	1st	21stR
1983-84	Division 1	19 November	Won	**3**	**1**	14 April	Lost	**0**	**2**	10th	15th
1984-85	Division 1	2 March	Lost	**0**	**1**	27 October	Lost	**0**	**5**	10th	15th
1985-86	Division 1	31 March	Won	**1**	**0**	26 December	Lost	**1**	**3**	16th	19th
1986-87	Division 1	1 November	Won	**2**	**0**	11 April	Drew	**1**	**1**	22ndR	20thR
1987-88	Division 2	6 February	Won	**2**	**1**	5 September	Won	**2**	**0**	2ndP	13th
1994-95	Premiership	22 February	Drew	**4**	**4**	3 December	Drew	**1**	**1**	18th	21stR
1996-97	Premiership	16 November	Lost	**1**	**3**	5 March	Lost	**0**	**1**	5th	9th
1997-98	Premiership	10 January	Drew	**1**	**1**	9 August	Lost	**0**	**1**	7th	10th
1998-99	Premiership	24 October	Drew	**1**	**1**	6 April	Drew	**2**	**2**	6th	10th
1999-00	Premiership	22 April	Drew	**2**	**2**	25 September	Lost	**1**	**3**	6th	8th
2000-01	Premiership	4 April	Won	**2**	**1**	19 August	Drew	**0**	**0**	8th	13th
2001-02	Premiership	1 December	Lost	**0**	**2**	20 April	Drew	**2**	**2**	8th	20thR
2003-04	Premiership	30 August	Won	**3**	**1**	31 January	Won	**5**	**0**	6th	18thR

FA Cup

Season	Round	Home Date	Result	Villa	Leicester	Away Date	Result	Villa	Leicester	Division Villa	Leicester
1904-05	Round 1	4 February	Won	**5**	**1**					Div 1	Div 2
1965-66	Round 3	22 January	Lost	**1**	**2**					Div 1	Div 1
1976-77	Round 3					8 January	Won	**1**	**0**	Div 1	Div 1
2000-01	Round 4	27 January	Lost	**1**	**2**					Prem	Prem

League Cup

Season	Round	Home Date	Result	Villa	Leicester	Away Date	Result	Villa	Leicester	Division Villa	Leicester
1981-82	Round 3	25 November	Won	**2**	**0**	11 November	Drew	**0**	**0**	Div 1	Div 2
1999-00	Semi-Final	25 January	Drew	**0**	**0**	2 February	Lost	**0**	**1**	Prem	Prem
2003-04	Round 3	29 October	Won	**1**	**0**					Prem	Prem

Summary	*P*	*W*	*D*	*L*	*F*	*A*
Villa's home league record:	41	19	9	13	83	61
Villa's away league record:	41	7	12	22	58	96
Villa's cup record:	9	4	2	3	11	6
TOTAL:	**91**	**30**	**23**	**38**	**152**	**165**

Villa's top scorers vs Leicester

George Brown 9
Billy Walker 7
Pongo Waring 6
Dai Astley, Joe Beresford 5
Derek Dougan, Peter Withe, Dicky York 4

Villa hat-tricks vs Leicester

28 Feb 1931 Joe Beresford
2 Jan 1932 George Brown (5)
19 Jan 1935 Dai Astley
21 Apr 1962 Bobby Thomson

Played for both clubs

David Skea	Villa 1892-93	Leicester 1894-96
John Baird	Villa 1891-95	Leicester 1895-96
Robert Gordon	Villa 1894-95	Leicester 1894-95
Billy Dorrell	Villa 1894-96	Leicester 1895-99
Fred Watkins	Leicester 1897-99	Villa 1899-1900

FACT FILE

- **In January 1932, Villa scored eight in an away league match for the only time. Also in this game, George Brown became the last man to score five goals in a top-flight game for Villa.**
- **Leicester also shared Villa's highest scoring Premiership draw (4-4 in 1995).**
- **From 1927 to 1931, the series produced eight successive home wins.**
- **From 1936 to 1961, Leicester won 10 and lost one of the sides' 12 meetings.**
- **Villa won only once in 17 matches against Leicester between 1994 and 2002.**
- **Villa recorded their biggest Premiership away win to date with a 5-0 win over Leicester in 2004.**

Billy Garraty	Villa 1897-1908	Leicester 1908-09
George Travers	Villa 1908-09	Leicester 1910-11
Brendel Anstey	Villa 1910-15	Leicester 1919-20
John Roxburgh	Leicester 1920-23	Villa 1922-23
Matt Moralee	Villa 1936-37	Leicester 1937-39
James Harrison	Leicester 1946-49	Villa 1949-50
Derek Dougan	Villa 1961-63	Leicester 1965-67
Brian Greenhalgh	Villa 1967-69	Leicester 1968-69
Andy Lochhead	Leicester 1968-70	Villa 1969-73
Dave Gibson	Leicester 1961-70	Villa 1970-72
Allan Evans	Villa 1977-89	Leicester 1989-90
Colin Gibson	Villa 1978-86	Leicester 1990-94
Paul Kerr	Villa 1983-87	Leicester 1993-94
Kevin Poole	Villa 1984-87	Leicester 1991-97
Steve Sims	Leicester 1975-79	Villa 1987-89
Ian Ormondroyd	Villa 1988-92	Leicester 1991-95
Mark Blake	Villa 1989-93	Leicester 1993-96
Garry Parker	Villa 1991-95	Leicester 1994-99
Graham Fenton	Villa 1993-96	Leicester 1997-2000
Franz Carr	Leicester 1994-95	Villa 1994-96
Gary Charles	Leicester 1988-89	Villa 1994-99
Mark Draper	Leicester 1994-95	Villa 1995-2000
Julian Joachim	Leicester 1992-96	Villa 1995-2001
Ricardo Scimeca	Villa 1995-99	Leicester 2003-04
Stan Collymore	Villa 1997-99	Leicester 1999-2001
Simon Grayson	Leicester 1991-97	Villa 1997-99

v. Leyton Orient

		Home					Away			Final Positions	
Season	League	Date	Result	Villa	Leyton	Date	Result	Villa	Leyton	Villa	Leyton
1959-60	Division 2	26 September	Won	**1**	**0**	13 February	Drew	**0**	**0**	1stP	10th
1962-63	Division 1	20 October	Won	**1**	**0**	9 March	Won	**2**	**0**	15th	22ndR
1972-73	Division 2	16 December	Won	**1**	**0**	24 February	Lost	**0**	**4**	3rd	15th
1973-74	Division 2	22 September	Drew	**2**	**2**	3 May	Drew	**1**	**1**	14th	4th
1974-75	Division 2	7 September	Won	**3**	**1**	22 March	Lost	**0**	**1**	2ndP	12th

FA Cup										Division	
1928-29	Round 4	26 January	Drew	**0**	**0**	30 January	Won	**8**	**0**	Div 1	Div 2

Summary	P	W	D	L	F	A
Villa's home league record:	5	4	1	0	8	3
Villa's away league record:	5	1	2	2	3	6
Villa's cup record:	2	1	1	0	8	0
TOTAL:	**12**	**6**	**4**	**2**	**19**	**9**

FACT FILE

- **Villa have not lost in their six home games in the series.**

Villa's top scorers vs Orient

Ray Graydon, Pongo Waring 3

Villa hat-tricks vs Orient

30 Jan 1929 Pongo Waring (cup)

Played for both clubs

Walter Leigh	Villa 1898-99	Orient 1905-06/07-08
Alf Gilson	Villa 1900-01	Orient 1905-06
Bert Kingaby	Orient 1905-06	Villa 1905-06
John Boden	Orient 1905-06	Villa 1905-07
Rowland Codling	Orient 1905-06	Villa 1905-09
Harold Halse	Orient 1905-06	Villa 1912-13
Joe Nicholson	Orient 1919-24	Villa 1926-27
Albert Surtees	Villa 1923-25	Orient 1927-28
Fred Tully	Villa 1927-29	Orient 1937-39
Oliver Tidman	Villa 1932-33	Orient 1937-38
Michael Pinner	Villa 1954-57	Orient 1962-65
Phil Woosnam	Orient 1954-59	Villa 1962-66
Harry Gregory	Orient 1962-66	Villa 1970-72
Mervyn Day	Orient 1979-83	Villa 1983-85
Steve Hodge	Villa 1985-87	Orient 1997-98
Les Sealey	Villa 1991-92	Orient 1996-97

v. Lincoln City

				Home					Away		Final Positions	
Season	*League*	*Date*	*Result*	Villa	Lincoln	*Date*	*Result*	Villa	Lincoln	Villa	Lincoln
1959-60	Division 2	1 March	Drew	**1**	**1**	3 October	Drew	**0**	**0**	1stP	13th

Summary	*P*	*W*	*D*	*L*	*F*	*A*
Villa's home league record:	1	0	1	0	1	1
Villa's away league record:	1	0	1	0	0	0
TOTAL:	**2**	**0**	**2**	**0**	**1**	**1**

FACT FILE

- **This is the only Villa series in which neither side has won a match.**

Played for both clubs

James Fleming	Villa 1892-93	Lincoln 1892-93
Willie Clarke	Villa 1901-05	Lincoln 1909-11
Billy Garraty	Villa 1897-1908	Lincoln 1910-11
Archie Campbell	Villa 1923-25	Lincoln 1925-27
Billy Dinsdale	Villa 1924-26	Lincoln 1926-29/30-31
Bob Iverson	Lincoln 1933-35	Villa 1936-48
Roy Chapman	Villa 1953-58	Lincoln 1957-62/64-67
Kenneth Barrett	Villa 1958-59	Lincoln 1959-63
Ken Fencott	Villa 1961-64	Lincoln 1964-67
Graham Parker	Villa 1963-68	Lincoln 1968-69
Colin Withers	Villa 1964-69	Lincoln 1969-70
John Burridge	Villa 1975-77	Lincoln 1993-94
Dave Hughes	Villa 1976-77	Lincoln 1977-81
Steve Sims	Villa 1987-89	Lincoln 1990-91
Lee Butler	Lincoln 1986-87	Villa 1988-91
John Fashanu	Lincoln 1983-85	Villa 1994-95

v. Liverpool

		Home					Away			Final Positions	
Season	League	Date	Result	Villa	Liverpool	Date	Result	Villa	Liverpool	Villa	Liverpool
1894-95	Division 1	27 October	Won	**5**	**0**	8 September	Won	**2**	**1**	3rd	16thR
1896-97	Division 1	13 March	Drew	**0**	**0**	25 December	Drew	**3**	**3**	1st	5th
1897-98	Division 1	30 October	Won	**3**	**1**	16 April	Lost	**0**	**4**	6th	9th
1898-99	Division 1	29 April	Won	**5**	**0**	15 October	Won	**3**	**0**	1st	2nd
1899-00	Division 1	24 March	Won	**1**	**0**	18 November	Drew	**3**	**3**	1st	10th
1900-01	Division 1	16 March	Lost	**0**	**2**	10 November	Lost	**1**	**5**	15th	1st
1901-02	Division 1	29 March	Lost	**0**	**1**	30 November	Lost	**0**	**1**	8th	11th
1902-03	Division 1	13 December	Lost	**1**	**2**	11 April	Lost	**1**	**2**	2nd	5th
1903-04	Division 1	28 November	Won	**2**	**1**	26 March	Drew	**1**	**1**	5th	17thR
1905-06	Division 1	11 September	Won	**5**	**0**	2 December	Lost	**0**	**3**	8th	1st
1906-07	Division 1	30 March	Won	**4**	**0**	24 November	Lost	**2**	**5**	5th	15th
1907-08	Division 1	4 April	Won	**5**	**1**	7 December	Lost	**0**	**5**	2nd	8th
1908-09	Division 1	25 December	Drew	**1**	**1**	1 September	Lost	**2**	**3**	7th	16th
1909-10	Division 1	18 December	Won	**3**	**1**	30 April	Lost	**0**	**2**	1st	2nd
1910-11	Division 1	24 December	Drew	**1**	**1**	29 April	Lost	**1**	**3**	2nd	13th
1911-12	Division 1	2 December	Won	**5**	**0**	6 April	Won	**2**	**1**	6th	17th
1912-13	Division 1	5 April	Lost	**1**	**3**	30 November	Lost	**0**	**2**	2nd	12th
1913-14	Division 1	6 December	Won	**2**	**1**	11 April	Won	**1**	**0**	2nd	16th
1914-15	Division 1	3 April	Won	**6**	**2**	28 November	Won	**6**	**3**	14th	13th
1919-20	Division 1	20 September	Lost	**0**	**1**	13 September	Lost	**1**	**2**	9th	4th
1920-21	Division 1	1 January	Lost	**0**	**2**	18 December	Lost	**1**	**4**	10th	4th
1921-22	Division 1	3 December	Drew	**1**	**1**	10 December	Lost	**0**	**2**	5th	1st
1922-23	Division 1	25 November	Lost	**0**	**1**	18 November	Lost	**0**	**3**	6th	1st
1923-24	Division 1	17 November	Drew	**0**	**0**	24 November	Won	**1**	**0**	6th	12th
1924-25	Division 1	21 January	Lost	**1**	**4**	30 August	Won	**4**	**2**	15th	4th
1925-26	Division 1	6 April	Won	**3**	**0**	1 January	Lost	**1**	**3**	6ht	7th
1926-27	Division 1	30 August	Drew	**1**	**1**	8 September	Lost	**1**	**2**	10th	9th
1927-28	Division 1	7 January	Lost	**3**	**4**	3 September	Drew	**0**	**0**	8th	16th
1928-29	Division 1	1 September	Won	**3**	**1**	5 January	Lost	**0**	**4**	3rd	5th
1929-30	Division 1	16 November	Lost	**2**	**3**	22 March	Lost	**0**	**2**	4th	12th
1930-31	Division 1	20 September	Won	**4**	**2**	24 January	Drew	**1**	**1**	2nd	9th
1931-32	Division 1	16 January	Won	**6**	**1**	5 September	Lost	**0**	**2**	5th	10th
1932-33	Division 1	21 January	Won	**5**	**2**	10 September	Drew	**0**	**0**	2nd	14th
1933-34	Division 1	9 September	Won	**4**	**2**	20 January	Won	**3**	**2**	13th	18th
1934-35	Division 1	13 April	Won	**4**	**2**	1 December	Lost	**1**	**3**	13th	7th
1935-36	Division 1	29 February	Won	**3**	**0**	9 November	Lost	**2**	**3**	21stR	19th
1938-39	Division 1	18 February	Won	**2**	**0**	15 October	Lost	**0**	**3**	12th	11th
1946-47	Division 1	26 April	Lost	**1**	**2**	21 December	Lost	**1**	**4**	8th	1st
1947-48	Division 1	24 April	Won	**2**	**1**	6 December	Drew	**3**	**3**	6th	11th
1948-49	Division 1	21 August	Won	**2**	**1**	18 December	Drew	**1**	**1**	10th	12th
1949-50	Division 1	11 March	Won	**2**	**0**	19 November	Lost	**1**	**2**	12th	8th
1950-51	Division 1	2 September	Drew	**1**	**1**	25 April	Drew	**0**	**0**	15th	9th
1951-52	Division 1	22 September	Won	**2**	**0**	26 January	Won	**2**	**1**	6th	11th
1952-53	Division 1	7 March	Won	**4**	**0**	18 October	Won	**2**	**0**	11th	17th

		Home				Away				Final Positions	
Season	*League*	*Date*	*Result*	Villa	Liverpool	*Date*	*Result*	Villa	Liverpool	Villa	Liverpool
1953-54	Division 1	27 February	Won	**2**	**1**	10 October	Lost	**1**	**6**	13th	22ndR
1959-60	Division 2	30 March	Drew	**4**	**4**	7 November	Lost	**1**	**2**	1stP	3rd
1962-63	Division 1	18 May	Won	**2**	**0**	13 February	Lost	**0**	**4**	15th	8th
1963-64	Division 1	19 February	Drew	**2**	**2**	5 October	Lost	**2**	**5**	19th	1st
1964-65	Division 1	6 February	Lost	**0**	**1**	26 September	Lost	**1**	**5**	16th	7th
1965-66	Division 1	26 March	Lost	**0**	**3**	2 October	Lost	**1**	**3**	16th	1st
1966-67	Division 1	1 October	Lost	**2**	**3**	11 February	Lost	**0**	**1**	21stR	5th
1975-76	Division 1	10 April	Drew	**0**	**0**	20 September	Lost	**0**	**3**	16th	1st
1976-77	Division 1	15 December	Won	**5**	**1**	30 October	Lost	**0**	**3**	4th	1st
1977-78	Division 1	1 April	Lost	**0**	**3**	5 November	Won	**2**	**1**	8th	2nd
1978-79	Division 1	16 April	Won	**3**	**1**	8 May	Lost	**0**	**3**	8th	1st
1979-80	Division 1	8 December	Lost	**1**	**3**	3 May	Lost	**1**	**4**	7th	1st
1980-81	Division 1	10 January	Won	**2**	**0**	22 November	Lost	**1**	**2**	1st	5th
1981-82	Division 1	30 January	Lost	**0**	**3**	19 September	Drew	**0**	**0**	11th	1st
1982-83	Division 1	18 December	Lost	**2**	**4**	7 May	Drew	**1**	**1**	6th	1st
1983-84	Division 1	20 January	Lost	**1**	**3**	17 September	Lost	**1**	**2**	10th	1st
1984-85	Division 1	15 December	Drew	**0**	**0**	11 May	Lost	**1**	**2**	10th	2nd
1985-86	Division 1	21 August	Drew	**2**	**2**	7 December	Lost	**0**	**3**	16th	1st
1986-87	Division 1	21 February	Drew	**2**	**2**	27 September	Drew	**3**	**3**	22ndR	2nd
1988-89	Division 1	10 September	Drew	**1**	**1**	3 January	Lost	**0**	**1**	17th	2nd
1989-90	Division 1	23 August	Drew	**1**	**1**	9 December	Drew	**1**	**1**	2nd	1st
1990-91	Division 1	12 January	Drew	**0**	**0**	1 September	Lost	**1**	**2**	17th	2nd
1991-92	Division 1	11 April	Won	**1**	**0**	14 September	Drew	**1**	**1**	7th	6th
1992-93	Premiership	19 September	Won	**4**	**2**	9 January	Won	**2**	**1**	2nd	6th
1993-94	Premiership	7 May	Won	**2**	**1**	28 November	Lost	**1**	**2**	10th	8th
1994-95	Premiership	6 May	Won	**2**	**0**	8 October	Lost	**2**	**3**	18th	4th
1995-96	Premiership	31 January	Lost	**0**	**2**	3 March	Lost	**0**	**3**	4th	3rd
1996-97	Premiership	2 March	Won	**1**	**0**	18 January	Lost	**0**	**3**	5th	4th
1997-98	Premiership	28 February	Won	**2**	**1**	22 September	Lost	**0**	**3**	7th	3rd
1998-99	Premiership	21 November	Lost	**2**	**4**	17 April	Won	**1**	**0**	6th	7th
1999-00	Premiership	2 October	Drew	**0**	**0**	15 March	Drew	**0**	**0**	6th	4th
2000-01	Premiership	13 January	Lost	**0**	**3**	6 September	Lost	**1**	**3**	8th	3rd
2001-02	Premiership	26 December	Lost	**1**	**2**	8 September	Won	**3**	**1**	8th	2th
2002-03	Premiership	18 August	Lost	**0**	**1**	11 January	Drew	**1**	**1**	16th	5th
2003-04	Premiership	24 August	Drew	**0**	**0**	10 January	Lost	**0**	**1**	6th	4th

FA Cup										*Division*	
1896-97	Semi-Final	20 March				Bramall Lane	Won	**3**	**0**	Div 1	Div 1
1913-14	Semi-Final	28 March				White Hart Lane	Lost	**0**	**2**	Div 1	Div 1
1966-67	Round 4					18 February	Lost	**0**	**1**	Div 1	Div 1
1984-85	Round 3					5 January	Lost	**0**	**3**	Div 1	Div 1
1987-88	Round 4	31 January	Lost	**0**	**2**					Div 2	Div 1
1991-92	Q'ter Final					8 March	Lost	**0**	**1**	Div 1	Div 1
1995-96	Semi-Final	31 March				Old Trafford	Lost	**0**	**3**	Prem	Prem

League Cup											
2002-03	Q'ter Final	18 December	Lost	**3**	**4**					Prem	Prem

Summary	P	W	D	L	F	A
Villa's home league record:	79	37	18	24	153	103
Villa's away league record:	79	14	16	49	84	175
Villa's cup record:	8	1	0	7	6	16
TOTAL:	**166**	**52**	**34**	**80**	**243**	**294**

FACT FILE

- **In common with virtually every side who has played there, Villa have had some bad experiences at Anfield over the years. Between 1953 and 1992, Villa won once and lost 20 times in 26 matches.**
- **Liverpool have won the last seven cup matches between the sides. Villa have failed to score in six of these.**
- **Villa have had happier times against Liverpool as well. In April 1899, the two title challengers met in the final game of the season for a title decider. Villa needed only a draw, but clearly had no thoughts of playing defensively, as they ripped Liverpool apart 5-0 for their fourth league title in six seasons.**
- **In a second division match in 1960, Liverpool were 4-0 up after an hour, only for Villa to score four times between the 66th and 85th minutes to snatch a draw.**
- **In 1976, Villa had been back in the top flight for only a year following an eight-year absence. Their first season back was unspectacular, but their second season really came to life when they beat the reigning champions 5-1, having led by that score at half-time. Some great years were just around the corner.**
- **Villa Park hosted six successive league draws between the sides from 1984 to 1991.**
- **Villa won seven successive home games from 1930 to 1939.**

Villa's Charlie Aitken could not prevent Roger Hunt's header from finding the back of the net at Anfield in September 1964, but the Liverpool man's effort was ruled offside. Liverpool, though, won the game 5-1 with Tony Hateley getting Villa's consolation.

Sam Hardy, who made 183 League and Cup appearances for Aston Villa including two FA Cup Finals, was the most famous English goalkeeper either side of World War One. Hardy began as a professional with his local club, Chesterfield, in 1903. Two years later he let in six against Liverpool but they were still impressed and signed him. He went on to make 239 League and Cup appearances for the Anfield club before being transferred to Villa in May 1912. He moved to Nottingham Forest in 1921 and his career ended three years later after he was injured playing against Newcastle. Hardy was capped 21 times for England and altogether made over 600 League and Cup appearances in his career.

Villa's top scorers vs Liverpool

Harry Hampton 15
Joe Bache 9
George Brown, Len Capewell, Jack Devey, Eric Houghton, Pongo Waring 6

Villa hat-tricks vs Liverpool

11 Sep 1905 Harry Hampton
4 Apr 1908 Joe Bache
3 Apr 1915 Harry Hampton
3 Apr 1915 Harry Nash
16 Jan 1932 George Brown (4)

Played for both clubs

Bert Goode	Liverpool 1908-10	Villa 1911-12
Sam Hardy	Liverpool 1905-12	Villa 1912-21
Jimmy Harrop	Liverpool 1907-12	Villa 1912-21
Tommy Gardner	Liverpool 1929-30	Villa 1933-38
Gordon Hodgson	Liverpool 1925-36	Villa 1935-37
David Hickson	Villa 1955-56	Liverpool 1959-61
Tony Hateley	Villa 1963-67	Liverpool 1967-69
Ian Ross	Liverpool 1966-72	Villa 1971-76
Alun Evans	Liverpool 1968-72	Villa 1972-74
Mark Walters	Villa 1981-88	Liverpool 1991-95
Steve McMahon	Villa 1983-86	Liverpool 1985-92
Steve Staunton	Liverpool 1988-91/98-2001	Villa 1991-98/2000-03
Ray Houghton	Liverpool 1987-92	Villa 1992-95
Dean Saunders	Liverpool 1991-93	Villa 1992-95
Stan Collymore	Liverpool 1995-97	Villa 1997-99
David James	Liverpool 1992-99	Villa 1999-2001
Oyvind Leonhardsen	Liverpool 1997-99	Villa 2002-03

v. Luton Town

		Home				Away				Final Positions	
Season	League	Date	Result	Villa	Luton	Date	Result	Villa	Luton	Villa	Luton
1937-38	Division 2	6 September	Won	**4**	**1**	1 September	Lost	**2**	**3**	1stP	12th
1955-56	Division 1	12 November	Won	**1**	**0**	24 March	Lost	**1**	**2**	20th	10th
1956-57	Division 1	27 April	Lost	**1**	**3**	5 September	Drew	**0**	**0**	10th	16th
1957-58	Division 1	14 September	Won	**2**	**0**	18 January	Lost	**0**	**3**	14th	8th
1958-59	Division 1	21 March	Won	**3**	**1**	1 November	Lost	**1**	**2**	21stR	17th
1972-73	Division 2	18 November	Lost	**0**	**2**	21 April	Drew	**0**	**0**	3rd	12th
1973-74	Division 2	2 February	Lost	**0**	**1**	15 December	Lost	**0**	**1**	14th	2ndP
1982-83	Division 1	8 September	Won	**4**	**1**	9 April	Lost	**1**	**2**	6th	18th
1983-84	Division 1	4 February	Drew	**0**	**0**	1 October	Lost	**0**	**1**	10th	16th
1984-85	Division 1	6 May	Lost	**0**	**1**	8 December	Lost	**0**	**1**	10th	13th
1985-86	Division 1	31 August	Won	**3**	**1**	18 January	Lost	**0**	**2**	16th	9th
1986-87	Division 1	3 September	Won	**2**	**1**	14 February	Lost	**1**	**2**	22ndR	7th
1988-89	Division 1	1 April	Won	**2**	**1**	17 December	Drew	**1**	**1**	17th	16th
1989-90	Division 1	10 March	Won	**2**	**0**	14 October	Won	**1**	**0**	2nd	17th
1990-91	Division 1	9 March	Lost	**1**	**2**	24 November	Lost	**0**	**2**	17th	18th
1991-92	Division 1	5 October	Won	**4**	**0**	25 April	Lost	**0**	**2**	7th	20thR

FA Cup

										Division	
1921-22	Round 2	28 January	Won	**1**	**0**					Div 1	Div 3S
1956-57	Round 3	7 January	Won	**2**	**0**	5 January	Drew	**2**	**2**	Div 1	Div 1

League Cup

1964-65	Round 2					23 September	Won	**1**	**0**	Div 1	Div 3
1978-79	Round 4	8 November	Lost	**0**	**2**					Div 1	Div 2
2002-03	Round 2	2 October	Won	**3**	**0**					Prem	Div 2

David Geddis had two spells with Luton Town.

Summary	P	W	D	L	F	A
Villa's home league record:	16	10	1	5	29	15
Villa's away league record:	16	1	3	12	8	24
Villa's cup record:	6	4	1	1	9	4
TOTAL:	**38**	**15**	**5**	**18**	**46**	**43**

FACT FILE

- **Kenilworth Road is one of Villa's least favourite grounds. The side have managed only two wins and 11 goals in 18 matches there.**
- **In contrast, Villa have won well over half of their home games against Luton.**

Villa's top scorers vs Luton

Johnny Dixon 5

Gerry Hitchens 3

Played for both clubs

George H. Stephenson	Villa 1931-32	Luton 1934-40
Leslie Jones	Luton 1950-58	Villa 1957-58
Jimmy Adam	Luton 1953-59	Villa 1959-61
Bruce Rioch	Luton 1964-69	Villa 1969-74
Chris Nicholl	Luton 1969-72	Villa 1971-77
Jake Findlay	Villa 1973-77	Luton 1978-85
David Geddis	Luton 1976-77/82-83	Villa 1979-83
Mervyn Day	Villa 1983-85	Luton 1991-92
Steve Foster	Villa 1983-85	Luton 1984-89
Paul Elliott	Luton 1982-86	Villa 1985-87
Mark Burke	Villa 1986-88	Luton 1993-94
Les Sealey	Luton 1983-89	Villa 1991-92
Garry Parker	Luton 1982-86	Villa 1991-95
Bryan Small	Villa 1991-95	Luton 1997-98

Bruce Rioch (and brother Neil) had just signed for Aston Villa from Luton when this 1969-70 photo was taken. Back row (left to right): Ian Hamilton, Barry Hole, Fred Turnbull, Barry Lynch, Keith Bradley. Middle row: Lionel Martin, Dave Simmonds, Dick Edwards, John Dunn, Neil Rioch, Charlie Aitken, Dave Rudge. Front row: Arthur Cox (trainer), Mick Wright, Mick Ferguson, Brian Tiler, Bruce Rioch, Willie Anderson, Tommy Docherty (manager).

v. Manchester City

				Home				Away		Final Positions	
Season	*League*	*Date*	*Result*	Villa	Man City	*Date*	*Result*	Villa	Man City	Villa	Man City
1899-00	Division 1	21 October	Won	**2**	**1**	19 March	Won	**2**	**0**	1st	7th
1900-01	Division 1	1 December	Won	**7**	**1**	27 April	Lost	**0**	**4**	15th	11th
1901-02	Division 1	31 March	Drew	**2**	**2**	17 February	Lost	**0**	**1**	8th	18thR
1903-04	Division 1	13 January	Lost	**0**	**1**	17 October	Lost	**0**	**1**	5th	2nd
1904-05	Division 1	29 April	Won	**3**	**2**	9 November	Lost	**1**	**2**	4th	3rd
1905-06	Division 1	21 October	Won	**2**	**1**	14 March	Won	**4**	**1**	8th	5th
1906-07	Division 1	23 February	Won	**4**	**1**	20 October	Lost	**2**	**4**	5th	17th
1907-08	Division 1	9 November	Drew	**2**	**2**	7 March	Lost	**2**	**3**	2nd	3rd
1908-09	Division 1	24 April	Won	**2**	**1**	19 December	Lost	**0**	**2**	7th	19thR
1910-11	Division 1	15 October	Won	**2**	**1**	18 February	Drew	**1**	**1**	2nd	17th
1911-12	Division 1	20 January	Won	**3**	**1**	16 September	Won	**6**	**2**	6th	15th
1912-13	Division 1	4 January	Won	**2**	**0**	14 September	Lost	**0**	**1**	2nd	6th
1913-14	Division 1	1 September	Drew	**1**	**1**	10 April	Lost	**1**	**3**	2nd	13th
1914-15	Division 1	21 April	Won	**4**	**1**	25 November	Lost	**0**	**1**	14th	5th
1919-20	Division 1	26 April	Lost	**0**	**1**	1 May	Drew	**2**	**2**	9th	7th
1920-21	Division 1	6 September	Won	**3**	**1**	30 August	Lost	**1**	**3**	10th	2nd
1921-22	Division 1	3 September	Won	**4**	**0**	27 August	Lost	**1**	**2**	5th	10th
1922-23	Division 1	3 February	Won	**2**	**0**	10 February	Drew	**1**	**1**	6th	8th
1923-24	Division 1	29 August	Won	**2**	**0**	5 September	Won	**2**	**1**	6th	11th
1924-25	Division 1	10 April	Won	**2**	**1**	13 April	Lost	**0**	**1**	15th	10th
1925-26	Division 1	28 November	Won	**3**	**1**	10 April	Lost	**2**	**4**	6th	21stR
1928-29	Division 1	19 December	Won	**5**	**1**	27 April	Lost	**0**	**3**	3rd	8th
1929-30	Division 1	25 December	Lost	**0**	**2**	26 December	Won	**2**	**1**	4th	3rd
1930-31	Division 1	25 April	Won	**4**	**2**	20 December	Lost	**1**	**3**	2nd	8th
1931-32	Division 1	9 April	Won	**2**	**1**	28 November	Drew	**3**	**3**	5th	14th
1932-33	Division 1	8 April	Drew	**1**	**1**	26 November	Lost	**2**	**5**	2nd	16th
1933-34	Division 1	7 March	Drew	**0**	**0**	21 October	Lost	**0**	**1**	13th	5th
1934-35	Division 1	27 October	Won	**4**	**2**	9 March	Lost	**1**	**4**	13th	4th
1935-36	Division 1	11 April	Drew	**2**	**2**	7 December	Lost	**0**	**5**	21stR	9th
1947-48	Division 1	30 August	Drew	**1**	**1**	3 January	Won	**2**	**0**	6th	10th
1948-49	Division 1	12 March	Won	**1**	**0**	16 October	Lost	**1**	**4**	10th	7th
1949-50	Division 1	17 December	Won	**1**	**0**	20 August	Drew	**3**	**3**	12th	21stR
1951-52	Division 1	29 December	Lost	**1**	**2**	1 September	Drew	**2**	**2**	6th	15th
1952-53	Division 1	25 October	Drew	**0**	**0**	14 March	Lost	**1**	**4**	11th	20th
1953-54	Division 1	24 August	Won	**3**	**0**	2 September	Won	**1**	**0**	13th	17th
1954-55	Division 1	30 April	Won	**2**	**0**	16 October	Won	**4**	**2**	6th	7th
1955-56	Division 1	17 December	Lost	**0**	**3**	20 August	Drew	**2**	**2**	20th	4th
1956-57	Division 1	4 February	Drew	**2**	**2**	25 August	Drew	**1**	**1**	10th	18th
1957-58	Division 1	14 December	Lost	**1**	**2**	26 April	Won	**2**	**1**	14th	5th
1958-59	Division 1	6 December	Drew	**1**	**1**	25 April	Drew	**0**	**0**	21stR	20th
1960-61	Division 1	3 December	Won	**5**	**1**	22 April	Lost	**1**	**4**	9th	13th
1961-62	Division 1	25 November	Won	**2**	**1**	14 April	Lost	**0**	**1**	7th	12th
1962-63	Division 1	8 May	Won	**3**	**1**	25 August	Won	**2**	**0**	15th	21stR
1966-67	Division 1	3 September	Won	**3**	**0**	19 April	Drew	**1**	**1**	21stR	15th

				Home				Away		Final Positions	
Season	*League*	*Date*	*Result*	Villa	Man City	*Date*	*Result*	Villa	Man City	Villa	Man City
1975-76	Division 1	27 August	Won	**1**	**0**	7 February	Lost	**1**	**2**	16th	8th
1976-77	Division 1	4 May	Drew	**1**	**1**	25 August	Lost	**0**	**2**	4th	2nd
1977-78	Division 1	24 August	Lost	**1**	**4**	31 December	Lost	**0**	**2**	8th	4th
1978-79	Division 1	4 November	Drew	**1**	**1**	15 May	Won	**3**	**2**	8th	15th
1979-80	Division 1	27 February	Drew	**2**	**2**	7 April	Drew	**1**	**1**	7th	17th
1980-81	Division 1	31 January	Won	**1**	**0**	23 August	Drew	**2**	**2**	1st	12th
1981-82	Division 1	1 May	Drew	**0**	**0**	5 December	Lost	**0**	**1**	11th	10th
1982-83	Division 1	22 January	Drew	**1**	**1**	18 September	Won	**1**	**0**	6th	20thR
1985-86	Division 1	1 January	Lost	**0**	**1**	29 March	Drew	**2**	**2**	16th	15th
1986-87	Division 1	4 April	Drew	**0**	**0**	8 November	Lost	**1**	**3**	22ndR	21stR
1987-88	Division 2	31 August	Drew	**1**	**1**	23 January	Won	**2**	**0**	2ndP	9th
1989-90	Division 1	1 April	Lost	**1**	**2**	22 October	Won	**2**	**0**	2nd	14th
1990-91	Division 1	23 April	Lost	**1**	**5**	5 September	Lost	**1**	**2**	17th	5th
1991-92	Division 1	7 December	Won	**3**	**1**	29 February	Lost	**0**	**2**	7th	5th
1992-93	Premiership	18 April	Won	**3**	**1**	19 December	Drew	**1**	**1**	2nd	9th
1993-94	Premiership	22 February	Drew	**0**	**0**	2 April	Lost	**0**	**3**	10th	16th
1994-95	Premiership	3 May	Drew	**1**	**1**	31 December	Drew	**2**	**2**	18th	17th
1995-96	Premiership	27 April	Lost	**0**	**1**	25 November	Lost	**0**	**1**	4th	18thR
2000-01	Premiership	16 December	Drew	**2**	**2**	31 March	Won	**3**	**1**	8th	18thR
2002-03	Premiership	28 August	Won	**1**	**0**	26 December	Lost	**1**	**3**	16th	9th
2003-04	Premiership	4 April	Drew	**1**	**1**	14 September	Lost	**1**	**4**	6th	16th

FA Cup										*Division*	
1899-00	Round 1	31 January	Won	**3**	**0**	27 January	Drew	**1**	**1**	Div 1	Div 1
1909-10	Round 3	19 February	Lost	**1**	**2**					Div 1	Div 2
1914-15	Round 2					30 January	Lost	**0**	**1**	Div 1	Div 1
1933-34	Semi-Final	17 March		Leeds Road, Huddersfield			Lost	**1**	**6**	Div 1	Div 1
1937-38	Q'ter Final	6 March	Won	**3**	**2**					Div 2	Div 1
1994-95	Round 4					28 January	Lost	**0**	**1**	Prem	Prem

Harry Morton cannot stop this effort from Manchester City's Fred Tilson in the 1934 FA Cup semi-final at Leeds Road, Huddersfield. It was a grim day for Aston Villa, who went down 6-1.

League Cup		Date	Result	Home Villa	Home Man City	Division Villa	Division Man City
1976-77	Round 2	1 September	Won	**3**	**0**	Div 1	Div 1
1983-84	Round 3	9 November	Won	**3**	**0**	Div 1	Div 2
2000-01	Round 3	1 November	Lost	**0**	**1**	Prem	Prem

Summary	*P*	*W*	*D*	*L*	*F*	*A*
Villa's home league record:	65	33	21	11	118	70
Villa's away league record:	65	15	15	35	84	126
Villa's cup record:	10	4	1	5	15	14
TOTAL:	**140**	**52**	**37**	**51**	**217**	**210**

FACT FILE

- **From 1905 to 1949, Villa lost twice in 28 home league games, a sequence that including seven straight wins.**
- **From 1912 to 1935, Villa lost 15 times in 20 matches against City away from Villa Park.**
- **All in all, this has been a very even series, with neither side putting together many wins in a row.**

Villa's top scorers vs Man City

Harry Hampton 13
Billy Garraty, Billy Walker 8
Joe Bache 7
Tommy Thompson, Pongo Waring 6
Eric Houghton, George Johnson 5

Villa hat-tricks vs Man City

1 Dec 1900 George Johnson (4)
16 Sep 1911 Joe Bache
16 Oct 1954 Tommy Thompson

Played for both clubs

Howard Harvey	Villa 1897-98	Man City 1899-1901
Albert Fisher	Villa 1902-03	Man City 1906-07
Rowland Codling	Villa 1905-09	Man City 1910-11
Jimmy McLuckie	Man City 1933-35	Villa 1934-36
Phil Woosnam	Man City 1952-53	Villa 1962-66
Stan Horne	Villa 1963-64	Man City 1965-68
Barry Stobart	Man City 1964-65	Villa 1964-68
Bobby McDonald	Villa 1972-76	Man City 1980-83
John Gidman	Villa 1972-80	Man City 1986-88
Frank Carrodus	Man City 1969-74	Villa 1974-79
John Burridge	Villa 1975-77	Man City 1994-95
Ken McNaught	Villa 1977-83	Man City 1984-85
Robert Hopkins	Villa 1979-83	Man City 1986-87
Steve McMahon	Villa 1983-86	Man City 1991-95
Mark Lillis	Man City 1985-86	Villa 1987-89
Adrian Heath	Villa 1989-90	Man City 1989-92
Dalian Atkinson	Villa 1991-95	Man City 1996-97
Earl Barrett	Man City 1985-87	Villa 1991-95
David James	Villa 1999-2001	Man City 2003-04
Peter Schmeichel	Villa 2001-02	Man City 2002-03

v. Manchester United

		Home					Away			Final Positions	
Season	League	Date	Result	Villa	Man Utd	Date	Result	Villa	Man Utd	Villa	Man Utd
1892-93	Division 1	6 March	Won	2	0	19 November	Lost	0	2	4th	16th
1893-94	Division 1	3 February	Won	5	1	16 December	Won	3	1	1st	16thR
1906-07	Division 1	26 December	Won	2	0	1 January	Lost	0	1	5th	8th
1907-08	Division 1	2 September	Lost	1	4	20 April	Won	2	1	2nd	1st
1908-09	Division 1	17 October	Won	3	1	31 March	Won	2	0	7th	13th
1909-10	Division 1	26 February	Won	7	1	16 October	Lost	0	2	1st	5th
1910-11	Division 1	22 April	Won	4	2	17 December	Lost	0	2	2nd	1st
1911-12	Division 1	30 March	Won	6	0	25 November	Lost	1	3	6th	13th
1912-13	Division 1	16 November	Won	4	2	22 March	Lost	0	4	2nd	4th
1913-14	Division 1	8 November	Won	3	1	14 March	Won	6	0	2nd	14th
1914-15	Division 1	19 December	Drew	3	3	26 April	Lost	0	1	14th	18th
1919-20	Division 1	6 December	Won	2	0	13 December	Won	2	1	9th	12th
1920-21	Division 1	25 December	Lost	3	4	27 December	Won	3	1	10th	13th
1921-22	Division 1	19 November	Won	3	1	26 November	Lost	0	1	5th	22ndR
1925-26	Division 1	7 September	Drew	2	2	2 September	Lost	0	3	6th	9th
1926-27	Division 1	19 February	Won	2	0	2 October	Lost	1	2	10th	15th
1927-28	Division 1	31 March	Won	3	1	19 November	Lost	1	5	8th	18th
1928-29	Division 1	27 August	Drew	0	0	1 January	Drew	2	2	3rd	12th
1929-30	Division 1	2 November	Won	1	0	8 March	Won	3	2	4th	17th
1930-31	Division 1	27 December	Won	7	0	30 August	Won	4	3	2nd	22ndR
1937-38	Division 2	2 April	Won	3	0	20 November	Lost	1	3	1stP	2ndP
1938-39	Division 1	5 November	Lost	0	2	11 March	Drew	1	1	12th	14th
1946-47	Division 1	2 November	Drew	0	0	8 March	Lost	1	2	8th	2nd
1947-48	Division 1	22 March	Lost	0	1	25 October	Lost	0	2	6th	2nd
1948-49	Division 1	19 February	Won	2	1	25 September	Lost	1	3	10th	2nd
1949-50	Division 1	15 October	Lost	0	4	8 March	Lost	0	7	12th	4th
1950-51	Division 1	4 September	Lost	1	3	13 September	Drew	0	0	15th	2nd
1951-52	Division 1	13 October	Lost	2	5	1 March	Drew	1	1	6th	1st
1952-53	Division 1	20 September	Drew	3	3	7 February	Lost	1	3	11th	8th
1953-54	Division 1	13 March	Drew	2	2	24 October	Lost	0	1	13th	4th
1954-55	Division 1	28 December	Won	2	1	27 December	Won	1	0	6th	5th
1955-56	Division 1	15 October	Drew	4	4	25 February	Lost	0	1	20th	1st
1956-57	Division 1	8 December	Lost	1	3	9 March	Drew	1	1	10th	1st
1957-58	Division 1	31 March	Won	3	2	5 October	Lost	1	4	14th	9th
1958-59	Division 1	27 December	Lost	0	2	26 December	Lost	1	2	21stR	2nd
1960-61	Division 1	17 September	Won	3	1	4 February	Drew	1	1	9th	7th
1961-62	Division 1	18 September	Drew	1	1	15 January	Lost	0	2	7th	15th
1962-63	Division 1	9 April	Lost	1	2	24 November	Drew	2	2	15th	19th
1963-64	Division 1	16 November	Won	4	0	6 April	Lost	0	1	19th	2nd
1964-65	Division 1	28 April	Won	2	1	24 October	Lost	0	7	16th	1st
1965-66	Division 1	6 April	Drew	1	1	9 May	Lost	1	6	16th	4th
1966-67	Division 1	3 December	Won	2	1	29 April	Lost	1	3	21stR	1st
1974-75	Division 2	22 February	Won	2	0	16 November	Lost	1	2	2ndP	1stP
1975-76	Division 1	21 February	Won	2	1	15 November	Lost	0	2	16th	3rd

		Home					Away			Final Positions	
Season	*League*	*Date*	*Result*	Villa	Man Utd	*Date*	*Result*	Villa	Man Utd	Villa	Man Utd
1976-77	Division 1	6 November	Won	**3**	**2**	1 January	Lost	**0**	**2**	4th	6th
1977-78	Division 1	29 October	Won	**2**	**1**	29 March	Drew	**1**	**1**	8th	10th
1978-79	Division 1	14 October	Drew	**2**	**2**	24 February	Drew	**1**	**1**	8th	9th
1979-80	Division 1	8 September	Lost	**0**	**3**	23 April	Lost	**1**	**2**	7th	2nd
1980-81	Division 1	14 March	Drew	**3**	**3**	8 October	Drew	**3**	**3**	1st	8th
1981-82	Division 1	12 September	Drew	**1**	**1**	6 February	Lost	**1**	**4**	11th	3rd
1982-83	Division 1	20 November	Won	**2**	**1**	1 January	Lost	**1**	**3**	6th	3rd
1983-84	Division 1	3 March	Lost	**0**	**3**	5 November	Won	**2**	**1**	10th	4th
1984-85	Division 1	6 October	Won	**3**	**0**	23 March	Lost	**0**	**4**	10th	4th
1985-86	Division 1	14 December	Lost	**1**	**3**	17 August	Lost	**0**	**4**	16th	4th
1986-87	Division 1	13 December	Drew	**3**	**3**	9 May	Lost	**1**	**3**	22ndR	11th
1988-89	Division 1	12 March	Drew	**0**	**0**	5 November	Drew	**1**	**1**	17th	11th
1989-90	Division 1	26 December	Won	**3**	**0**	17 April	Lost	**0**	**2**	2nd	13th
1990-91	Division 1	6 April	Drew	**1**	**1**	29 December	Drew	**1**	**1**	17th	6th
1991-92	Division 1	21 August	Lost	**0**	**1**	22 January	Lost	**0**	**1**	7th	2nd
1992-93	Premiership	7 November	Won	**1**	**0**	14 March	Drew	**1**	**1**	2nd	1st
1993-94	Premiership	23 August	Lost	**1**	**2**	19 December	Lost	**1**	**3**	10th	1st
1994-95	Premiership	6 November	Lost	**1**	**2**	4 February	Lost	**0**	**1**	18th	2nd
1995-96	Premiership	19 August	Won	**3**	**1**	13 January	Drew	**0**	**0**	4th	1st
1996-97	Premiership	21 September	Drew	**0**	**0**	1 January	Drew	**0**	**0**	5th	1st
1997-98	Premiership	18 February	Lost	**0**	**2**	15 December	Lost	**0**	**1**	7th	2nd
1998-99	Premiership	5 December	Drew	**1**	**1**	1 May	Lost	**1**	**2**	6th	1st
1999-00	Premiership	14 May	Lost	**0**	**1**	30 October	Lost	**0**	**3**	6th	1st
2000-01	Premiership	26 December	Lost	**0**	**1**	20 January	Lost	**0**	**2**	8th	1st
2001-02	Premiership	26 August	Drew	**1**	**1**	23 February	Lost	**0**	**1**	8th	3rd
2002-03	Premiership	15 March	Lost	**0**	**1**	26 October	Drew	**1**	**1**	16th	1st
2003-04	Premiership	15 May	Lost	**0**	**2**	6 December	Lost	**0**	**4**	6th	3rd

FA Cup										*Division*	
1905-06	Round 3					24 February	Lost	**1**	**5**	Div 1	Div 2
1907-08	Round 3	22 February	Lost	**0**	**2**					Div 1	Div 1
1910-11	Round 2					4 February	Lost	**1**	**2**	Div 1	Div 1
1919-20	Round 2					31 January	Won	**2**	**1**	Div 1	Div 1
1947-48	Round 3	10 January	Lost	**4**	**6**					Div 1	Div 1
1956-57	Final	4 May		Wembley			Won	**2**	**1**	Div 1	Div 1
1962-63	Round 4					11 March	Lost	**0**	**1**	Div 1	Div 1
1976-77	Q'ter Final					19 March	Lost	**1**	**2**	Div 1	Div 1
2001-02	Round 3	6 January	Lost	**2**	**3**					Prem	Prem
2003-04	Round 3	4 January	Lost	**1**	**2**					Prem	Prem

League Cup											
1970-71	Semi-Final	23 December	Won	**2**	**1**	16 December	Drew	**1**	**1**	Div 3	Div 1
1975-76	Round 3	8 October	Lost	**1**	**2**					Div 1	Div 1
1992-93	Round 3	28 October	Won	**1**	**0**					Prem	Prem
1993-94	Final	27 March		Wembley			Won	**3**	**1**	Prem	Prem
1999-00	Round 3	13 October	Won	**3**	**0**					Prem	Prem

Summary	P	W	D	L	F	A
Villa's home league record:	71	32	18	21	136	102
Villa's away league record:	71	10	16	45	63	146
Villa's cup record:	16	6	1	9	25	30
TOTAL:	**158**	**48**	**35**	**75**	**224**	**278**

FACT FILE

- **Since the war, Villa have lost by seven goals on two occasions in all matches. Both of these defeats came at the hands of Manchester United, the last in 1964.**
- **Villa's joint biggest away win in league football came against United in 1914.**
- **Villa have not won in their last 17 Premiership matches against United.**
- **Villa have won only once in their last 43 away matches against United. This win came in 1983, when Peter Withe scored both goals.**
- **The sides have met twice in cup finals. Both times United were favourites, and both times Villa won. In 1957, United were striving to become the first team since Villa themselves 60 years earlier to win the double, but two goals from Peter McParland ensured that they left disappointed.**
- **In 1994, United were striving to become the first team ever to win the domestic treble, but were outplayed in a 3-1 defeat to Villa. The domestic treble has still never been done.**
- **Villa won nine of their first 10 home league games against United.**

Villa's top scorers vs United

Harry Hampton 13
Clem Stephenson 11
Pongo Waring 9
Johnny Dixon, Peter Withe 7
Joe Bache, Andy Gray, Billy Walker 5

Villa hat-tricks vs United

3 Feb 1894 Jack Devey
26 Feb 1910 Joe Walters
30 Mar 1912 Clem Stephenson
14 Mar 1914 Joe Bache
31 Aug 1930 Pongo Waring (4)

Played for both clubs

Jimmy Warner	Villa 1888-92	Man United 1892-93
Jimmy Whitehouse	Villa 1896-98	Man United 1900-03
Tom Wilson	Villa 1900-02	Man United 1907-08
George Travers	Villa 1908-09	Man United 1913-15
Harold Halse	Man United 1907-12	Villa 1912-13
George Hunter	Villa 1908-12	Man United 1913-15
Frank Mann	Villa 1911-12	Man United 1922-30
Frank Barson	Villa 1919-22	Man United 1922-28
Reg Chester	Villa 1925-35	Man United 1935-36

Michael Pinner	Villa 1954-57	Man United 1960-61
Stanley Crowther	Man United 1957-59	Villa 1956-58
George Graham	Villa 1962-64	Man United 1972-75
Willie Anderson	Man United 1963-67	Villa 1966-73
John Gidman	Villa 1972-80	Man United 1981-86
Jimmy Rimmer	Man United 1967-63	Villa 1977-83
Colin Gibson	Villa 1978-86	Man United 1985-90
Paul McGrath	Man United 1982-89	Villa 1989-96
Dwight Yorke	Villa 1989-99	Man United 1998-2002
Les Sealey	Man United 1989-91	Villa 1991-92
Mark Bosnich	Man United 1989-91/99-2000	Villa 1991-99
Dion Dublin	Man United 1992-94	Villa 1998-2004
Peter Schmeichel	Man United 1991-99	Villa 2001-02
Ronny Johnsen	Man United 1996-2002	Villa 2002-04

Skipper Johnny Dixon holds aloft the FA Cup after Villa's controversial victory over Manchester United in 1957.

v. Mansfield Town

Season	League	Date	Result	Home Villa	Home Mansfield	Date	Result	Away Villa	Away Mansfield	Final Positions Villa	Final Positions Mansfield
1970-71	Division 3	31 August	Lost	**0**	**1**	26 April	Lost	**0**	**2**	4th	7th
1971-72	Division 3	22 September	Lost	**0**	**1**	24 April	Drew	**1**	**1**	1stP	21stR

Summary	*P*	*W*	*D*	*L*	*F*	*A*
Villa's home league record:	2	0	0	2	0	2
Villa's away league record:	2	0	1	1	1	3
TOTAL:	**4**	**0**	**1**	**3**	**1**	**5**

FACT FILE

- **Mansfield are the only team to remain unbeaten against Villa after more than two matches.**

Played for both clubs

Ginger Phoenix	Villa 1924-25	Mansfield 1931-32
George Blackburn	Villa 1920-26	Mansfield 1931-32
Fred Biddlestone	Villa 1929-39	Mansfield 1939-40
Frank Shell	Villa 1937-39	Mansfield 1947-48
Roy Chapman	Villa 1953-58	Mansfield 1961-65
Raymond Hogg	Villa 1954-57	Mansfield 1958-60
Tommy Mitchinson	Mansfield 1965-68	Villa 1967-69
Dick Edwards	Mansfield 1966-68/73-74	Villa 1967-70
David Hunt	Villa 1987-89	Mansfield 1989-90
Mark Blake	Villa 1989-93	Mansfield 1999-2001
Colin Calderwood	Mansfield 1981-85	Villa 1998-2000

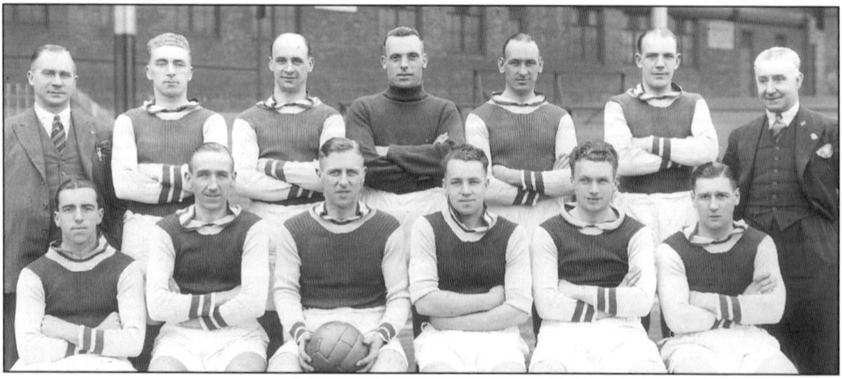

Aston Villa's line-up in the 1937-38 season with two players who were to transfer to Mansfield. Back row (left to right): H. Bourne (trainer), Alex Massie, Mush Callaghan, Fred Biddlestone, Bob Iverson, Tommy Cummings, Jimmy Hogan (manager). Front row: Frank Broome, Freddie Haycock, Jimmy Allen, Frank Shell, Ronnie Starling, Eric Houghton. That season Villa reached the semi-finals of the FA Cup and won promotion back to the top flight as champions of Division Two.

v. Middlesbrough

		Home					Away				Final Positions	
Season	*League*	*Date*	*Result*	Villa	Middlesb'gh	*Date*	*Result*	Villa	Middlesb'gh		Villa	Middlesb'gh
1902-03	Division 1	27 April	Won	**5**	**0**	22 November	Won	**2**	**1**		2nd	13th
1903-04	Division 1	19 March	Won	**2**	**1**	21 November	Lost	**1**	**2**		5th	10th
1904-05	Division 1	10 December	Drew	**0**	**0**	8 April	Lost	**1**	**3**		4th	15th
1905-06	Division 1	4 November	Won	**4**	**1**	10 March	Won	**2**	**1**		8th	18th
1906-07	Division 1	27 October	Lost	**2**	**3**	2 March	Lost	**0**	**1**		5th	11th
1907-08	Division 1	14 December	Won	**6**	**0**	11 April	Won	**1**	**0**		2nd	6th
1908-09	Division 1	12 December	Lost	**0**	**3**	17 April	Lost	**0**	**1**		7th	9th
1909-10	Division 1	25 March	Won	**4**	**2**	28 March	Lost	**2**	**3**		1st	17th
1910-11	Division 1	26 November	Won	**5**	**0**	1 April	Won	**1**	**0**		2nd	16th
1911-12	Division 1	4 November	Won	**2**	**1**	9 March	Won	**2**	**1**		6th	7th
1912-13	Division 1	2 November	Won	**5**	**1**	9 April	Drew	**1**	**1**		2nd	16th
1913-14	Division 1	25 April	Lost	**1**	**3**	20 December	Lost	**2**	**5**		2nd	3rd
1914-15	Division 1	13 March	Won	**5**	**0**	7 November	Drew	**1**	**1**		14th	12th
1919-20	Division 1	1 November	Won	**5**	**3**	25 October	Won	**4**	**1**		9th	13th
1920-21	Division 1	2 April	Lost	**0**	**1**	26 March	Won	**4**	**1**		10th	8th
1921-22	Division 1	29 October	Won	**6**	**2**	22 October	Lost	**0**	**5**		5th	8th
1922-23	Division 1	23 September	Drew	**2**	**2**	30 September	Drew	**2**	**2**		6th	18th
1923-24	Division 1	1 December	Drew	**0**	**0**	8 December	Won	**2**	**0**		6th	22ndR
1927-28	Division 1	8 October	Won	**5**	**1**	21 March	Drew	**0**	**0**		8th	22ndR
1929-30	Division 1	29 March	Won	**4**	**2**	23 November	Won	**3**	**2**		4th	16th
1930-31	Division 1	31 January	Won	**8**	**1**	27 September	Lost	**1**	**3**		2nd	7th
1931-32	Division 1	25 December	Won	**7**	**1**	26 December	Drew	**1**	**1**		5th	18th
1932-33	Division 1	31 December	Won	**3**	**1**	27 August	Won	**2**	**0**		2nd	17th
1933-34	Division 1	11 November	Won	**3**	**0**	24 March	Won	**2**	**1**		13th	16th
1934-35	Division 1	27 April	Lost	**0**	**3**	15 December	Lost	**1**	**4**		13th	20th
1935-36	Division 1	9 September	Lost	**2**	**7**	4 September	Won	**2**	**1**		21stR	14th
1938-39	Division 1	6 May	Drew	**1**	**1**	31 August	Drew	**1**	**1**		12th	4th
1939-40	Division 1	26 August	Won	**2**	**0**							
1946-47	Division 1	31 August	Lost	**0**	**1**	28 December	Won	**2**	**1**		8th	11th
1947-48	Division 1	13 December	Drew	**1**	**1**	1 May	Won	**3**	**1**		6th	16th
1948-49	Division 1	7 May	Drew	**1**	**1**	11 December	Lost	**0**	**6**		10th	19th
1949-50	Division 1	21 January	Won	**4**	**0**	17 September	Won	**2**	**0**		12th	9th
1950-51	Division 1	4 November	Lost	**0**	**1**	24 March	Lost	**1**	**2**		15th	6th
1951-52	Division 1	24 November	Won	**2**	**0**	12 April	Lost	**0**	**2**		6th	18th
1952-53	Division 1	11 October	Won	**1**	**0**	4 March	Lost	**0**	**1**		11th	13th
1953-54	Division 1	14 November	Won	**5**	**3**	3 April	Lost	**1**	**2**		13th	21stR
1959-60	Division 2	17 October	Won	**1**	**0**	5 March	Won	**1**	**0**		1stP	5th
1967-68	Division 2	10 February	Lost	**0**	**1**	30 September	Drew	**1**	**1**		16th	6th
1968-69	Division 2	23 November	Won	**1**	**0**	4 March	Drew	**0**	**0**		18th	4th
1969-70	Division 2	8 April	Won	**2**	**0**	30 August	Lost	**0**	**1**		21stR	4th
1972-73	Division 2	28 October	Drew	**1**	**1**	24 March	Drew	**1**	**1**		3rd	4th
1973-74	Division 2	12 January	Drew	**1**	**1**	15 September	Drew	**0**	**0**		14th	1stP
1975-76	Division 1	24 April	Won	**2**	**1**	4 October	Drew	**0**	**0**		16th	13th
1976-77	Division 1	5 April	Won	**1**	**0**	27 December	Lost	**2**	**3**		4th	12th

		Home				Away				Final Positions	
Season	League	Date	Result	Villa	Middlesb'gh	Date	Result	Villa	Middlesb'gh	Villa	Middlesb'gh
1977-78	Division 1	12 November	Lost	**0**	**1**	17 December	Lost	**0**	**1**	8th	14th
1978-79	Division 1	27 October	Lost	**0**	**2**	10 March	Lost	**0**	**2**	8th	12th
1979-80	Division 1	19 March	Lost	**0**	**2**	29 September	Drew	**0**	**0**	7th	9th
1980-81	Division 1	25 April	Won	**3**	**0**	6 December	Lost	**1**	**2**	1st	14th
1981-82	Division 1	17 April	Won	**1**	**0**	21 November	Drew	**3**	**3**	11th	22ndR
1987-88	Division 2	2 May	Lost	**0**	**1**	28 November	Lost	**1**	**2**	2ndP	3rdP
1988-89	Division 1	29 April	Drew	**1**	**1**	10 December	Drew	**3**	**3**	17th	18thR
1992-93	Premiership	17 January	Won	**5**	**1**	26 September	Won	**3**	**2**	2nd	21stR
1995-96	Premiership	19 March	Drew	**0**	**0**	1 January	Won	**2**	**0**	4th	12th
1996-97	Premiership	30 November	Won	**1**	**0**	3 May	Lost	**2**	**3**	5th	19thR
1998-99	Premiership	23 August	Won	**3**	**1**	9 January	Drew	**0**	**0**	6th	9th
1999-00	Premiership	28 August	Won	**1**	**0**	14 February	Won	**4**	**0**	6th	12th
2000-01	Premiership	10 February	Drew	**1**	**1**	23 September	Drew	**1**	**1**	8th	14th
2001-02	Premiership	17 November	Drew	**0**	**0**	6 April	Lost	**1**	**2**	8th	12th
2002-03	Premiership	28 December	Won	**1**	**0**	28 January	Won	**5**	**2**	16th	11th
2003-04	Premiership	8 November	Lost	**0**	**2**	24 April	Won	**2**	**1**	6th	11th

FA Cup

										Division	
1949-50	Round 3	7 January	Drew	**2**	**2**	11 January	Drew*	**0**	**0**	Div 1	Div 1
		16 January		Elland Road (2nd replay)			Lost	**0**	**3**		
1952-53	Round 3	10 January	Won	**3**	**1**					Div 1	Div 1
1956-57	Round 4					26 January	Won	**3**	**2**	Div 1	Div 2

League Cup

1987-88	Round 2	7 October	Won	**1**	**0**	23 September	Won	**1**	**0**	Div 2	Div 2
1990-91	Round 4	28 November	Won	**3**	**2**					Div 1	Div 2
1994-95	Round 3	26 October	Won	**1**	**0**					Prem	Div 1

Summary	*P*	*W*	*D*	*L*	*F*	*A*
Villa's home league record:	60	34	12	14	129	63
Villa's away league record:	59	21	16	22	83	87
Villa's cup record:	9	6	2	1	14	10
TOTAL:	**128**	**61**	**30**	**37**	**226**	**160**

Scorer of a hat-trick against Middlesbrough in 1919, when they won 5-3, Clem Stephenson was a clever forward who scored 96 goals in 216 senior appearances for Aston Villa between 1910 and 1921. He joined them from Durham City and it was a surprise when he left for Huddersfield Town 11 years later. In between, Stephenson had won two FA Cup winners' medals – in 1913 and 1920 – and played in two England trials. With Huddersfield, Stephenson went on to even greater things, winning League championship medals, playing in another two Cup Finals (one as a winner) and at last gaining an England cap. As their manager, he later took Town to two more Cup Finals. He was equally at home as an inside-forward or on the wing. His brother, George, also played for Villa, scoring 22 goals in 95 appearances between 1921 and 1927.

FACT FILE

- **Villa are unbeaten in 11 home games from 1989 to 2002.**
- **When the sides met at the Riverside in January 2003, Villa had yet to win away and Boro had yet to lose at home that season. The fact that Villa scored five goals in a Premiership away match for the first time is thus somewhat surprising.**
- **There were eight successive league home wins in the series from 1951 to 1959.**
- **The sides met twice at Villa Park in the calendar year of 1931. Villa scored 15 goals.**
- **From 1967 to 1988, Villa failed to win in 14 away league games.**

Villa's top scorers vs Middlesbrough

Harry Hampton 14

Joe Bache, Eric Houghton 10

Joe Beresford, Clem Stephenson, Billy Walker 8

Villa hat-tricks vs Middlesbrough

25 Mar 1910 Harry Hampton

26 Nov 1910 Joe Bache

25 Oct 1919 Walter Boyman

1 Nov 1919 Clem Stephenson

8 Oct 1927 Billy Cook

25 Dec 1931 Eric Houghton

25 Dec 1931 Joe Beresford

14 Nov 1953 Tommy Thompson

Eric Houghton (left) and Joe Beresford are both included in Villa's top scorers and scored hat-tricks in the 7-1 defeat of Middlesbrough in 1931, with Mort completing the rout.

Played for both clubs

James Suddick	Villa 1897-98	Middlesbrough 1903-04
Tommy Niblo	Middlesbrough 1899-1900	Villa 1901-04
Willie Macaulay	Villa 1900-01	Middlesbrough 1902-03
Billy Brawn	Villa 1901-06	Middlesbrough 1905-08
Joe Hisbent	Villa 1905-06	Middlesbrough 1911-15
Arthur Layton	Villa 1908-11	Middlesbrough 1911-12
Edmund Eyre	Villa 1908-11	Middlesbrough 1911-14
Charlie Slade	Villa 1913-14	Middlesbrough 1922-25
Ian Dickson	Villa 1920-24	Middlesbrough 1923-25
Norman Swales	Middlesbrough 1925-26	Villa 1928-30
Arthur Cunliffe	Villa 1932-36	Middlesbrough 1935-37
Tom Griffiths	Middlesbrough 1932-36	Villa 1935-37
Willie Hamilton	Middlesbrough 1960-62	Villa 1965-67
Pat Heard	Villa 1979-83	Middlesbrough 1985-86
Paul Kerr	Villa 1983-87	Middlesbrough 1986-91
Dean Glover	Villa 1984-87	Middlesbrough 1987-89
Kevin Poole	Villa 1984-87	Middlesbrough 1987-90
Mark Burke	Villa 1986-88	Middlesbrough 1987-90
Ugo Ehiogu	Villa 1991-2001	Middlesbrough 2000-04
Neil Cox	Villa 1991-94	Middlesbrough 1994-97
Andy Townsend	Villa 1993-98	Middlesbrough 1997-2000
Alan Wright	Villa 1994-2003	Middlesbrough 2003-04
Gareth Southgate	Villa 1995-2001	Middlesbrough 2001-04
Paul Merson	Middlesbrough 1997-99	Villa 1998-2002
Benito Carbone	Villa 1999-2000	Middlesbrough 2001-02
George Boateng	Villa 1999-2002	Middlesbrough 2002-04

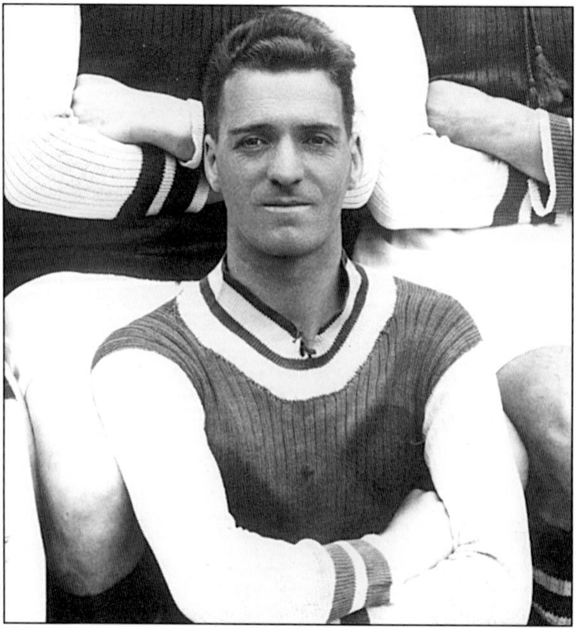

Arthur Cunliffe moved from Blackburn Rovers to join Villa in May 1933 and, after playing 75 games with 13 goals, joined Middlesbrough in December 1935.

v. Millwall

Season	League	Date	Result	Home Villa	Home Millwall	Date	Result	Away Villa	Away Millwall	Final Positions Villa	Final Positions Millwall
1967-68	Division 2	2 March	Won	**3**	**1**	14 October	Won	**2**	**1**	16th	7th
1968-69	Division 2	19 August	Drew	**1**	**1**	4 April	Won	**1**	**0**	18th	10th
1969-70	Division 2	6 September	Drew	**2**	**2**	16 March	Lost	**0**	**2**	21stR	10th
1972-73	Division 2	30 September	Won	**1**	**0**	23 April	Drew	**1**	**1**	3rd	11th
1973-74	Division 2	1 January	Drew	**0**	**0**	1 September	Drew	**1**	**1**	14th	12th
1974-75	Division 2	21 September	Won	**3**	**0**	1 April	Won	**3**	**1**	2ndP	20thR
1987-88	Division 2	7 November	Lost	**1**	**2**	2 April	Lost	**1**	**2**	2ndP	1stP
1988-89	Division 1	27 August	Drew	**2**	**2**	18 March	Lost	**0**	**2**	17th	10th
1989-90	Division 1	21 April	Won	**1**	**0**	16 December	Lost	**0**	**2**	2nd	20thR

FA Cup

Season	Round	Date	Result	Home Villa	Home Millwall	Date	Result	Away Villa	Away Millwall	Division Villa	Division Millwall
1899-00	Q'ter Final	28 February	Drew*	**0**	**0**	24 February	Drew	**1**	**1**	Div 1	Non L
		5 March				Elm Park, Reading (2nd replay)	Lost	**1**	**2**	Div 1	Non L
1900-01	Round 1	26 January	Won	**5**	**0**						
1945-46	Round 4	28 January	Won	**9**	**1**	26 January	Won	**4**	**2**	Div 1	Div 2
1967-68	Round 3	27 January	Won	**3**	**0**					Div 2	Div 2
1985-86	Round 4	25 January	Drew	**1**	**1**	29 January	Lost	**0**	**1**	Div 1	Div 2

League Cup

Season	Round	Date	Result	Home Villa	Home Millwall	Division Villa	Division Millwall
1976-77	Q'ter Final	1 December	Won	**2**	**0**	Div 1	Div 2
1988-89	Round 3	2 November	Won	**3**	**1**	Div 1	Div 1
1990-91	Round 3	31 October	Won	**2**	**0**	Div 1	Div 2

Summary

	P	*W*	*D*	*L*	*F*	*A*
Villa's home league record:	9	4	4	1	14	8
Villa's away league record:	9	3	2	4	9	12
Villa's cup record:	12	7	3	2	31	9
TOTAL:	**30**	**14**	**9**	**7**	**54**	**29**

Joining Millwall in 1997, Nigel Spink had played in only one Football League game before he was plunged into the 1982 European Cup Final. Back in December 1979 Spink had been called up for the away game at Nottingham Forest, but realistically he was third-choice goalkeeper at Villa. But named as subsutute 'keeper for the game against Bayern Munich in Rotterdam, he had to come on after only ten minutes when Rimmer hurt his neck. Spink performed like a veteran, Villa scored the only goal of the game and he stepped up to collect a well-earned medal. Essex-born, Spink played for Chelmsford City in the Southern League before Villa signed him in January 1977. After his memorable night in Rotterdam, Spink at last won a regular place and went on to appear in 451 senior games for Villa before moving to West Brom on a free transfer in 1986. He was later a manager of Forest Green Rovers.

Big centre-forward Tony Cascarino, a hugely successful signing from Millwall.

FACT FILE

- **Villa have lost only once in 17 home games against Millwall.**
- **Villa have lost their last four away games to Millwall.**

Villa's top scorers vs Millwall

George Johnson 4

Willie Anderson 4

Ray Graydon 4

Villa hat-tricks vs Millwall

26 Jan 1901 George Johnson (cup)

28 Jan 1946 Frank Broome (cup)

21 Sep 1974 Ray Graydon

Played for both clubs

George Travers	Villa 1908-09	Millwall 1920-21
Joe Walters	Villa 1905-12	Millwall 1921-22
Joseph Tyrell	Villa 1953-56	Millwall 1955-57
Pat Saward	Millwall 1951-55	Villa 1955-61
Dennis Jackson	Villa 1956-59	Millwall 1959-61
Nigel Spink	Villa 1979-96	Millwall 1997-2000
Paul Kerr	Villa 1983-87	Millwall 1990-92
Malcolm Allen	Villa 1987-88	Millwall 1989-93
Andy Gray	Villa 1987-89	Millwall 1997-99
Tony Cascarino	Millwall 1987-90	Villa 1989-91
John Fashanu	Millwall 1984-86	Villa 1994-95
Dion Dublin	Villa 1998-2004	Millwall 2001-02

v. Newcastle United

		Home					Away				Final Positions	
Season	League	Date	Result	Villa	Newcastle	Date	Result	Villa	Newcastle	Villa	Newcastle
1898-99	Division 1	26 December	Won	1	0	1 October	Drew	1	1	1st	13th
1899-00	Division 1	4 November	Won	2	1	10 March	Lost	2	3	1st	5th
1900-01	Division 1	17 November	Drew	2	2	17 April	Lost	0	3	15th	6th
1901-02	Division 1	7 December	Drew	0	0	5 April	Lost	1	2	8th	3rd
1902-03	Division 1	29 November	Won	7	0	28 March	Lost	0	2	2nd	14th
1903-04	Division 1	7 November	Won	3	1	2 September	Drew	1	1	5th	4th
1904-05	Division 1	26 November	Lost	0	1	5 April	Lost	0	2	4th	1st
1905-06	Division 1	18 November	Lost	0	3	24 March	Lost	1	3	8th	4th
1906-07	Division 1	10 November	Drew	0	0	16 March	Lost	2	3	5th	1st
1907-08	Division 1	30 November	Drew	3	3	8 April	Won	5	2	2nd	4th
1908-09	Division 1	26 April	Won	3	0	21 November	Won	2	0	7th	1st
1909-10	Division 1	27 April	Won	4	0	11 December	Lost	0	1	1st	4th
1910-11	Division 1	12 November	Won	3	2	18 March	Lost	0	1	2nd	8th
1911-12	Division 1	20 April	Won	2	0	16 December	Lost	2	6	6th	3rd
1912-13	Division 1	21 December	Won	3	1	26 April	Won	3	2	2nd	14th
1913-14	Division 1	4 April	Lost	1	3	29 November	Drew	2	2	2nd	11th
1914-15	Division 1	31 October	Won	2	1	28 April	Lost	0	3	14th	15th
1919-20	Division 1	5 April	Won	4	0	1 January	Lost	0	2	9th	8th
1920-21	Division 1	11 December	Drew	0	0	4 December	Lost	1	2	10th	5th
1921-22	Division 1	24 December	Won	1	0	17 December	Won	2	1	5th	7th
1922-23	Division 1	16 December	Drew	1	1	23 December	Drew	0	0	6th	4th
1923-24	Division 1	21 April	Won	6	1	1 January	Lost	1	4	6th	9th
1924-25	Division 1	6 September	Drew	0	0	3 January	Lost	1	4	15th	6th
1925-26	Division 1	12 September	Drew	2	2	23 January	Drew	2	2	6th	10th
1926-27	Division 1	15 January	Lost	1	2	28 August	Lost	0	4	10th	1st
1927-28	Division 1	29 October	Won	3	0	10 March	Lost	5	7	8th	9th
1928-29	Division 1	15 September	Drew	1	1	13 March	Lost	1	2	3rd	10th
1929-30	Division 1	12 April	Won	2	0	7 December	Drew	2	2	4th	19th
1930-31	Division 1	7 April	Won	4	3	1 January	Lost	0	2	2nd	17th
1931-32	Division 1	28 December	Won	3	0	1 January	Lost	1	3	5th	11th
1932-33	Division 1	18 April	Won	3	0	17 April	Lost	1	3	2nd	5th
1933-34	Division 1	25 November	Lost	2	3	7 April	Drew	1	1	13th	21stR
1936-37	Division 2	30 March	Lost	0	2	26 March	Won	2	0	9th	4th
1937-38	Division 2	16 October	Won	2	0	26 February	Lost	0	2	1stP	19th
1948-49	Division 1	13 September	Lost	2	4	8 September	Lost	1	2	10th	4th
1949-50	Division 1	31 December	Lost	0	1	3 September	Lost	2	3	12th	5th
1950-51	Division 1	7 October	Won	3	0	4 April	Won	1	0	15th	4th
1951-52	Division 1	8 December	Drew	2	2	26 April	Lost	1	6	6th	8th
1952-53	Division 1	1 May	Lost	0	1	13 December	Lost	1	2	11th	16th
1953-54	Division 1	17 October	Lost	1	2	6 March	Won	1	0	13th	15th
1954-55	Division 1	13 September	Lost	1	2	8 September	Lost	3	5	6th	8th
1955-56	Division 1	29 October	Won	3	0	10 March	Won	3	2	20th	11th
1956-57	Division 1	13 October	Won	3	1	20 April	Won	2	1	10th	17th
1957-58	Division 1	19 October	Won	4	3	1 March	Won	4	2	14th	19th

			Home					Away		*Final Positions*	
Season	*League*	*Date*	*Result*	Villa	Newcastle	*Date*	*Result*	Villa	Newcastle	Villa	Newcastle
1958-59	Division 1	4 October	Won	**2**	**1**	21 February	Lost	**0**	**1**	21stR	11th
1960-61	Division 1	8 October	Won	**2**	**0**	25 February	Lost	**1**	**2**	9th	21stR
1965-66	Division 1	1 January	Won	**4**	**2**	9 October	Lost	**0**	**1**	16th	15th
1966-67	Division 1	20 August	Drew	**1**	**1**	17 December	Won	**3**	**0**	21stR	20th
1975-76	Division 1	17 January	Drew	**1**	**1**	6 September	Lost	**0**	**3**	16th	15th
1976-77	Division 1	18 December	Won	**2**	**1**	14 May	Lost	**2**	**3**	4th	5th
1977-78	Division 1	17 April	Won	**2**	**0**	8 April	Drew	**1**	**1**	8th	21stR
1984-85	Division 1	22 December	Won	**4**	**0**	1 September	Lost	**0**	**3**	10th	14th
1985-86	Division 1	26 October	Lost	**1**	**2**	9 April	Drew	**2**	**2**	16th	11th
1986-87	Division 1	25 October	Won	**2**	**0**	7 March	Lost	**1**	**2**	22ndR	17th
1988-89	Division 1	14 January	Won	**3**	**1**	8 April	Won	**2**	**1**	17th	20thR
1993-94	Premiership	2 October	Lost	**0**	**2**	27 April	Lost	**1**	**5**	10th	3rd
1994-95	Premiership	1 October	Lost	**0**	**2**	25 February	Lost	**1**	**3**	18th	6th
1995-96	Premiership	18 November	Drew	**1**	**1**	14 April	Lost	**0**	**1**	4th	2nd
1996-97	Premiership	11 January	Drew	**2**	**2**	30 September	Lost	**3**	**4**	5th	2nd
1997-98	Premiership	1 February	Lost	**0**	**1**	23 August	Lost	**0**	**1**	7th	13th
1998-99	Premiership	9 September	Won	**1**	**0**	30 January	Lost	**1**	**2**	6th	13th
1999-00	Premiership	4 December	Lost	**0**	**1**	7 August	Won	**1**	**0**	6th	11th
2000-01	Premiership	2 December	Drew	**1**	**1**	19 May	Lost	**0**	**3**	8th	11th
2001-02	Premiership	2 April	Drew	**1**	**1**	3 November	Lost	**0**	**3**	8th	4th
2002-03	Premiership	7 December	Lost	**0**	**1**	21 April	Drew	**1**	**1**	16th	3rd
2003-04	Premiership	18 April	Drew	**0**	**0**	1 November	Drew	**1**	**1**	6th	5th

FA Cup										*Division*	
1894-95	Round 2	16 February	Won	**7**	**1**					Div 1	Div 2
1896-97	Round 1	30 January	Won	**5**	**0**					Div 1	Div 2
1904-05	Final	15 April		Crystal Palace			Won	**2**	**0**	Div 1	Div 1
1923-24	Final	26 April		Wembley			Lost	**0**	**2**	Div 1	Div 1
1951-52	Round 3					12 January	Lost	**2**	**4**	Div 1	Div 1
2000-01	Round 3	17 January	Won	**1**	**0**	6 January	Drew	**1**	**1**	Prem	Prem

The 1905 Cup Final and Newcastle goalkeeper Lawrence is again beaten by Harry Hampton as the Villa man scores his second goal to give his side the FA Cup. The game was described as 'the finest Cup Final ever witnessed'.

Summary	P	W	D	L	F	A
Villa's home league record:	66	32	17	17	120	70
Villa's away league record:	66	13	11	42	82	144
Villa's cup record:	7	4	1	2	18	8
TOTAL:	**139**	**49**	**29**	**61**	**220**	**222**

FACT FILE

- **In March 1928 Villa, for the only time in their history, scored five goals in a game and still lost.**
- **From 1955 to 1984, Villa were unbeaten in 11 home games.**
- **Villa lost on their first six Premiership visits to St. James' Park.**
- **Neither side won away in the first 14 matches between the sides.**
- **Newcastle are one of two sides Villa have met more than once in FA Cup finals. West Bromwich Albion are the other.**

Villa's top scorers vs Newcastle

Joe Bache 13

Billy Walker 12

Harry Hampton, Charlie Wallace 11

Johnny Dixon 10

Jack Devey, Arthur Dorrell, Eric Houghton, Pongo Waring, Dicky York 6

George Brown 5

Villa hat-tricks vs Newcastle

7 Nov 1903 Joe Bache

5 Apr 1920 Billy Walker

21 Apr 1924 Billy Walker

22 Dec 1984 Paul Rideout

30 Sep 1996 Dwight Yorke

Played for both clubs

James Logan	Villa 1892-94	Newcastle 1895-96
Tommy Niblo	Newcastle 1897-1902	Villa 1901-04
Bobby Templeton	Villa 1898-1903	Newcastle 1902-05
Ronnie Starling	Newcastle 1930-31	Villa 1936-47
Tommy Thompson	Newcastle 1947-50	Villa 1950-55
Trevor Hockey	Newcastle 1963-66	Villa 1973-74
John Burridge	Villa 1975-77	Newcastle 1989-91
Alex Cropley	Villa 1976-80	Newcastle 1979-80
Tommy Craig	Newcastle 1974-78	Villa 1977-79
Pat Heard	Villa 1979-83	Newcastle 1984-85
Peter Withe	Newcastle 1978-80	Villa 1980-85
Malcolm Allen	Villa 1987-88	Newcastle 1993-95
Franz Carr	Newcastle 1991-93	Villa 1994-96
Alan Thompson	Newcastle 1991-93	Villa 1998-2000
Steve Watson	Newcastle 1990-99	Villa 1998-2000
David Ginola	Newcastle 1995-97	Villa 2000-02
Nolberto Solano	Newcastle 1998-2004	Villa 2003-04

v. Northampton Town

Season	League	Date (Home)	Result	Villa	North'ton	Date (Away)	Result	Villa	North'ton	Final Positions Villa	Final Positions North'ton
1965-66	Division 1	2 April	Lost	**1**	**2**	6 November	Lost	**1**	**2**	16th	21stR

FA Cup										Division	
1982-83	Round 3	8 January	Won	**1**	**0**					Div 1	Div 4

League Cup											
1967-68	Round 2					13 September	Lost	**1**	**3**	Div 2	Div 3
1970-71	Round 3	13 October	Won	**3**	**0**	6 October	Drew	**1**	**1**	Div 3	Div 4

Summary	P	W	D	L	F	A
Villa's home league record:	1	0	0	1	1	2
Villa's away league record:	1	0	0	1	1	2
Villa's cup record:	4	2	1	1	6	4
TOTAL:	**6**	**2**	**1**	**3**	**8**	**8**

FACT FILE

- **Villa lost their first three matches against the Cobblers.**

Villa's top scorers vs Northampton

Andy Lochhead 2

Played for both clubs

Joe Eccles	Villa 1924-25	Northampton 1928-29
Billy Simpson	Villa 1931-35	Northampton 1936-37
Larry Canning	Villa 1948-54	Northampton 1956-57
Lew Chatterley	Villa 1962-71	Northampton 1971-72
Bobby Park	Villa 1964-69	Northampton 1972-74
Neil Rioch	Villa 1969-75	Northampton 1971-72
Ian Ross	Villa 1971-76	Northampton 1976-77
John Gregory	Northampton 1972-77	Villa 1977-79
Andy Blair	Villa 1981-84/85-88	Northampton 1988-89
Kevin Poole	Northampton 1984-85	Villa 1984-87
David Norton	Villa 1984-88	Northampton 1994-96
Phil Robinson	Villa 1986-87	Northampton 1994-95
Garry Thompson	Villa 1986-89	Northampton 1994-97
Bernard Gallacher	Villa 1986-91	Northampton 1993-94
Gareth Williams	Villa 1987-90	Northampton 1994-96
Derek Mountfield	Villa 1988-92	Northampton 1995-96
Darren Byfield	Villa 1997-98	Northampton 1999-2000
Richard Walker	Villa 1997-2000	Northampton 2003-04

v. Norwich City

		Home				Away				Final Positions	
Season	*League*	*Date*	*Result*	Villa	Norwich	*Date*	*Result*	Villa	Norwich	Villa	Norwich
1936-37	Division 2	19 December	Won	**3**	**0**	24 April	Lost	**1**	**5**	9th	17th
1937-38	Division 2	7 May	Won	**2**	**0**	16 September	Lost	**0**	**1**	1stP	14th
1967-68	Division 2	16 December	Won	**4**	**2**	19 August	Lost	**0**	**1**	16th	9th
1968-69	Division 2	21 December	Won	**2**	**1**	19 October	Drew	**1**	**1**	18th	13th
1969-70	Division 2	9 August	Lost	**0**	**1**	14 February	Lost	**1**	**3**	21stR	11th
1974-75	Division 2	24 August	Drew	**1**	**1**	30 April	Won	**4**	**1**	2ndP	3rdP
1975-76	Division 1	13 December	Won	**3**	**2**	23 August	Lost	**3**	**5**	16th	10th
1976-77	Division 1	23 April	Won	**1**	**0**	27 November	Drew	**1**	**1**	4th	16th
1977-78	Division 1	15 October	Won	**3**	**0**	11 March	Lost	**1**	**2**	8th	13th
1978-79	Division 1	16 December	Drew	**1**	**1**	21 April	Won	**2**	**1**	8th	16th
1979-80	Division 1	26 March	Won	**2**	**0**	1 December	Drew	**1**	**1**	7th	12th
1980-81	Division 1	20 August	Won	**1**	**0**	12 November	Won	**3**	**1**	1st	20thR
1982-83	Division 1	5 March	Won	**3**	**2**	23 October	Lost	**0**	**1**	6th	14th
1983-84	Division 1	10 September	Won	**1**	**0**	11 February	Lost	**1**	**3**	10th	14th
1984-85	Division 1	20 October	Drew	**2**	**2**	9 March	Drew	**2**	**2**	10th	20thR
1986-87	Division 1	20 September	Lost	**1**	**4**	28 February	Drew	**1**	**1**	22ndR	5th
1988-89	Division 1	3 December	Won	**3**	**1**	22 April	Drew	**2**	**2**	17th	4th
1989-90	Division 1	28 April	Drew	**3**	**3**	11 November	Lost	**0**	**2**	2nd	10th
1990-91	Division 1	8 May	Won	**2**	**1**	17 November	Lost	**0**	**2**	17th	15th
1991-92	Division 1	28 March	Won	**1**	**0**	1 January	Lost	**1**	**2**	7th	18th
1992-93	Premiership	28 November	Lost	**2**	**3**	24 March	Lost	**0**	**1**	2nd	3rd
1993-94	Premiership	4 April	Drew	**0**	**0**	29 December	Won	**2**	**1**	10th	12th
1994-95	Premiership	15 October	Drew	**1**	**1**	14 May	Drew	**1**	**1**	18th	20thR

FA Cup										*Division*	
1937-38	Round 3					8 January	Won	**3**	**2**	Div 2	Div 2
1983-84	Round 3	7 January	Drew	**1**	**1**	11 January	Lost	**0**	**3**	Div 1	Div 1

League Cup											
1962-63	Q'ter Final	3 December	Won	**4**	**1**					Div 1	Div 2
1974-75	Final	1 March		Wembley			Won	**1**	**0**	Div 2	Div 2
1976-77	Round 3	21 September	Won	**2**	**1**					Div 1	Div 1
1983-84	Q'ter Final					17 January	Won	**2**	**0**	Div 1	Div 1

Summary	*P*	*W*	*D*	*L*	*F*	*A*
Villa's home league record:	23	14	6	3	42	25
Villa's away league record:	23	4	7	12	28	41
Villa's cup record:	7	5	1	1	13	8
TOTAL:	**53**	**23**	**14**	**16**	**83**	**74**

FACT FILE

- **From 1974 to 1984, Villa were unbeaten in 12 home matches against the Canaries.**
- **From 1982 to 1993, Norwich were unbeaten in nine home league games.**
- **In 1984, Villa knocked Norwich out of the League Cup just six days after Norwich had knocked Villa out of the FA Cup.**

Villa's top scorers vs Norwich

Gary Shaw 6

Ray Graydon 5

Allan Evans, Peter Withe 4

Played for both clubs

George Travers	Villa 1908-09	Norwich 1920-21
Percy Varco	Villa 1923-25	Norwich 1927-30
Teddy Bowen	Villa 1923-34	Norwich 1934-38
George Edwards	Norwich 1935-38	Villa 1938-51
Kevin Keelan	Villa 1959-60	Norwich 1963-80
Mike Kenning	Villa 1960-61	Norwich 1966-68
Trevor Hockey	Norwich 1972-73	Villa 1973-74
John Deehan	Villa 1975-80	Norwich 1981-86
Malcolm Allen	Villa 1987-88	Norwich 1988-90
Andy Townsend	Norwich 1988-90	Villa 1993-98
John Fashanu	Norwich 1981-83	Villa 1994-95
Peter Crouch	Villa 2001-04	Norwich 2003-04

The 1975 League Cup Final between Aston Villa and Norwich City was a mediocre affair settled by Ray Graydon's second attempt after his penalty had been saved by Kevin Keelan.

v. Nottingham Forest

Season	League	Home Date	Home Result	Home Villa	Home Forest	Away Date	Away Result	Away Villa	Away Forest	Final Positions Villa	Final Positions Forest
1892-93	Division 1	15 October	Won	**1**	**0**	12 November	Won	**5**	**4**	4th	10th
1893-94	Division 1	14 April	Won	**3**	**1**	7 October	Won	**2**	**1**	1st	7th
1894-95	Division 1	24 November	Won	**4**	**1**	6 October	Lost	**1**	**2**	3rd	7th
1895-96	Division 1	25 January	Won	**3**	**1**	3 April	Won	**2**	**0**	1st	13th
1896-97	Division 1	19 December	Won	**3**	**2**	6 March	Won	**4**	**2**	1st	11th
1897-98	Division 1	30 April	Won	**2**	**0**	26 March	Lost	**1**	**3**	6th	8th
1898-99	Division 1	22 October	Won	**3**	**0**	18 February	Lost	**0**	**1**	1st	11th
1899-00	Division 1	9 December	Drew	**2**	**2**	14 April	Drew	**1**	**1**	1st	8th
1900-01	Division 1	15 December	Won	**2**	**1**	20 April	Lost	**1**	**3**	15th	4th
1901-02	Division 1	28 December	Won	**3**	**0**	1 April	Drew	**1**	**1**	8th	5th
1902-03	Division 1	10 January	Won	**3**	**1**	13 September	Lost	**0**	**2**	2nd	10th
1903-04	Division 1	16 April	Won	**3**	**1**	19 December	Won	**7**	**3**	5th	9th
1904-05	Division 1	17 September	Won	**2**	**0**	14 January	Drew	**1**	**1**	4th	16th
1905-06	Division 1	17 February	Won	**3**	**1**	14 October	Drew	**2**	**2**	8th	19thR
1907-08	Division 1	25 December	Won	**4**	**0**	26 December	Drew	**2**	**2**	2nd	9th
1908-09	Division 1	9 January	Lost	**1**	**2**	12 September	Won	**2**	**1**	7th	14th
1909-10	Division 1	25 September	Drew	**0**	**0**	1 January	Won	**4**	**1**	1st	14th
1910-11	Division 1	11 February	Won	**3**	**1**	8 October	Lost	**1**	**3**	2nd	20thR
1922-23	Division 1	27 January	Won	**4**	**0**	20 January	Lost	**1**	**3**	6th	20th
1923-24	Division 1	19 April	Won	**2**	**0**	12 April	Drew	**0**	**0**	6th	20th
1924-25	Division 1	2 May	Won	**2**	**0**	2 October	Won	**2**	**0**	15th	22ndR
1936-37	Division 2	7 September	Drew	**1**	**1**	2 September	Drew	**1**	**1**	9th	18th
1937-38	Division 2	9 March	Lost	**1**	**2**	23 October	Won	**2**	**0**	1stP	20th
1957-58	Division 1	30 April	Drew	**1**	**1**	23 November	Lost	**1**	**4**	14th	10th
1958-59	Division 1	6 September	Lost	**2**	**3**	20 April	Lost	**0**	**2**	21stR	13th
1960-61	Division 1	1 April	Lost	**1**	**2**	10 December	Lost	**0**	**2**	9th	14th
1961-62	Division 1	23 April	Won	**5**	**1**	24 April	Lost	**0**	**2**	7th	19th
1962-63	Division 1	4 May	Lost	**0**	**2**	22 September	Lost	**1**	**3**	15th	9th
1963-64	Division 1	14 December	Won	**3**	**0**	24 August	Won	**1**	**0**	19th	13th
1964-65	Division 1	20 March	Won	**2**	**1**	7 November	Lost	**2**	**4**	16th	5th
1965-66	Division 1	15 January	Won	**3**	**0**	23 October	Won	**2**	**1**	16th	18th
1966-67	Division 1	19 November	Drew	**1**	**1**	15 April	Lost	**0**	**3**	21stR	2nd
1972-73	Division 2	26 December	Drew	**2**	**2**	23 September	Drew	**1**	**1**	3rd	14th
1973-74	Division 2	24 April	Won	**3**	**1**	27 October	Won	**2**	**1**	14th	7th
1974-75	Division 2	2 October	Won	**3**	**0**	8 March	Won	**3**	**2**	2ndP	16th
1977-78	Division 1	5 April	Lost	**0**	**1**	17 September	Lost	**0**	**2**	8th	1st
1978-79	Division 1	30 September	Lost	**1**	**2**	4 April	Lost	**0**	**4**	8th	2nd
1979-80	Division 1	5 April	Won	**3**	**2**	26 December	Lost	**1**	**2**	7th	5th
1980-81	Division 1	18 April	Won	**2**	**0**	27 December	Drew	**2**	**2**	1st	7th
1981-82	Division 1	28 November	Won	**3**	**1**	24 April	Drew	**1**	**1**	11th	12th
1982-83	Division 1	11 September	Won	**4**	**1**	5 February	Won	**2**	**1**	6th	5th
1983-84	Division 1	17 March	Won	**1**	**0**	7 September	Drew	**2**	**2**	10th	3rd
1984-85	Division 1	5 September	Lost	**0**	**5**	29 December	Lost	**2**	**3**	10th	9th
1985-86	Division 1	12 October	Lost	**1**	**2**	15 March	Drew	**1**	**1**	16th	8th

		Home				Away				Final Positions	
Season	*League*	*Date*	*Result*	Villa	Forest	*Date*	*Result*	Villa	Forest	Villa	Forest
1986-87	Division 1	3 January	Drew	**0**	**0**	13 September	Lost	**0**	**6**	22ndR	8th
1988-89	Division 1	24 September	Drew	**1**	**1**	21 January	Lost	**0**	**4**	17th	3rd
1989-90	Division 1	2 December	Won	**2**	**1**	19 August	Drew	**1**	**1**	2nd	9th
1990-91	Division 1	10 November	Drew	**1**	**1**	23 February	Drew	**2**	**2**	17th	8th
1991-92	Division 1	21 September	Won	**3**	**1**	18 April	Lost	**0**	**2**	7th	8th
1992-93	Premiership	12 December	Won	**2**	**1**	4 April	Won	**1**	**0**	2nd	22ndR
1994-95	Premiership	22 October	Lost	**0**	**2**	21 January	Won	**2**	**1**	18th	3rd
1995-96	Premiership	23 September	Drew	**1**	**1**	10 December	Drew	**1**	**1**	4th	9th
1996-97	Premiership	2 November	Won	**2**	**0**	22 February	Drew	**0**	**0**	5th	20thR
1998-99	Premiership	24 April	Won	**2**	**0**	28 November	Drew	**2**	**2**	6th	20thR

FA Cup

										Division	
1880-81	Round 2					4 December	Won	**2**	**1**		
1881-82	Round 1	5 November	Won	**4**	**1**						
1894-95	Q'ter Final	2 March	Won	**6**	**1**					Div 1	Div 1
1898-99	Round 1					28 January	Lost	**1**	**2**	Div 1	Div 1
1900-01	Round 2	23 February	Drew	**0**	**0**	27 February	Won*	**3**	**1**	Div 1	Div 1
1908-09	Round 1					16 January	Lost	**0**	**2**	Div 1	Div 1
1958-59	Semi-Final	14 March		Hillsborough			Lost	**0**	**1**	Div 1	Div 1
1978-79	Round 3					10 January	Lost	**0**	**2**	Div 1	Div 1
1995-96	Q'ter Final					13 March	Won	**1**	**0**	Prem	Prem

League Cup

1972-73	Round 2					5 September	Won	**1**	**0**	Div 2	Div 2
1977-78	Round 4					29 November	Lost	**2**	**4**	Div 1	Div 1

The second game of the 1936-37 season, Villa's first ever outside the top flight of English football, and Nottingham Forest's Roy Brown scores at the City Ground. Villa, though, drew 1-1 thanks to a goal from Frank Broome.

Summary	P	W	D	L	F	A
Villa's home league record:	54	34	10	10	110	53
Villa's away league record:	54	16	17	21	76	99
Villa's cup record:	12	6	1	5	20	15
TOTAL:	**120**	**56**	**28**	**36**	**206**	**167**

FACT FILE

- **Villa recorded 16 wins and two draws from their first 18 home matches against Forest.**
- **Forest were unbeaten in nine matches between 1984 and 1989.**
- **Villa are undefeated in the sides' last eight meetings.**

Villa's top scorers vs Forest

Jack Devey 14
Joe Bache 11
Billy Garraty 9
Charlie Athersmith, Harry Hampton, Peter Withe 7
Harry Burrows, Ray Graydon, Tony Hateley 5

Villa hat-tricks vs Forest

12 Nov 1892 Charlie Athersmith
19 Dec 1903 Tommy Niblo
19 Dec 1903 Joe Bache
25 Dec 1907 Joe Bache (4)
1 Jan 1910 Harry Hampton

Played for both clubs

James Suddick	Villa 1897-98	Forest 1898-99
Tommy Niblo	Villa 1901-04	Forest 1904-06
Harry Hadley	Villa 1905-06	Forest 1905-07
Sam Hardy	Villa 1912-21	Forest 1921-25
Walter Boyman	Villa 1919-22	Forest 1921-23
Jack Maund	Villa 1935-38	Forest 1939-40
George Pritty	Villa 1936-38	Forest 1938-48
Frank O'Donnell	Villa 1938-40	Forest 1946-47
Sailor Brown	Forest 1946-48	Villa 1947-49
Geoff Vowden	Forest 1959-65	Villa 1970-74
Trevor Hockey	Forest 1961-64	Villa 1973-74
Kenny Swain	Villa 1978-83	Forest 1982-85
Peter Withe	Forest 1976-79	Villa 1980-85
Steve Hodge	Forest 1981-86/88-91	Villa 1985-87
Stuart Gray	Forest 1980-83	Villa 1987-91
David Platt	Villa 1987-91	Forest 1999-2001
Garry Parker	Forest 1987-92	Villa 1991-95
Dean Saunders	Villa 1992-95	Forest 1996-98
Franz Carr	Forest 1985-91	Villa 1994-96
Gary Charles	Forest 1988-93	Villa 1994-99
Carl Tiler	Forest 1991-95	Villa 1995-97
Ricardo Scimeca	Villa 1995-99	Forest 1999-2003
Stan Collymore	Forest 1993-95	Villa 1997-99
Colin Calderwood	Villa 1998-2000	Forest 1999-2001
Steve Stone	Forest 1991-99	Villa 1998-2002

v. Notts County

Season	League	Home Date	Home Result	Home Villa	Home Notts C	Away Date	Away Result	Away Villa	Away Notts C	Final Positions Villa	Final Positions Notts C
1888-89	Division 1	29 September	Won	9	1	8 December	Won	4	2	2nd	11th
1889-90	Division 1	14 September	Drew	1	1	9 November	Drew	1	1	8th	10th
1890-91	Division 1	13 September	Won	3	2	29 November	Lost	1	7	9th	3rd
1891-92	Division 1	7 November	Won	5	1	2 January	Lost	2	5	4th	8th
1892-93	Division 1	18 March	Won	3	1	31 December	Won	4	1	4th	14thR
1897-98	Division 1	16 October	Won	4	2	11 September	Won	3	2	6th	13th
1898-99	Division 1	22 April	Won	6	1	24 December	Lost	0	1	1st	5th
1899-00	Division 1	17 February	Won	6	2	14 October	Won	4	1	1st	15th
1900-01	Division 1	13 October	Lost	1	2	16 February	Lost	0	2	15th	3rd
1901-02	Division 1	9 September	Won	2	0	2 November	Won	3	0	8th	13th
1902-03	Division 1	15 April	Won	2	1	8 November	Lost	1	2	2nd	15th
1903-04	Division 1	24 October	Won	4	0	1 April	Drew	0	0	5th	13th
1904-05	Division 1	12 November	Won	4	2	11 March	Won	2	1	4th	18th
1905-06	Division 1	21 April	Won	2	1	16 December	Lost	1	2	8th	16th
1906-07	Division 1	13 April	Drew	0	0	8 December	Drew	1	1	5th	18th
1907-08	Division 1	2 March	Won	5	1	2 November	Won	3	0	2nd	18th
1908-09	Division 1	14 November	Drew	1	1	20 March	Drew	1	1	7th	15th
1909-10	Division 1	4 December	Drew	1	1	16 April	Won	3	2	1st	9th
1910-11	Division 1	10 December	Won	3	1	15 April	Won	2	1	2nd	11th
1911-12	Division 1	16 March	Won	5	1	13 March	Lost	0	2	6th	16th
1912-13	Division 1	15 March	Won	1	0	9 November	Drew	1	1	2nd	19thR
1914-15	Division 1	2 September	Won	2	1	5 April	Drew	1	1	14th	16th
1919-20	Division 1	3 April	Won	3	1	10 April	Lost	1	2	9th	21stR
1923-24	Division 1	3 November	Drew	0	0	10 November	Won	1	0	6th	10th
1924-25	Division 1	21 March	Drew	0	0	15 November	Drew	0	0	15th	9th
1925-26	Division 1	26 September	Won	2	1	6 February	Lost	0	1	6th	22ndR
1971-72	Division 3	13 November	Won	1	0	4 March	Won	3	0	1stP	4th
1973-74	Division 2	22 December	Drew	1	1	29 September	Lost	0	2	14th	10th

Ian Ross was on the fringes of a hugely talented squad at Liverpool before he joined Aston Villa in February 1972 for £70,000. By the end of that season he had helped Villa to the Third Division championship. A sound defender, Ross captained the team which won the League Cup and promotion to the top flight in 1975. After 204 appearances in the first team, Ross joined Peterborough United in December 1976, having earlier been on loan to Notts County and Northampton. He later served as player-coach at Wolves and then as a coach back at Villa Park. Thereafter he worked in numerous coaching positions both at home and abroad.

		Home				Away				Final Positions	
Season	League	Date	Result	Villa	Notts C	Date	Result	Villa	Notts C	Villa	Notts C
1974-75	Division 2	9 November	Lost	**0**	**1**	1 February	Won	**3**	**1**	2ndP	14th
1981-82	Division 1	29 August	Lost	**0**	**1**	16 January	Lost	**0**	**1**	11th	15th
1982-83	Division 1	8 March	Won	**2**	**0**	9 October	Lost	**1**	**4**	6th	15th
1983-84	Division 1	28 April	Won	**3**	**1**	26 November	Lost	**2**	**5**	10th	21stR
1991-92	Division 1	16 November	Won	**1**	**0**	10 March	Drew	**0**	**0**	7th	21stR

FA Cup										Division	
1880-81	Round 3	12 February	Won	**3**	**1**						
1881-82	Round 3	31 December	Drew*	**2**	**2**	7 January	Drew*	**2**	**2**		
		14 January	Won	**4**	**1**	(2nd replay)					
1882-83	Q'ter Final					3 March	Lost	**3**	**4**		
1889-90	Round 2					1 February	Lost	**1**	**4**	Div 1	Div 1
1896-97	Round 2	13 February	Won	**2**	**1**					Div 1	Div 2
1920-21	Round 2	2 February	Won	**1**	**0**	29 January	Drew	**0**	**0**	Div 1	Div 2
1921-22	Q'ter Final	8 March	Lost	**3**	**4**	4 March	Drew	**2**	**2**	Div 1	Div 2
1981-82	Round 3					5 January	Won	**6**	**0**	Div 1	Div 1
1996-97	Round 3	22 January	Won	**3**	**0**	14 January	Drew	**0**	**0**	Prem	Div 2

League Cup											
1970-71	Round 1	19 August	Won	**4**	**0**					Div 3	Div 4
1982-83	Round 2	6 October	Lost	**1**	**2**	26 October	Lost	**0**	**1**	Div 1	Div 1

Summary	*P*	*W*	*D*	*L*	*F*	*A*
Villa's home league record:	33	23	7	3	83	29
Villa's away league record:	33	12	8	13	49	52
Villa's cup record:	17	7	5	5	37	24
TOTAL:	**83**	**42**	**20**	**21**	**169**	**105**

FACT FILE

- **Villa lost only one of their first 28 home league matches against Notts County.**
- **Villa have not won on their last six visits to Meadow Lane.**
- **In December 1910, Villa won a club record ninth successive league game when they beat County 3-1 at Villa Park.**

Villa's top scorers vs Notts County

Jack Devey, Harry Hampton 12
Billy Garraty 10
Joe Bache 9
Archie Hunter 6
George Johnson 5

Villa hat-tricks vs Notts County

29 Sep 1888 Albert Allen
22 Apr 1899 Jack Devey
14 Oct 1899 George Johnson
17 Feb 1900 Billy Garraty
2 Mar 1908 Joe Bache
5 Jan 1982 David Geddis (cup)

Played for both clubs

James Logan	Villa 1892-94	Notts Co 1893-95
Will Devey	Villa 1892-94	Notts Co 1896-98

George Kinsey	Villa 1894-95	Notts Co 1896-97
Billy Matthews	Villa 1903-07	Notts Co 1906-12
Jimmy Cantrell	Villa 1904-08	Notts Co 1907-13
Rowland Harper	Villa 1907-08	Notts Co 1907-09
Horace Henshall	Villa 1910-12	Notts Co 1912-22
Arthur Davis	Villa 1919-22	Notts Co 1923-28
Lew Price	Villa 1920-22	Notts Co 1922-28
George Jakeman	Villa 1924-29	Notts Co 1929-33
Ken Tewkesbury	Notts Co 1932-33	Villa 1932-33
Eric Houghton	Villa 1929-47	Notts Co 1946-49
Frank Broome	Villa 1934-37	Notts Co 1949-53
William Evans	Villa 1946-49	Notts Co 1949-53
Edward Lowe	Villa 1946-50	Notts Co 1963-65
Harold Chapman	Villa 1947-48	Notts Co 1948-51
Derek Pace	Villa 1950-58	Notts Co 1964-66
Roy Pritchard	Villa 1955-58	Notts Co 1957-58
Jackie Sewell	Notts Co 1946-51	Villa 1955-60
Ron Wylie	Notts Co 1951-59	Villa 1958-65
Jimmy McMorran	Villa 1960-62	Notts Co 1969-70
Tony Hateley	Notts Co 1958-63/70-72	Villa 1963-67
Dick Edwards	Notts Co 1959-67	Villa 1967-70
Ian Ross	Villa 1971-76	Notts Co 1976-77
Andy Gray	Villa 1975-79/85-87	Notts Co 1987-88
Gary Shelton	Villa 1978-82	Notts Co 1979-80
Paul Rideout	Villa 1983-85	Notts Co 1991-92
David Norton	Villa 1984-88	Notts Co 1988-91
Phil Robinson	Villa 1986-87	Notts Co 1989-92/96-98
David Hunt	Notts Co 1977-87	Villa 1987-89
Steve Sims	Notts Co 1984-87	Villa 1987-89
Phil King	Notts Co 1993-94	Villa 1994-95
Tommy Johnson	Notts Co 1988-92	Villa 1994-97
Mark Draper	Notts Co 1988-94	Villa 1994-97
Simon Grayson	Villa 1997-99	Notts Co 2001-02
Colin Calderwood	Villa 1998-2000	Notts Co 2000-01
Jonathan Bewers	Villa 1999-2000	Notts Co 2003-04

Inside-forward Freddie Haycock was a key figure in the club's revival after Aston Villa were relegated from the top flight in 1936. Born in Liverpool in 1911, Haycock played for Bootle Boys and he later played for Waterford and for an Irish representative team after spending family holidays in Ireland. He was playing for Prescot Cables when Villa signed him in 1934 and in the last three seasons before World War Two he was outstanding. He had scored 33 goals in 110 senior games when the League was suspended and during the war he guested for Plymouth, Northampton, Wolves, Forest and Notts County. In 1946 he was transferred to Wrexham but retired a year later.

v. Oldbury Town

Away

FA Cup		Date	Result	Villa	Oldbury
1887-88	Round 1	15 October	Won	**4**	**0**

Summary	P	W	D	L	F	A
Villa's cup record:	1	1	0	0	4	0
TOTAL:	**1**	**1**	**0**	**0**	**4**	**0**

Villa's top scorers vs Oldbury

Albert Brown 2

v. Oldham Athletic

Season	League	Date	Result	Home Villa	Home Oldham	Date	Result	Away Villa	Away Oldham	Final Positions Villa	Final Positions Oldham
1910-11	Division 1	3 September	Drew	**1**	**1**	13 December	Drew	**1**	**1**	2nd	7th
1911-12	Division 1	26 December	Won	**6**	**1**	8 April	Won	**2**	**1**	6th	18th
1912-13	Division 1	26 December	Won	**7**	**1**	9 September	Drew	**2**	**2**	2nd	9th
1913-14	Division 1	18 March	Drew	**0**	**0**	1 November	Won	**1**	**0**	2nd	4th
1914-15	Division 1	17 April	Drew	**0**	**0**	12 December	Drew	**3**	**3**	14th	2nd
1919-20	Division 1	20 December	Won	**3**	**0**	27 December	Won	**3**	**0**	9th	17th
1920-21	Division 1	25 September	Won	**3**	**0**	2 October	Drew	**1**	**1**	10th	19th
1921-22	Division 1	29 April	Won	**2**	**0**	6 May	Lost	**1**	**3**	5th	19th
1922-23	Division 1	11 November	Won	**3**	**0**	4 November	Won	**2**	**0**	6th	22ndR
1971-72	Division 3	10 April	Won	**1**	**0**	27 November	Won	**6**	**0**	1stP	11th
1974-75	Division 2	12 April	Won	**5**	**0**	5 October	Won	**2**	**1**	2ndP	18th
1987-88	Division 2	4 April	Lost	**1**	**2**	14 November	Won	**1**	**0**	2ndP	10th
1991-92	Division 1	22 February	Won	**1**	**0**	30 November	Lost	**2**	**3**	7th	17th
1992-93	Premiership	2 May	Lost	**0**	**1**	24 October	Drew	**1**	**1**	2nd	19th
1993-94	Premiership	19 March	Lost	**1**	**2**	25 September	Drew	**1**	**1**	10th	21stR

FA Cup

Season	Round	Date	Result	Villa	Oldham	Date / Venue	Result	Villa	Oldham	Division Villa	Division Oldham
1909-10	Round 1					15 January	Won	**2**	**1**	Div 1	Div 2
1912-13	Semi-Final	29 March				Ewood Park	Won	**1**	**1**	Div 1	Div 1
1974-75	Round 3					4 January	Won	**3**	**0**	Div 2	Div 2
1989-90	Q'ter Final					14 March	Lost	**0**	**3**	Div 1	Div 2

League Cup

Season	Round	Date	Result	Villa	Oldham	Date	Result	Villa	Oldham	Division Villa	Division Oldham
1975-76	Round 2	10 September	Won	**2**	**0**					Div 1	Div 2

Much-travelled Tony Hateley, scorer of 86 goals in 148 games for Villa. Derby-born, he played for Notts County, Chelsea, Liverpool, Coventry, Birmingham and Notts County again before finishing his League career at Oldham, by which time his goals amounted to 211 and appearances to 434. His son, Mark, followed his father into football and enjoyed a successful career, including England caps.

Summary	P	W	D	L	F	A
Villa's home league record:	15	9	3	3	34	8
Villa's away league record:	15	7	6	2	29	17
Villa's cup record:	5	4	0	1	8	4
TOTAL:	**35**	**20**	**9**	**6**	**71**	**29**

FACT FILE

- **Villa were unbeaten in their first 12 home matches against Oldham. Oldham failed to score in any of the last nine of these.**
- **Villa were unbeaten in their first 17 matches home and away against Oldham.**
- **The home defeat to Oldham in May 1993 ended Villa's hopes of winning the inaugural Premier League title.**
- **The 6-0 win in 1971 is Villa's joint highest away win in league football.**

Villa's top scorers vs Oldham

Harry Hampton 9
Clem Stephenson 8
Billy Kirton 6
Billy Walker 5
Brian Little 4

Villa hat-tricks vs Oldham

26 Dec 1911 Harry Hampton (4)
26 Dec 1912 Harry Hampton
27 Nov 1971 Andy Lochhead
12 Apr 1975 Brian Little

Played for both clubs

George Hunter	Villa 1908-12	Oldham 1911-13
Joe Walters	Villa 1905-12	Oldham 1912-20
Charlie Wallace	Villa 1907-21	Oldham 1921-23
John Sleeuwenhoek	Villa 1960-68	Oldham 1971-72
Tony Hateley	Villa 1963-67	Oldham 1973-74
Andy Lochhead	Villa 1969-73	Oldham 1973-75
Simon Stainrod	Oldham 1978-81	Villa 1985-88
Ian Olney	Villa 1988-92	Oldham 1992-96
Ian Ormondroyd	Oldham 1986-87/96-98	Villa 1988-92
Earl Barrett	Oldham 1987-92	Villa 1991-95

v. Oxford United

		Home					Away			Final Positions	
Season	League	Date	Result	Villa	Oxford	Date	Result	Villa	Oxford	Villa	Oxford
1968-69	Division 2	28 September	Won	**2**	**0**	5 April	Lost	**0**	**1**	18th	20th
1969-70	Division 2	31 March	Drew	**0**	**0**	25 October	Drew	**2**	**2**	21stR	15th
1972-73	Division 2	31 March	Won	**2**	**1**	25 November	Lost	**0**	**2**	3rd	8th
1973-74	Division 2	8 September	Won	**2**	**0**	29 December	Lost	**1**	**2**	14th	18th
1974-75	Division 2	29 November	Drew	**0**	**0**	18 January	Won	**2**	**1**	2ndP	11th
1985-86	Division 1	2 November	Won	**2**	**0**	5 April	Drew	**1**	**1**	16th	18th
1986-87	Division 1	6 September	Lost	**1**	**2**	20 December	Drew	**2**	**2**	22ndR	18th

League Cup										Division	
1985-86	Semi-Final	4 March	Drew	**2**	**2**	12 March	Lost	**1**	**2**	Div 1	Div 1
1992-93	Round 2	7 October	Won	**2**	**1**	23 September	Won	**2**	**1**	Prem	Div 1
2002-03	Round 3					6 November	Won	**3**	**0**	Prem	Div 3

Summary	*P*	*W*	*D*	*L*	*F*	*A*
Villa's home league record:	7	4	2	1	9	3
Villa's away league record:	7	1	3	3	8	11
Villa's cup record:	5	3	1	1	10	6
TOTAL:	**19**	**8**	**6**	**5**	**27**	**20**

FACT FILE

- **Villa have lost only once in their nine home games against Oxford.**

Villa's top scorers vs Oxford

Simon Stainrod 4

Pat McMahon 3

Played for both clubs

Ray Graydon	Villa 1971-77	Oxford 1978-81
Bobby McDonald	Villa 1972-76	Oxford 1983-87
Gary Shelton	Villa 1978-82	Oxford 1987-89
Terry Donovan	Villa 1979-82	Oxford 1982-83
Steve Foster	Villa 1983-85	Oxford 1989-92
Ray Houghton	Oxford 1985-88	Villa 1992-95
Dean Saunders	Oxford 1986-89	Villa 1992-95
Richard Walker	Villa 1997-2000	Oxford 2003-04
Neil Cutler	Villa 1999-2000	Oxford 2000-01

v. Peterborough United

FA Cup		Home Date	Result	Villa	Pet'borough	Away Date	Result	Villa	Pet'borough	Division Villa	Pet'borough
1960-61	Round 4	1 February	Won	**2**	**1**	28 January	Drew	**1**	**1**	Div 1	Div 4

League Cup

1962-63	Round 2	24 September	Won	**6**	**1**					Div 1	Div 3
1995-96	Round 2	20 September	Won	**6**	**0**	3 October	Drew	**1**	**1**	Prem	Div 2

Summary	*P*	*W*	*D*	*L*	*F*	*A*
Villa's cup record:	5	3	2	0	16	4
TOTAL:	**5**	**3**	**2**	**0**	**16**	**4**

Villa's top scorers vs Peterborough

Derek Dougan 3

Peter McParland, Dwight Yorke 2

Villa hat-tricks vs Peterborough

24 Sep 1962 Derek Dougan (cup)

Played for both clubs

Raymond Hogg	Villa 1954-57	Peterborough 1960-61
Vic Crowe	Villa 1954-64	Peterborough 1964-67
Nigel Sims	Villa 1955-64	Peterborough 1964-65
Derek Dougan	Villa 1961-63	Peterborough 1963-65
Bobby Park	Villa 1964-69	Peterborough 1972-73
Keith Bradley	Villa 1964-72	Peterborough 1972-76
Ian Ross	Villa 1971-76	Peterborough 1976-79
Ivor Linton	Villa 1976-82	Peterborough 1982-84
Martin Carruthers	Villa 1991-93	Peterborough 1996-99
Dave Farrell	Villa 1992-94	Peterborough 1997-2004
Guy Whittingham	Villa 1993-95	Peterborough 2000-01

When he took over as manager from Tommy Docherty in January 1970, Vic Crowe was already a great name in Aston Villa's history. As a wing-half Crowe made 351 senior appearances for the club after signing from junior football in June 1952. He missed only one game when Villa won the Second Division championship in 1960 and the following year helped them win the League Cup. In 1963 he played in another League Cup Final for the club. A Welsh international who also played with Peterborough, as a manager Crowe took Villa to the 1971 League Cup Final, guided them back to the Second Division in 1972 and built a side which won the League Cup and regained Villa's top-flight status. After leaving Villa in May 1974, Crowe went to work in American soccer.

v. Plymouth Argyle

Season	League	Home Date	Home Result	Villa	Plymouth	Away Date	Away Result	Villa	Plymouth	Final Positions Villa	Final Positions Plymouth
1936-37	Division 2	13 February	Won	**5**	**4**	10 October	Drew	**2**	**2**	9th	5th
1937-38	Division 2	23 February	Won	**3**	**0**	2 October	Won	**3**	**0**	1stP	13th
1959-60	Division 2	31 October	Won	**2**	**0**	30 April	Lost	**0**	**3**	1stP	19th
1967-68	Division 2	28 August	Lost	**0**	**1**	23 August	Lost	**1**	**2**	16th	22ndR
1970-71	Division 3	22 August	Drew	**1**	**1**	19 December	Drew	**1**	**1**	4th	15th
1971-72	Division 3	14 August	Won	**3**	**1**	16 October	Lost	**2**	**3**	1stP	8th
1987-88	Division 2	27 February	Won	**5**	**2**	3 October	Won	**3**	**1**	2ndP	16th

FA Cup

Season	Round	Home Date	Home Result	Villa	Plymouth	Away Date	Away Result	Villa	Plymouth	Division Villa	Division Plymouth
1905-06	Round 2	3 February	Drew	**0**	**0**	7 February	Won	**5**	**1**	Div 1	Non L

League Cup

Season	Round	Home Date	Home Result	Villa	Plymouth	Away Date	Away Result	Villa	Plymouth	Division Villa	Division Plymouth
1960-61	Round 4	13 December	Drew	**3**	**3**	6 February	Won	**5**	**3**	Div 1	Div 2

Summary	P	W	D	L	F	A
Villa's home league record:	7	5	1	1	19	9
Villa's away league record:	7	2	2	3	12	12
Villa's cup record:	4	2	2	0	13	7
TOTAL:	**18**	**9**	**5**	**4**	**44**	**28**

FACT FILE

- **Villa have lost only once in nine home games against Plymouth.**
- **Villa's league cup replay on 19 December 1960 was abandoned at 0-0 after 90 minutes as the pitch was unfit for extra-time.**

Villa's top scorers vs Plymouth

Frank Broome 6
Eric Houghton 4
Gerry Hitchens, Peter McParland 3

Villa hat-tricks vs Plymouth

13 Feb 1937 Eric Houghton
6 Feb 1961 Gerry Hitchens (cup)

Played for both clubs

Norman Mackay	Villa 1923-24	Plymouth 1927-34
Peter McParland	Villa 1952-62	Plymouth 1962-64
Harry Burrows	Villa 1959-65	Plymouth 1973-75
Alan O'Neill	Villa 1960-63	Plymouth 1962-64
Neil Rioch	Villa 1969-75	Plymouth 1975-76
Geoff Crudgington	Villa 1970-72	Plymouth 1979-88
John Gregory	Villa 1977-79	Plymouth 1989-90
Andy Comyn	Villa 1989-91	Plymouth 1993-95
Les Sealey	Plymouth 1984-85	Villa 1991-92

v. Port Vale

		Home					Away			Final Positions	
Season	League	Date	Result	Villa	Port Vale	Date	Result	Villa	Port Vale	Villa	Port Vale
1970-71	Division 3	16 January	Won	**1**	**0**	19 October	Lost	**0**	**2**	4th	17th
1971-72	Division 3	26 February	Won	**2**	**0**	6 November	Drew	**4**	**4**	1stP	15th

FA Cup										Division	
1924-25	Round 1	10 January	Won	**7**	**2**					Div 1	Div 2
1959-60	Round 5					20 February	Won	**2**	**1**	Div 2	Div 3
1976-77	Round 5	26 February	Won	**3**	**0**					Div 1	Div 3
1989-90	Round 4	27 January	Won	**6**	**0**					Div 1	Div 2

Summary	P	W	D	L	F	A
Villa's home league record:	2	2	0	0	3	0
Villa's away league record:	2	0	1	1	4	6
Villa's cup record:	4	4	0	0	18	3
TOTAL:	**8**	**6**	**1**	**1**	**25**	**9**

FACT FILE

- **Villa have a 100% record in their five home games, winning them by an aggregate 19-2 margin.**

England international right-winger Dickie York was born in Handsworth in 1899 and when Villa won the FA Cup in 1913 he was playing for England Schoolboys. After wartime service in the Royal Flying Corps – and a few games guesting for Chelsea – York signed for Villa, his local club, in May 1919. Initially he appeared at right-half before switching to the wing. He developed quickly after that, playing twice for England and appearing in the 1924 Cup Final. In June 1931 he and Villa's Arthur Dorrell both moved to Port Vale. A year later York had gone to Brierley Hill Alliance before he retired in 1934. He made 390 senior appearances for Aston Villa, scoring 86 goals.

Villa's top scorers vs Port Vale

Len Capewell 4

Billy Walker 3

Villa hat-tricks vs Port Vale

10 Jan 1925 Billy Walker (cup)

10 Jan 1925 Len Capewell (4) (cup)

Played for both clubs

Lewis Campbell	Villa 1889-93	Port Vale 1893-94
Alf Wood	Port Vale 1892-95	Villa 1900-05
Howard Harvey	Villa 1897-98	Port Vale 1898-1900
Tommy Lyons	Villa 1907-15	Port Vale 1919-21
John Hampson	Villa 1919-21	Port Vale 1921-24
Arthur Dorrell	Villa 1919-30	Port Vale 1931-32
Jack Mandley	Port Vale 1928-30	Villa 1929-34
Dicky York	Villa 1919-31	Port Vale 1931-32
Keith Jones	Villa 1947-57	Port Vale 1957-59
Ivor Powell	Villa 1948-51	Port Vale 1951-52
Roy Chapman	Villa 1953-58	Port Vale 1967-69
Roy Pritchard	Villa 1955-58	Port Vale 1958-60
John Woodward	Villa 1966-69	Port Vale 1972-75
Sammy Morgan	Port Vale 1969-73	Villa 1973-76
Tony Betts	Villa 1974-75	Port Vale 1975-76
Lee Jenkins	Villa 1978-80	Port Vale 1980-81
Colin Gibson	Villa 1978-86	Port Vale 1990-91
Ray Walker	Villa 1982-86	Port Vale 1984-85/86-97
Paul Kerr	Villa 1983-87	Port Vale 1992-94
Dean Glover	Villa 1984-87	Port Vale 1988-98
Mark Burke	Villa 1986-88	Port Vale 1994-95
Ian Taylor	Port Vale 1992-94	Villa 1994-2003

Bought from Port Vale, Sammy Morgan enjoyed three years at Villa before leaving for Brighton.

v. Portsmouth

		Home				Away					Final Positions	
Season	League	Date	Result	Villa	Portsmouth	Date	Result	Villa	Portsmouth	Villa	Portsmouth
1927-28	Division 1	5 September	Won	7	2	31 August	Lost	1	3	8th	20th
1928-29	Division 1	26 December	Won	3	2	25 December	Lost	2	3	3rd	20th
1929-30	Division 1	21 April	Lost	0	1	18 April	Won	2	1	4th	13th
1930-31	Division 1	3 December	Drew	2	2	4 April	Lost	0	5	2nd	4th
1931-32	Division 1	27 February	Lost	0	1	17 October	Won	3	0	5th	8th
1932-33	Division 1	4 February	Won	4	1	24 September	Won	4	2	2nd	9th
1933-34	Division 1	10 February	Drew	1	1	30 September	Lost	2	3	13th	10th
1934-35	Division 1	26 November	Won	5	4	6 April	Won	1	0	13th	14th
1935-36	Division 1	4 January	Won	4	2	7 September	Lost	0	3	21stR	10th
1938-39	Division 1	1 October	Won	2	0	4 February	Drew	0	0	12th	17th
1946-47	Division 1	12 October	Drew	1	1	15 February	Lost	2	3	8th	12th
1947-48	Division 1	27 March	Won	2	1	8 November	Won	4	2	6th	8th
1948-49	Division 1	9 October	Drew	1	1	5 March	Lost	0	3	10th	1st
1949-50	Division 1	5 September	Won	1	0	6 May	Lost	1	5	12th	1st
1950-51	Division 1	14 April	Drew	3	3	25 November	Drew	3	3	15th	7th
1951-52	Division 1	9 February	Won	2	0	29 September	Lost	0	2	6th	4th
1952-53	Division 1	18 February	Won	6	0	27 September	Drew	1	1	11th	15th
1953-54	Division 1	16 January	Drew	1	1	5 September	Lost	1	2	13th	14th
1954-55	Division 1	4 September	Won	1	0	27 April	Drew	2	2	6th	3rd
1955-56	Division 1	26 December	Lost	1	3	27 December	Drew	2	2	20th	12th
1956-57	Division 1	18 February	Drew	2	2	6 October	Lost	1	5	10th	19th
1957-58	Division 1	2 November	Won	2	1	15 March	Lost	0	1	14th	20th
1958-59	Division 1	25 August	Won	3	2	3 September	Lost	2	5	21stR	22ndR
1959-60	Division 2	14 September	Won	5	2	9 September	Won	2	1	1stP	20th
1967-68	Division 2	16 April	Won	1	0	15 April	Drew	2	2	16th	5th
1968-69	Division 2	1 February	Won	2	0	16 November	Lost	0	2	18th	15th
1969-70	Division 2	17 January	Lost	3	5	27 September	Drew	0	0	21stR	17th
1972-73	Division 2	17 March	Won	2	0	21 October	Won	1	0	3rd	17th
1973-74	Division 2	23 March	Won	4	1	10 November	Lost	0	2	14th	15th
1974-75	Division 2	23 November	Won	2	0	18 February	Won	3	2	2ndP	17th
2003-04	Premiership	6 January	Won	2	1	16 August	Lost	1	2	6th	13th

Tony Barton also scored plenty of goals in his career, for Fulham, Forest and Portsmouth, and he was in the same side as Ron Saunders when Pompey won the Third Division title in 1962. When Saunders resigned in February 1982, Barton took over, initially as caretaker boss, and guided Villa to their European Cup triumph. He was sacked, however, at the end of the 1983-84 season, when Villa finished tenth in Division One, but later built a promotion-winning side for Northampton Town before suffering a heart attack. He later became assistant to former Villa player Chris Nicholl at Southampton but sadly died following further heart problems.

FA Cup

										Division	
1910-11	Round 1					14 January	Won	**4**	**1**	Div 1	Non L
1928-29	Semi-Final	23 March	Highbury				Lost	**0**	**1**	Div 1	Div 1
1931-32	Round 4	27 January	Lost	**0**	**1**	23 January	Drew	**1**	**1**	Div 1	Div 1
1985-86	Round 3	13 January	Won*	**3**	**2**	4 January	Drew	**2**	**2**	Div 1	Div 2
1997-98	Round 3	14 January	Won	**1**	**0**	3 January	Drew	**2**	**2**	Prem	Div 1

League Cup

1983-84	Round 2	26 October	Won*	**3**	**2**	4 October	Drew	**2**	**2**	Div 1	Div 2

Summary	*P*	*W*	*D*	*L*	*F*	*A*
Villa's home league record:	31	20	7	4	75	40
Villa's away league record:	31	8	7	16	43	67
Villa's cup record:	10	4	4	2	18	14
TOTAL:	**72**	**32**	**18**	**22**	**136**	**121**

FACT FILE

- **From 1933 to 1954, Villa were undefeated in 14 home games against Portsmouth.**
- **Villa failed to win at Fratton Park in 11 matches between 1949 and 1958.**
- **Villa have lost once in their last 11 games with Pompey.**

Villa's top scorers vs Portsmouth

Dai Astley, Joe Beresford, Johnny Dixon 7
Eric Houghton 5
Peter McParland, Billy Walker, David Walsh, Pongo Waring 4

Villa hat-tricks vs Portsmouth

5 Sep 1927 Joe Beresford

Played for both clubs

Jimmy Allen	Portsmouth 1930-34	Villa 1934-40
Derek Dougan	Portsmouth 1957-59	Villa 1961-63
George Graham	Villa 1962-64	Portsmouth 1974-77
Jimmy Brown	Villa 1969-75	Portsmouth 1979-80
Alex Cropley	Villa 1976-80	Portsmouth 1981-82
Kenny Swain	Villa 1978-83	Portsmouth 1985-88
Noel Blake	Villa 1979-82	Portsmouth 1984-88
Steve Foster	Portsmouth 1975-79	Villa 1983-85
Warren Aspinall	Villa 1986-88	Portsmouth 1988-94
Chris Price	Villa 1988-92	Portsmouth 1992-94
Mark Blake	Villa 1989-93	Portsmouth 1993-94
Guy Whittingham	Portsmouth 1989-93/98-2001	Villa 1993-95
Carl Tiler	Villa 1995-97	Portsmouth 2000-03
Paul Merson	Villa 1998-2002	Portsmouth 2002-03
Steve Stone	Villa 1998-2002	Portsmouth 2002-04
Peter Crouch	Portsmouth 2001-02	Villa 2001-04

v. Preston North End

		Home					Away			Final Positions	
Season	League	Date	Result	Villa	Preston NE	Date	Result	Villa	Preston NE	Villa	Preston NE
1888-89	Division 1	9 February	Lost	**0**	**2**	10 November	Drew	**1**	**1**	2nd	1st
1889-90	Division 1	21 September	Won	**5**	**3**	25 December	Lost	**2**	**3**	8th	1st
1890-91	Division 1	9 March	Lost	**0**	**1**	24 January	Lost	**1**	**4**	9th	2nd
1891-92	Division 1	16 April	Won	**3**	**1**	19 September	Won	**1**	**0**	4th	2nd
1892-93	Division 1	26 November	Won	**3**	**1**	21 October	Lost	**1**	**4**	4th	2nd
1893-94	Division 1	25 November	Won	**2**	**0**	18 January	Won	**5**	**2**	1st	14th
1894-95	Division 1	10 November	Won	**4**	**1**	12 January	Won	**1**	**0**	3rd	4th
1895-96	Division 1	11 January	Won	**1**	**0**	7 December	Lost	**3**	**4**	1st	9th
1896-97	Division 1	22 February	Won	**3**	**1**	26 April	Won	**1**	**0**	1st	4th
1897-98	Division 1	5 February	Won	**4**	**0**	6 November	Lost	**1**	**3**	6th	12th
1898-99	Division 1	8 October	Won	**4**	**2**	4 February	Lost	**0**	**2**	1st	15th
1899-00	Division 1	7 April	Won	**3**	**1**	2 December	Won	**5**	**0**	1st	16th
1900-01	Division 1	3 September	Won	**4**	**0**	20 October	Won	**2**	**0**	15th	17thR
1904-05	Division 1	1 September	Lost	**1**	**2**	3 December	Won	**3**	**2**	4th	8th
1905-06	Division 1	17 March	Lost	**0**	**1**	11 November	Lost	**0**	**2**	8th	2nd
1906-07	Division 1	24 December	Won	**3**	**0**	3 November	Lost	**0**	**2**	5th	14th
1907-08	Division 1	14 March	Won	**3**	**0**	16 November	Lost	**0**	**3**	2nd	12th
1908-09	Division 1	10 April	Lost	**2**	**4**	5 December	Lost	**2**	**3**	7th	10th
1909-10	Division 1	9 April	Won	**3**	**0**	27 November	Lost	**0**	**1**	1st	12th
1910-11	Division 1	8 April	Lost	**0**	**2**	3 December	Won	**1**	**0**	2nd	14th
1911-12	Division 1	9 December	Won	**1**	**0**	13 April	Lost	**1**	**4**	6th	19thR
1913-14	Division 1	22 November	Won	**3**	**0**	1 April	Lost	**2**	**3**	2nd	19thR
1919-20	Division 1	18 October	Lost	**2**	**4**	11 October	Lost	**0**	**3**	9th	19th
1920-21	Division 1	9 October	Won	**1**	**0**	16 October	Lost	**1**	**6**	10th	16th
1921-22	Division 1	17 September	Won	**2**	**0**	10 September	Lost	**0**	**1**	5th	16th
1922-23	Division 1	30 December	Won	**1**	**0**	6 January	Lost	**2**	**3**	6th	16th
1923-24	Division 1	29 September	Won	**5**	**1**	22 September	Drew	**2**	**2**	6th	18th
1924-25	Division 1	18 April	Won	**1**	**0**	13 December	Lost	**2**	**3**	15th	21stR
1934-35	Division 1	29 September	Won	**4**	**2**	9 February	Drew	**0**	**0**	13th	11th
1935-36	Division 1	14 September	Won	**5**	**1**	18 January	Lost	**0**	**3**	21stR	7th
1938-39	Division 1	1 April	Won	**3**	**0**	26 November	Lost	**2**	**3**	12th	9th
1946-47	Division 1	17 May	Won	**4**	**2**	26 October	Lost	**1**	**3**	8th	7th
1947-48	Division 1	1 November	Won	**4**	**1**	20 March	Lost	**0**	**3**	6th	7th
1948-49	Division 1	9 April	Won	**2**	**0**	13 November	Won	**1**	**0**	10th	21stR
1951-52	Division 1	27 October	Won	**3**	**2**	15 March	Drew	**2**	**2**	6th	7th
1952-53	Division 1	8 November	Won	**1**	**0**	28 March	Won	**3**	**1**	11th	2nd
1953-54	Division 1	24 April	Won	**1**	**0**	5 December	Drew	**1**	**1**	13th	11th
1954-55	Division 1	20 November	Lost	**1**	**3**	23 April	Won	**3**	**0**	6th	14th
1955-56	Division 1	10 December	Won	**3**	**2**	21 April	Won	**1**	**0**	20th	19th
1956-57	Division 1	30 March	Won	**2**	**0**	17 November	Drew	**3**	**3**	10th	3rd
1957-58	Division 1	30 November	Drew	**2**	**2**	12 April	Drew	**1**	**1**	14th	2nd
1958-59	Division 1	22 November	Won	**2**	**0**	11 April	Lost	**2**	**4**	21stR	12th
1960-61	Division 1	15 April	Won	**1**	**0**	12 November	Drew	**1**	**1**	9th	22ndR
1967-68	Division 2	9 September	Won	**1**	**0**	18 March	Lost	**1**	**2**	16th	20th

		Home						Away			Final Positions
Season	*League*	*Date*	*Result*	Villa	Preston NE	*Date*	*Result*	Villa	Preston NE	Villa	Preston NE
1968-69	Division 2	9 November	Lost	**0**	**1**	18 January	Lost	**0**	**1**	18th	14th
1969-70	Division 2	4 October	Drew	**0**	**0**	31 January	Drew	**1**	**1**	21stR	22ndR
1970-71	Division 3	19 September	Won	**2**	**0**	24 April	Drew	**0**	**0**	4th	1stP
1972-73	Division 2	17 February	Drew	**1**	**1**	12 August	Won	**1**	**0**	3rd	19th
1973-74	Division 2	25 August	Won	**2**	**0**	19 January	Drew	**0**	**0**	14th	21stR

FA Cup										*Division*	
1887-88	Round 5	7 January	Lost	**1**	**3**						
1896-97	Q'ter Final	3 March	Drew	**0**	**0**	27 February	Drew	**1**	**1**	Div 1	Div 1
		10 March				Bramall Lane (2nd replay)	Won	**3**	**2**		
1937-38	Semi-Final	26 March				Bramall Lane	Lost	**1**	**2**	Div 2	Div 1
1938-39	Round 4					21 January	Lost	**0**	**2**	Div 1	Div 1
1959-60	Q'ter Final	12 March	Won	**2**	**0**					Div 2	Div 1
1966-67	Round 3					28 January	Won	**1**	**0**	Div 1	Div 2

League Cup											
1960-61	Round 3	23 November	Won	**3**	**1**	15 November	Drew	**3**	**3**	Div 1	Div 1
1962-63	Round 4	12 November	Won	**6**	**2**					Div 1	Div 2
2002-03	Round 4	4 December	Won	**5**	**0**					Prem	Div 1

Summary	*P*	*W*	*D*	*L*	*F*	*A*
Villa's home league record:	49	37	3	9	108	44
Villa's away league record:	49	13	11	25	64	90
Villa's cup record:	12	6	3	3	26	16
TOTAL:	**110**	**56**	**17**	**37**	**198**	**150**

Tommy Docherty, a former Scottish international wing-half who played for Celtic, Preston, Chelsea and Arsenal, is one of the game's most colourful characters. After great success as manager of Chelsea he took over at Villa Park in December 1968 but he could not repeat his performance with Villa who were at the foot of the Second Division when Docherty was sacked in January 1970.

FACT FILE

- **Villa won 10 successive home league games against Preston between 1891 and 1900.**
- **However, they bettered this with an incredible 14 straight home wins from 1920 to 1954.**
- **Villa are undefeated in their last nine games against Preston.**
- **Preston were unbeaten in 14 home games against Villa from 1912 to 1948.**

Villa's top scorers vs Preston

Jack Devey 15
Billy Walker 12
Billy Garraty 6
Dai Astley, Jimmy Cowan, Harry Hampton, Peter McParland, Charlie Wallace 5

Villa hat-tricks vs Preston

2 Dec 1899 Steve Smith
4 Sep 1900 Jack Devey
29 Sep 1923 Billy Walker
29 Sep 1934 Dai Astley

Played for both clubs

Archie Goodall	Preston 1888-89	Villa 1888-89
John Cowan	Preston 1892-94	Villa 1895-99
George Smith	Preston 1899-1901	Villa 1901-02
Arthur Brown	Villa 1900-01	Preston 1904-06
Arthur Lockett	Villa 1902-05	Preston 1905-08
Billy Gerrish	Villa 1909-12	Preston 1912-13
George T. Stephenson	Villa 1921-28	Preston 1933-34
Jackie Palethorpe	Preston 1933-35	Villa 1935-36
Joe Beresford	Villa 1927-36	Preston 1935-38
Frank O'Donnell	Preston 1935-38	Villa 1938-40
Jack Hindle	Preston 1947-48	Villa 1950-51
Tommy Thompson	Villa 1950-55	Preston 1955-61
Brian Greenhalgh	Preston 1965-68	Villa 1967-69
Brian Godfrey	Preston 1963-68	Villa 1967-71
Jimmy Brown	Villa 1969-75	Preston 1975-78
Tony Morley	Preston 1972-76	Villa 1979-84
Paul Birch	Villa 1983-91	Preston 1995-96
Kevin Gage	Villa 1987-91	Preston 1995-97
Shaun Teale	Villa 1991-95	Preston 1996-97
Darren Byfield	Villa 1997-98	Preston 1998-99

v. Queen's Park Rangers

Season	League	Home Date	Home Result	Home Villa	Home QPR	Away Date	Away Result	Away Villa	Away QPR	Final Positions Villa	Final Positions QPR
1967-68	Division 2	11 May	Lost	**1**	**2**	5 September	Lost	**0**	**3**	16th	2ndP
1969-70	Division 2	1 November	Drew	**1**	**1**	28 February	Lost	**2**	**4**	21stR	9th
1972-73	Division 2	14 October	Lost	**0**	**1**	10 March	Lost	**0**	**1**	3rd	2ndP
1975-76	Division 1	31 January	Lost	**0**	**2**	19 August	Drew	**1**	**1**	16th	2nd
1976-77	Division 1	20 May	Drew	**1**	**1**	11 September	Lost	**1**	**2**	4th	14th
1977-78	Division 1	2 January	Drew	**1**	**1**	20 August	Won	**2**	**1**	8th	19th
1978-79	Division 1	20 March	Won	**3**	**1**	23 September	Lost	**0**	**1**	8th	20thR
1983-84	Division 1	31 December	Won	**2**	**1**	3 September	Lost	**1**	**2**	10th	5th
1984-85	Division 1	27 April	Won	**5**	**2**	24 November	Lost	**0**	**2**	10th	19th
1985-86	Division 1	24 August	Lost	**1**	**2**	17 December	Won	**1**	**0**	16th	13th
1986-87	Division 1	7 February	Lost	**0**	**1**	30 August	Lost	**0**	**1**	22ndR	16th
1988-89	Division 1	26 December	Won	**2**	**1**	17 March	Lost	**0**	**1**	17th	9th
1989-90	Division 1	23 September	Lost	**1**	**3**	20 March	Drew	**1**	**1**	2nd	11th
1990-91	Division 1	22 September	Drew	**2**	**2**	10 April	Lost	**1**	**2**	17th	12th
1991-92	Division 1	14 March	Lost	**0**	**1**	2 November	Won	**1**	**0**	7th	11th
1992-93	Premiership	1 November	Won	**2**	**0**	9 May	Lost	**1**	**2**	2nd	5th
1993-94	Premiership	14 August	Won	**4**	**1**	4 December	Drew	**2**	**2**	10th	9th
1994-95	Premiership	14 January	Won	**2**	**1**	29 October	Lost	**0**	**2**	18th	8th
1995-96	Premiership	9 March	Won	**4**	**2**	23 December	Lost	**0**	**1**	4th	19thR

FA Cup						Division	
1919-20	Round 1	10 January	Won	**2**	**1**	Div 1	Non L
1968-69	Round 3	4 January	Won	**2**	**1**	Div 2	Div 1

League Cup											
1976-77	Semi-Final	16 February	Drew*	**2**	**2**	1 February	Drew	**0**	**0**	Div 1	Div 1
		22 February		Highbury (replay)			Won	**3**	**0**		
1977-78	Round 3	26 October	Won	**1**	**0**					Div 1	Div 1
1984-85	Round 3					30 October	Lost	**0**	**1**	Div 1	Div 1
1995-96	Round 4	29 November	Won	**1**	**0**					Prem	Prem

Summary	*P*	*W*	*D*	*L*	*F*	*A*
Villa's home league record:	19	8	4	7	32	26
Villa's away league record:	19	3	3	13	14	29
Villa's cup record:	8	5	2	1	11	5
TOTAL:	**46**	**16**	**9**	**21**	**57**	**60**

FACT FILE

- **Villa's record against QPR is surprisingly poor. They failed to win in their first 10 league games against the London club.**
- **Villa have, however, won their last five home games in the series.**

Villa's top scorers vs QPR

Brian Little 4

Dalian Atkinson, Peter Withe, Dwight Yorke 3

Villa hat-tricks vs QPR

22 Feb 1977 Brian Little (cup)

Played for both clubs

Jimmy Birch	Villa 1911-12	QPR 1920-26
Harold Edgley	Villa 1911-20	QPR 1921-23
Jimmy Stephenson	Villa 1914-21	QPR 1927-28
Jimmy Leach	Villa 1912-22	QPR 1922-23
Arthur Davis	Villa 1919-22	QPR 1922-24
Lew Price	Villa 1920-22	QPR 1928-29
Percy Varco	Villa 1923-25	QPR 1926-27
George Clarke	Villa 1924-25	QPR 1933-34
John Yates	Villa 1927-29	QPR 1929-30
Ivor Powell	QPR 1938-49	Villa 1948-51
Michael Pinner	Villa 1954-57	QPR 1959-60
Jimmy Dugdale	Villa 1955-62	QPR 1962-63
Mike Ferguson	Villa 1968-70	QPR 1969-73
John Burridge	Villa 1975-77	QPR 1980-82
John Gregory	Villa 1977-79	QPR 1981-86
Steve Hodge	Villa 1985-87	QPR 1994-95
Simon Stainrod	QPR 1980-85	Villa 1985-88
Garry Thompson	Villa 1986-89	QPR 1991-93
Andy Gray	Villa 1987-89	QPR 1988-89
Gary Penrice	Villa 1990-92	QPR 1991-96
Peter Crouch	QPR 2000-01	Villa 2001-04

Action from the QPR-Villa game in September 1978. Tommy Cunningham clears the ball from Villa's Gary Shelton. Villa lost 0-1.

v. Queen's Park, Glasgow

FA Cup		Date	Result	Away Villa	Away Queen's Park
1883-84	Round 4	19 January	Lost	**1**	**6**

Summary	P	W	D	L	F	A
Villa's cup record:	1	0	0	1	1	6
TOTAL:	**1**	**0**	**0**	**1**	**1**	**6**

FACT FILE

- **They may currently play in the Scottish third division, but in the 19th century, Queen's Park were a force to be reckoned with, reaching consecutive FA Cup finals in 1884 and 1885. They are one of two non-English sides to reach the FA Cup final (Cardiff City are the other).**

v. Glasgow Rangers

FA Cup		Home Date	Result	Villa	Glasgow R'rs	Away Date	Result	Villa	Glasgow R'rs
1886-87	Semi-Final	5 March	Nantwich Road, Crewe				Won	3	1

Summary	P	W	D	L	F	A
Villa's cup record:	1	1	0	0	3	1
TOTAL:	**1**	**1**	**0**	**0**	**3**	**1**

FACT FILE

- **This was Nantwich Road's only ever FA Cup semi-final, and qualified Villa for the first of their 10 FA Cup final appearances.**

Villa's top scorers vs Rangers
Archie Hunter 2

v. Reading

Season	League	Home Date	Home Result	Home Villa	Home Reading	Away Date	Away Result	Away Villa	Away Reading	Final Positions Villa	Final Positions Reading
1970-71	Division 3	4 May	Won	**2**	**1**	31 October	Won	**5**	**3**	4th	21stR
1987-88	Division 2	31 October	Won	**2**	**1**	19 March	Won	**2**	**0**	2ndP	22ndR

FA Cup

Season	Round	Home Date	Home Result	Villa	Reading	Away Date	Away Result	Villa	Reading	Division Villa	Division Reading
1911-12	Round 2	3 February	Drew	**1**	**1**	7 February	Lost	**0**	**1**	Div 1	Non L
1928-29	Round 5					16 February	Won	**3**	**1**	Div 1	Div 2
1929-30	Round 3	11 January	Won	**5**	**1**					Div 1	Div 2

League Cup

Season	Round	Home Date	Home Result	Villa	Reading	Away Date	Away Result	Villa	Reading	Division Villa	Division Reading
1964-65	Round 4	4 November	Won	**3**	**1**					Div 1	Div 3
1986-87	Round 2	8 October	Won	**4**	**1**	24 September	Drew	**1**	**1**	Div 1	Div 2
2001-02	Round 3	10 October	Won	**1**	**0**					Prem	Div 2

Summary	*P*	*W*	*D*	*L*	*F*	*A*
Villa's home league record:	2	2	0	0	4	2
Villa's away league record:	2	2	0	0	7	3
Villa's cup record:	8	5	2	1	18	7
TOTAL:	**12**	**9**	**2**	**1**	**29**	**12**

FACT FILE

- **The defeat to Reading in 1912 was the last time Villa were knocked out of the FA Cup by non-league opposition.**
- **This, however, remains Reading's only victory over Aston Villa in 12 attempts.**
- **Villa have won their last six home games against the Royals.**

Villa's top scorers vs Reading

Willie Anderson, Andy Gray, Tony Hateley, Steve Hodge, Eric Houghton, Pongo Waring 2

Played for both clubs

Les Dennington	Villa 1924-25	Reading 1926-29
Jock Johnstone	Villa 1921-27	Reading 1928-29
Jackie Palethorpe	Reading 1930-33	Villa 1935-36
Dennis Watkin	Villa 1932-36	Reading 1936-39
Ronnie Dix	Villa 1932-37	Reading 1947-49
Neale Cooper	Villa 1986-88	Reading 1991-92
Ray Houghton	Villa 1992-95	Reading 1997-99
Scott Murray	Villa 1995-97	Reading 2003-04

v. Rochdale

			Home				Away			Final Positions	
Season	*League*	*Date*	*Result*	Villa	Rochdale	*Date*	*Result*	Villa	Rochdale	Villa	Rochdale
1970-71	Division 3	17 April	Won	**1**	**0**	10 October	Drew	**1**	**1**	4th	16th
1971-72	Division 3	28 August	Won	**2**	**0**	8 January	Lost	**0**	**1**	1stP	18th

Summary	*P*	*W*	*D*	*L*	*F*	*A*
Villa's home league record:	2	2	0	0	3	0
Villa's away league record:	2	0	1	1	1	2
TOTAL:	**4**	**2**	**1**	**1**	**4**	**2**

Villa's top scorers vs Rochdale

Andy Lochhead 2

Played for both clubs

Joe Walters	Villa 1905-12	Rochdale 1922-23
Tommy Mort	Rochdale 1921-22	Villa 1921-35
Arthur Cunliffe	Villa 1932-36	Rochdale 1946-47
John Graham	Villa 1946-49	Rochdale 1952-53
John Cordell	Villa 1951-53	Rochdale 1953-55
Doug Winston	Villa 1958-61	Rochdale 1961-64
Brian Handley	Villa 1959-60	Rochdale 1965-66
Stan Horne	Villa 1963-64	Rochdale 1973-75
Mike Ferguson	Villa 1968-70	Rochdale 1974-76
Gary Shelton	Villa 1978-82	Rochdale 1993-94
David Norton	Villa 1984-88	Rochdale 1990-91

Full-back Tommy Mort was a semi-professional with Altrincham before Rochdale signed him as a full-timer in June 1921. Less than a year later Mort was transferred to Aston Villa and began a career which saw him make 368 senior appearances, many of them as a defensive partner to Tommy Smart when the pair struck up a famous full-back partnership. Mort won three England caps – against Wales, France and Scotland – and played in the 1924 FA Cup Final against Newcastle United. After retiring in 1935, Mort left Villa Park to return to his native Lancashire where he went into business.

v. Rotherham United

Season	League	Home Date	Home Result	Home Villa	Home Rotherham	Away Date	Away Result	Away Villa	Away Rotherham	Final Positions Villa	Final Positions Rotherham
1959-60	Division 2	23 April	Won	**3**	**0**	5 December	Lost	**1**	**2**	1stP	8th
1967-68	Division 2	26 August	Won	**3**	**1**	23 December	Won	**2**	**0**	18th	21stR
1970-71	Division 3	13 February	Won	**1**	**0**	23 January	Drew	**1**	**1**	4th	8th
1971-72	Division 3	9 October	Lost	**1**	**2**	11 March	Won	**2**	**0**	1stP	5th

FA Cup

Season	Round	Home Date	Home Result	Home Villa	Home Rotherham	Away Date	Away Result	Away Villa	Away Rotherham	Division Villa	Division Rotherham
1952-53	Round 5					14 February	Won	**3**	**1**	Div 1	Div 2
1958-59	Round 3	10 January	Won	**2**	**1**					Div 1	Div 2
1967-68	Round 4	17 February	Lost	**0**	**1**					Div 2	Div 2

League Cup

Season	Round	Home Date	Home Result	Home Villa	Home Rotherham	Away Date	Away Result	Away Villa	Away Rotherham	Division Villa	Division Rotherham
1961	Final	5 September	Won*	**3**	**0**	22 August	Lost	**0**	**2**	Div 1	Div 2

Summary	*P*	*W*	*D*	*L*	*F*	*A*
Villa's home league record:	4	3	0	1	8	3
Villa's away league record:	4	2	1	1	6	3
Villa's cup record:	5	3	0	2	8	5
TOTAL:	**13**	**8**	**1**	**4**	**22**	**11**

FACT FILE

- **Aston Villa and Rotherham United contested the first ever League Cup final, which was played at the start of the following season. Villa were favourites, but, having lost the first leg 2-0, they were still 2-0 down on aggregate with 25 minutes left at Villa Park. However, O'Neill and Burrows brought the tie level, and McParland, hero of the FA Cup final four years earlier, popped up with the winner in extra time.**

Villa's top scorers vs Rotherham

Willie Anderson, Andy Lochhead, Bobby Thomson

David Walsh 2

Played for both clubs

Howard Humphries	Villa 1914-22	Rotherham 1921-23
Billy Cook	Rotherham 1922-23	Villa 1926-29
William Myerscough	Villa 1956-59	Rotherham 1959-60
Norman Ashe	Villa 1959-62	Rotherham 1962-63
Graham Parker	Villa 1963-68	Rotherham 1967-68
Brian Tiler	Rotherham 1962-69	Villa 1968-73
Terry Donovan	Villa 1979-82	Rotherham 1983-85
Pat Heard	Villa 1979-83	Rotherham 1988-90
Gareth Farrelly	Rotherham 1994-95/2002-03	Villa 1995-97
Darren Byfield	Villa 1997-98	Rotherham 2001-04

v. Scunthorpe United

		Home					Away			Final Positions	
Season	League	Date	Result	Villa	Scunthorpe	Date	Result	Villa	Scunthorpe	Villa	Scunthorpe
1959-60	Division 2	28 November	Won	**5**	**0**	19 March	Won	**2**	**1**	1stP	15th

League Cup										Division	
1984-85	Round 2	10 October	Won	**3**	**1**	24 September	Won	**3**	**2**	Div 1	Div 4

Summary	P	W	D	L	F	A
Villa's home league record:	1	1	0	0	5	0
Villa's away league record:	1	1	0	0	2	1
Villa's cup record:	2	2	0	0	6	3
TOTAL:	**4**	**4**	**0**	**0**	**13**	**4**

Villa's top scorers vs Scunthorpe

Gerry Hitchens 4

Played for both clubs

Jeff Barker	Villa 1937-38	Scunthorpe 1950-52
Geoff Sidebottom	Villa 1960-65	Scunthorpe 1964-67
John Woodward	Villa 1966-69	Scunthorpe 1975-76
Brian Godfrey	Scunthorpe 1960-64	Villa 1967-71
Barrie Lynch	Villa 1968-70	Scunthorpe 1973-75
Dave Hughes	Villa 1976-77	Scunthorpe 1981-82
Mark Lillis	Villa 1987-89	Scunthorpe 1989-91
Lee Butler	Villa 1988-91	Scunthorpe 1995-96
Ian Ormondroyd	Villa 1988-92	Scunthorpe 1997-98
Martin Carruthers	Villa 1991-93	Scunthorpe 2000-03
Neil Cox	Scunthorpe 1990-91	Villa 1991-94
Dave Farrell	Scunthorpe 1992-93	Villa 1992-94

Mark Lillis signed from Derby County and spent a couple of seasons with Villa before joining Scunthorpe.

v. Shankhouse

FA Cup		Date	Result	Away Villa	Away Shankhouse
1887-88	Round 4	17 December	Won	**9**	**0**

Summary	P	W	D	L	F	A
Villa's cup record:	1	1	0	0	9	0
TOTAL:	**1**	**1**	**0**	**0**	**9**	**0**

FACT FILE

- **This is Villa's biggest ever away win in the FA Cup.**

Villa's top scorers vs Shankhouse

Albert Allen, Albert Brown, Tommy Green, Archie Hunter 2

v. Sheffield United

		Home				Away				Final Positions	
Season	*League*	*Date*	*Result*	Villa	Sheff Utd	*Date*	*Result*	Villa	Sheff Utd	Villa	Sheff Utd
1893-94	Division 1	30 October	Won	**4**	**0**	2 October	Lost	**0**	**3**	1st	10th
1894-95	Division 1	12 November	Won	**5**	**0**	22 October	Lost	**1**	**2**	3rd	6th
1895-96	Division 1	16 November	Drew	**2**	**2**	14 September	Lost	**1**	**2**	1st	12th
1896-97	Division 1	12 September	Drew	**2**	**2**	3 October	Drew	**0**	**0**	1st	2nd
1897-98	Division 1	15 January	Lost	**1**	**2**	8 January	Lost	**0**	**1**	6th	1st
1898-99	Division 1	24 September	Drew	**1**	**1**	21 January	Won	**3**	**1**	1st	16th
1899-00	Division 1	3 March	Drew	**1**	**1**	8 October	Lost	**1**	**2**	1st	2nd
1900-01	Division 1	30 March	Drew	**0**	**0**	24 November	Drew	**2**	**2**	15th	14th
1901-02	Division 1	16 September	Lost	**1**	**2**	1 January	Lost	**0**	**6**	8th	10th
1902-03	Division 1	18 April	Won	**4**	**2**	20 December	Won	**4**	**2**	2nd	4th
1903-04	Division 1	27 February	Won	**6**	**1**	31 October	Won	**2**	**1**	5th	7th
1904-05	Division 1	18 March	Won	**3**	**0**	19 November	Won	**3**	**0**	4th	6th
1905-06	Division 1	9 December	Won	**4**	**1**	14 April	Drew	**1**	**1**	8th	13th
1906-07	Division 1	15 December	Won	**5**	**1**	20 April	Drew	**0**	**0**	5th	4th
1907-08	Division 1	18 April	Won	**1**	**0**	21 December	Drew	**1**	**1**	2nd	17th
1908-09	Division 1	9 April	Won	**3**	**0**	6 February	Lost	**1**	**3**	7th	12th
1909-10	Division 1	27 December	Won	**2**	**1**	25 December	Won	**1**	**0**	1st	6th
1910-11	Division 1	14 April	Won	**3**	**0**	28 December	Lost	**1**	**2**	2nd	9th
1911-12	Division 1	23 December	Won	**1**	**0**	23 October	Won	**1**	**0**	6th	14th
1912-13	Division 1	28 April	Won	**4**	**2**	14 December	Lost	**2**	**3**	2nd	15th
1913-14	Division 1	26 December	Won	**3**	**0**	1 January	Lost	**0**	**3**	2nd	10th
1914-15	Division 1	14 November	Won	**1**	**0**	20 March	Lost	**0**	**3**	14th	6th
1919-20	Division 1	29 November	Won	**4**	**0**	22 November	Won	**2**	**1**	9th	14th
1920-21	Division 1	23 October	Won	**4**	**0**	30 October	Drew	**0**	**0**	10th	20th
1921-22	Division 1	27 December	Won	**5**	**3**	26 December	Won	**3**	**2**	5th	11th
1922-23	Division 1	9 December	Lost	**0**	**1**	2 December	Drew	**1**	**1**	6th	10th
1923-24	Division 1	22 December	Drew	**2**	**2**	15 December	Lost	**1**	**2**	6th	5th
1924-25	Division 1	17 January	Drew	**1**	**1**	13 September	Drew	**2**	**2**	15th	14th
1925-26	Division 1	20 March	Drew	**2**	**2**	7 November	Lost	**1**	**4**	6th	5th
1926-27	Division 1	25 December	Won	**4**	**0**	27 December	Lost	**1**	**3**	10th	8th
1927-28	Division 1	11 February	Won	**1**	**0**	1 October	Won	**3**	**0**	8th	13th
1928-29	Division 1	20 February	Won	**3**	**2**	6 October	Won	**3**	**1**	3rd	11th
1929-30	Division 1	14 December	Won	**5**	**1**	19 April	Drew	**3**	**3**	4th	20th
1930-31	Division 1	11 April	Won	**4**	**0**	6 December	Won	**4**	**3**	2nd	15th
1931-32	Division 1	23 April	Won	**5**	**0**	12 December	Lost	**4**	**5**	5th	7th
1932-33	Division 1	15 October	Won	**3**	**0**	24 April	Lost	**0**	**1**	2nd	10th
1933-34	Division 1	2 April	Won	**3**	**0**	1 January	Drew	**3**	**3**	13th	22ndR
1936-37	Division 2	6 March	Won	**2**	**1**	31 October	Lost	**1**	**5**	9th	7th
1937-38	Division 2	27 November	Won	**1**	**0**	9 April	Drew	**0**	**0**	1stP	3rd
1946-47	Division 1	30 November	Lost	**2**	**3**	5 April	Won	**2**	**1**	8th	6th
1947-48	Division 1	18 October	Won	**2**	**0**	6 March	Lost	**1**	**3**	6th	12th
1948-49	Division 1	2 October	Won	**4**	**3**	26 February	Won	**1**	**0**	10th	22ndR
1953-54	Division 1	26 September	Won	**4**	**0**	26 April	Lost	**1**	**2**	13th	20th
1954-55	Division 1	16 April	Won	**3**	**1**	27 November	Won	**3**	**1**	6th	13th

Season	League	Home Date	Result	Villa	Sheff Utd	Away Date	Result	Villa	Sheff Utd	Final Positions Villa	Sheff Utd
1955-56	Division 1	14 April	Won	**3**	**2**	3 December	Drew	**2**	**2**	20th	22ndR
1959-60	Division 2	27 February	Lost	**1**	**3**	10 October	Drew	**1**	**1**	1stP	4th
1961-62	Division 1	13 January	Drew	**0**	**0**	2 September	Won	**2**	**0**	7th	5th
1962-63	Division 1	15 September	Lost	**1**	**2**	1 May	Lost	**1**	**2**	15th	10th
1963-64	Division 1	28 September	Lost	**0**	**1**	8 February	Drew	**1**	**1**	19th	12th
1964-65	Division 1	17 April	Won	**2**	**1**	5 December	Lost	**2**	**4**	16th	19th
1965-66	Division 1	29 January	Lost	**0**	**2**	21 August	Lost	**0**	**1**	16th	9th
1966-67	Division 1	22 October	Drew	**0**	**0**	18 March	Drew	**3**	**3**	21stR	10th
1968-69	Division 2	1 March	Won	**3**	**1**	10 August	Lost	**1**	**3**	18th	9th
1969-70	Division 2	13 April	Won	**1**	**0**	22 November	Lost	**0**	**5**	21stR	6th
1975-76	Division 1	8 November	Won	**5**	**1**	14 February	Lost	**1**	**2**	16th	22ndR
1987-88	Division 2	26 September	Drew	**1**	**1**	26 December	Drew	**1**	**1**	2ndP	21stR
1990-91	Division 1	1 December	Won	**2**	**1**	2 March	Lost	**1**	**2**	17th	13th
1991-92	Division 1	31 March	Drew	**1**	**1**	14 December	Lost	**0**	**2**	7th	9th
1992-93	Premiership	27 January	Won	**3**	**1**	29 August	Won	**2**	**0**	2nd	14th
1993-94	Premiership	20 November	Won	**1**	**0**	16 April	Won	**2**	**1**	10th	20thR

FA Cup										*Division*	
1900-01	Semi-Final	6 April				City Ground, Nottingham	Drew	**2**	**2**	Div 1	Div 1
		11 April				Baseball Ground, Derby (replay)	Lost	**0**	**3**		
1964-65	Round 4					30 January	Won	**2**	**0**	Div 1	Div 1
1974-75	Round 4	25 January	Won	**4**	**1**					Div 2	Div 1
1995-96	Round 4					28 January	Won	**1**	**0**	Prem	Div 1

Summary	*P*	*W*	*D*	*L*	*F*	*A*
Villa's home league record:	60	40	12	8	145	55
Villa's away league record:	60	17	16	27	85	111
Villa's cup record:	5	3	1	1	9	6
TOTAL:	**125**	**60**	**29**	**36**	**239**	**172**

Villa's Welsh international goalkeeper Keith Jones tips over the bar from Sheffield United's Alf Ringstead at Bramall Lane in November 1954. Irish international centre-half Con Martin looks on. The other Blades player is Jimmy Hagan. Villa won the game 3-1 on their way to finishing sixth in Division One.

FACT FILE

- **Villa won 16 games in a row at Villa Park between 1903 and 1921.**
- **Villa won 10 home games in a row at Villa Park between 1926 and 1937.**
- **Villa have won the last five matches.**
- **Between 1963 and 1991, United were unbeaten in 11 league matches at home.**

Villa's top scorers vs Sheffield Utd

Billy Walker 10
Pongo Waring 10
Eric Houghton 10
Harry Hampton 9
Len Capewell 8
Billy Garraty 7
Jasper McLuckie 7

Villa hat-tricks vs Sheffield Utd

30 Oct 1893 Charlie Hare
18 Apr 1903 Jasper McLuckie
15 Dec 1906 Jimmy Cantrell
29 Nov 1919 Clem Stephenson (4)
27 Dec 1921 Ian Dickson
14 Dec 1929 Billy Walker (4)
14 Apr 1956 Derek Pace

Played for both clubs

Billy Brawn	Sheffield U 1899-1902	Villa 1901-06
Robert Evans	Villa 1906-08	Sheffield U 1908-15
Peter Kyle	Villa 1907-09	Sheffield U 1908-09
Jimmy Harrop	Villa 1912-21	Sheffield U 1920-22
John Roxburgh	Villa 1922-23	Sheffield U 1925-27
Derek Pace	Villa 1950-58	Sheffield U 1957-65
Willie Hamilton	Sheffield U 1956-61	Villa 1965-67
Bruce Rioch	Villa 1969-74	Sheffield U 1978-79
Ian Hamilton	Villa 1969-76	Sheffield U 1976-78
Trevor Hockey	Sheffield U 1970-73	Villa 1973-74
Bobby Campbell	Villa 1973-75	Sheffield U 1977-78
John Burridge	Villa 1975-77	Sheffield U 1984-87
Dennis Mortimer	Villa 1975-85	Sheffield U 1984-85
Gordon Cowans	Villa 1975-86/88-92/93-94	Sheffield U 1995-96
Ken McNaught	Villa 1977-83	Sheffield U 1985-86
Peter Withe	Villa 1980-85	Sheffield U 1985-88
Mervyn Day	Villa 1983-85	Sheffield U 1991-92
Dean Glover	Villa 1984-87	Sheffield U 1986-87
Simon Stainrod	Sheffield U 1975-79	Villa 1985-88
Kevin Gage	Villa 1987-91	Sheffield U 1991-96
Adrian Heath	Villa 1989-90	Sheffield U 1995-96
Paul McGrath	Villa 1989-96	Sheffield U 1997-98
Earl Barrett	Villa 1991-95	Sheffield U 1997-98
Dean Saunders	Villa 1992-95	Sheffield U 1997-99
Franz Carr	Sheffield U 1992-94	Villa 1994-96
Alan Wright	Villa 1994-2003	Sheffield U 2003-04
Carl Tiler	Villa 1995-97	Sheffield U 1996-98

v. Sheffield Wednesday

		Home					Away			Final Positions	
Season	League	Date	Result	Villa	Sheff W	Date	Result	Villa	Sheff W	Villa	Sheff W
1892-93	Division 1	7 January	Won	**5**	**1**	3 December	Lost	**3**	**5**	4th	12th
1893-94	Division 1	9 December	Won	**3**	**0**	6 January	Drew	**2**	**2**	1st	12th
1894-95	Division 1	3 December	Won	**3**	**1**	3 November	Lost	**0**	**1**	3rd	8th
1895-96	Division 1	14 March	Won	**2**	**1**	18 January	Won	**3**	**1**	1st	7th
1896-97	Division 1	21 November	Won	**4**	**0**	14 November	Won	**3**	**1**	1st	6th
1897-98	Division 1	1 September	Won	**5**	**2**	27 September	Lost	**0**	**3**	6th	5th
1898-99	Division 1	25 March	Won	**3**	**1**	13 March	Lost	**1**	**4**	1st	18thR
1900-01	Division 1	9 March	Won	**2**	**1**	3 November	Lost	**2**	**3**	15th	8th
1901-02	Division 1	26 October	Won	**4**	**1**	22 February	Lost	**0**	**1**	8th	9th
1902-03	Division 1	26 December	Won	**1**	**0**	1 January	Lost	**0**	**4**	2nd	1st
1903-04	Division 1	26 December	Won	**2**	**1**	23 April	Lost	**2**	**4**	5th	1st
1904-05	Division 1	21 January	Lost	**0**	**2**	24 September	Lost	**2**	**3**	4th	9th
1905-06	Division 1	7 October	Won	**3**	**0**	10 February	Drew	**2**	**2**	8th	3rd
1906-07	Division 1	9 February	Won	**8**	**1**	6 October	Lost	**1**	**2**	5th	13th
1907-08	Division 1	15 February	Won	**5**	**0**	19 October	Won	**3**	**2**	2nd	5th
1908-09	Division 1	5 September	Drew	**1**	**1**	2 January	Lost	**2**	**4**	7th	5th
1909-10	Division 1	12 March	Won	**5**	**0**	30 October	Lost	**2**	**3**	1st	11th
1910-11	Division 1	29 October	Won	**2**	**1**	4 March	Lost	**0**	**1**	2nd	6th
1911-12	Division 1	21 October	Lost	**2**	**3**	24 February	Lost	**0**	**3**	6th	5th
1912-13	Division 1	5 October	Won	**10**	**0**	8 February	Drew	**1**	**1**	2nd	3rd
1913-14	Division 1	11 October	Won	**2**	**0**	14 February	Won	**3**	**2**	2nd	18th
1914-15	Division 1	16 January	Drew	**0**	**0**	12 September	Lost	**2**	**5**	14th	7th
1919-20	Division 1	17 April	Won	**3**	**1**	29 April	Won	**1**	**0**	9th	22ndR
1926-27	Division 1	20 November	Drew	**2**	**2**	9 April	Lost	**1**	**3**	10th	16th
1927-28	Division 1	24 December	Won	**5**	**4**	5 May	Lost	**0**	**2**	8th	14th
1928-29	Division 1	4 May	Won	**4**	**1**	22 December	Lost	**1**	**4**	3rd	1st
1929-30	Division 1	14 September	Lost	**1**	**3**	18 January	Lost	**0**	**3**	4th	1st
1930-31	Division 1	1 September	Won	**2**	**0**	2 May	Lost	**0**	**3**	2nd	3rd
1931-32	Division 1	24 February	Won	**3**	**1**	3 October	Lost	**0**	**1**	5th	3rd
1932-33	Division 1	3 December	Lost	**3**	**6**	15 April	Won	**2**	**0**	2nd	3rd
1933-34	Division 1	4 September	Won	**1**	**0**	28 August	Won	**2**	**1**	13th	11th
1934-35	Division 1	10 November	Won	**4**	**0**	23 March	Lost	**1**	**2**	13th	3rd
1935-36	Division 1	31 August	Lost	**1**	**2**	28 December	Lost	**2**	**5**	21stR	20th
1937-38	Division 2	29 January	Won	**4**	**3**	18 September	Won	**2**	**1**	1stP	17th
1950-51	Division 1	31 March	Won	**2**	**1**	11 November	Lost	**2**	**3**	15th	21stR
1952-53	Division 1	18 April	Won	**4**	**3**	29 November	Drew	**2**	**2**	11th	18th
1953-54	Division 1	31 March	Won	**2**	**1**	7 September	Lost	**1**	**3**	13th	19th
1954-55	Division 1	1 January	Drew	**0**	**0**	28 August	Lost	**3**	**6**	6th	22ndR
1956-57	Division 1	13 April	Won	**5**	**0**	1 December	Lost	**1**	**2**	10th	14th
1957-58	Division 1	19 April	Won	**2**	**0**	7 December	Won	**5**	**2**	14th	22ndR
1960-61	Division 1	29 April	Won	**4**	**1**	26 November	Won	**2**	**1**	9th	2nd
1961-62	Division 1	16 October	Won	**1**	**0**	3 March	Lost	**0**	**3**	7th	6th
1962-63	Division 1	13 April	Lost	**0**	**2**	10 November	Drew	**0**	**0**	15th	6th
1963-64	Division 1	7 March	Drew	**2**	**2**	26 October	Lost	**0**	**1**	19th	6th

		Home				Away				Final Positions	
Season	*League*	*Date*	*Result*	Villa	Sheff W	*Date*	*Result*	Villa	Sheff W	Villa	Sheff W
1964-65	Division 1	19 September	Won	**2**	**0**	15 March	Lost	**1**	**3**	16th	8th
1965-66	Division 1	30 October	Won	**2**	**0**	27 April	Lost	**0**	**2**	16th	17th
1966-67	Division 1	22 August	Lost	**0**	**1**	31 August	Lost	**0**	**2**	21stR	11th
1972-73	Division 2	24 April	Won	**2**	**1**	23 December	Drew	**2**	**2**	3rd	10th
1973-74	Division 2	3 November	Won	**1**	**0**	1 April	Won	**4**	**2**	14th	19th
1974-75	Division 2	26 October	Won	**3**	**1**	23 April	Won	**4**	**0**	2ndP	22ndR
1984-85	Division 1	6 April	Won	**3**	**0**	26 December	Drew	**1**	**1**	10th	8th
1985-86	Division 1	16 November	Drew	**1**	**1**	19 April	Lost	**0**	**2**	16th	5th
1986-87	Division 1	4 May	Lost	**1**	**2**	6 December	Lost	**1**	**2**	22ndR	13th
1988-89	Division 1	4 February	Won	**2**	**0**	1 October	Lost	**0**	**1**	17th	15th
1989-90	Division 1	10 February	Won	**1**	**0**	16 September	Lost	**0**	**1**	2nd	18thR
1991-92	Division 1	18 January	Lost	**0**	**1**	17 August	Won	**3**	**2**	7th	3rd
1992-93	Premiership	20 March	Won	**2**	**0**	5 December	Won	**2**	**1**	2nd	7th
1993-94	Premiership	8 December	Drew	**2**	**2**	18 August	Drew	**0**	**0**	10th	7th
1994-95	Premiership	27 November	Drew	**1**	**1**	18 February	Won	**2**	**1**	18th	13th
1995-96	Premiership	6 March	Won	**3**	**2**	16 March	Lost	**0**	**2**	4th	15th
1996-97	Premiership	29 January	Lost	**0**	**1**	17 August	Lost	**1**	**2**	5th	7th
1997-98	Premiership	27 September	Drew	**2**	**2**	2 May	Won	**3**	**1**	7th	16th
1998-99	Premiership	28 December	Won	**2**	**1**	29 August	Won	**1**	**0**	6th	12th
1999-00	Premiership	18 December	Won	**2**	**1**	5 April	Won	**1**	**0**	6th	19thR

FA Cup

										Division	
1893-94	Q'ter Final					24 February	Lost*	**2**	**3**	Div 1	Div 1
1913-14	Q'ter Final					7 March	Won	**1**	**0**	Div 1	Div 1

League Cup

1978-79	Round 2	30 August	Won	**1**	**0**					Div 1	Div 3
1987-88	Round 4	18 November	Lost	**1**	**2**					Div 2	Div 1
2001-02	Round 4	28 November	Lost	**0**	**1**					Prem	Div 1

FACT FILE

- **Villa won their first 11 home matches against Wednesday.**
- **Villa have won their last five league matches against Wednesday.**
- **From 1897 to 1904, Villa lost seven away games in a row in the series.**
- **Wednesday are one of four teams against whom Villa have reached double figures in a league match.**
- **In the 1898-99 season English league history was created when, for the first and only time, a match started and ended on different days. On 26 November the match was abandoned after 79 minutes with Wednesday leading 3-1. The final 11 minutes, during which Wednesday scored again, were played on 13 March.**

Summary	P	W	D	L	F	A
Villa's home league record:	64	45	9	10	159	67
Villa's away league record:	64	18	8	38	88	132
Villa's cup record:	5	2	0	3	5	6
TOTAL:	**133**	**65**	**17**	**51**	**252**	**205**

Villa's top scorers vs Wednesday

Harry Hampton 17
Joe Bache 14
Johnny Dixon, Pongo Waring, Fred Wheldon 6
Dai Astley, Jack Devey, Billy Garraty, Gerry Hitchens, Brian Little, Peter McParland, Clem Stephenson 5

Villa hat-tricks vs Wednesday

1 Sep 1897 Fred Wheldon
9 Feb 1907 Harry Hampton
15 Feb 1908 Joe Bache
5 Oct 1912 Harry Hampton (5)
24 Dec 1927 Joe Beresford

Played for both clubs

Horace Henshall	Villa 1910-12	Wednesday 1922-23
George T Stephenson	Villa 1921-28	Wednesday 1930-33
George Beeson	Wednesday 1929-34	Villa 1934-37
Joe Nibloe	Villa 1932-34	Wednesday 1934-38
Jackie Palethorpe	Wednesday 1934-36	Villa 1935-36
Ronnie Starling	Wednesday 1932-37	Villa 1936-47
Frank Moss jr	Wednesday 1936-38	Villa 1938-55
Michael Pinner	Villa 1954-57	Wednesday 1957-59
Jackie Sewell	Wednesday 1950-56	Villa 1955-60
Tommy Craig	Wednesday 1968-75	Villa 1977-79
Gary Shelton	Villa 1978-82	Wednesday 1981-87
Pat Heard	Villa 1979-83	Wednesday 1982-85
Andy Blair	Villa 1981-84/85-88	Wednesday 1984-86
Simon Stainrod	Wednesday 1984-86	Villa 1985-88
Garry Thompson	Wednesday 1985-86	Villa 1986-89
Dalian Atkinson	Wednesday 1989-90	Villa 1991-95
Earl Barrett	Villa 1991-95	Wednesday 1997-99
Guy Whittingham	Villa 1993-95	Wednesday 1994-99
Ian Taylor	Wednesday 1994-95	Villa 1994-2003
Phil King	Wednesday 1989-94	Villa 1994-95
Franz Carr	Wednesday 1989-90	Villa 1994-96
Tommy Johnson	Villa 1994-97	Wednesday 2001-02
Simon Grayson	Villa 1997-99	Wednesday 2000-01
Benito Carbone	Wednesday 1996-2000	Villa 1999-2000
Gilles De Bilde	Wednesday 1999-2001	Villa 2000-01

Action from the Boxing Day 1904 League game against Sheffield Wednesday. Villa won 2-1 with goals from Tommy Niblo and Billy Brawn.

v. Shrewsbury Town

Season	League	Date	Result	Home Villa	Home Shrewsbury	Date	Result	Away Villa	Away Shrewsbury	Final Positions Villa	Final Positions Shrewsbury
1970-71	Division 3	26 December	Won	**2**	**0**	10 April	Lost	**1**	**2**	4th	13th
1971-72	Division 3	19 January	Won	**3**	**0**	15 March	Drew	**1**	**1**	1stP	12th
1987-88	Division 2	23 April	Won	**1**	**0**	3 November	Won	**2**	**1**	2ndP	18th

Summary	*P*	*W*	*D*	*L*	*F*	*A*
Villa's home league record:	3	3	0	0	6	0
Villa's away league record:	3	1	1	1	4	4
TOTAL:	6	4	1	1	10	4

Villa's top scorers vs Shrewsbury

Warren Aspinall 2

Played for both clubs

Alan Wakeman	Villa 1938-50	Shrewsbury 1952-54
Gordon Lee	Villa 1958-65	Shrewsbury 1966-67
Terry Morrall	Villa 1959-61	Shrewsbury 1960-63
Mike Kenning	Villa 1960-61	Shrewsbury 1961-63
Dave Poutney	Shrewsbury 1957-64/67-70	Villa 1963-68
Barry Stobart	Villa 1964-68	Shrewsbury 1967-69
Dave Roberts	Villa 1965-68	Shrewsbury 1967-74
Peter Broadbent	Shrewsbury 1964-67	Villa 1966-69
John Phillips	Shrewsbury 1968-70	Villa 1969-70
Brendan Ormsby	Villa 1978-86	Shrewsbury 1989-90
Gary Shaw	Villa 1978-88	Shrewsbury 1990-91
Noel Blake	Villa 1979-82	Shrewsbury 1981-82
David Geddis	Villa 1979-83	Shrewsbury 1986-89
Robert Hopkins	Villa 1979-83	Shrewsbury 1991-92
Chris Boden	Villa 1993-94	Shrewsbury 1995-96
David Hughes	Villa 1996-97	Shrewsbury 1999-2001

Gary Shaw was the only Birmingham-born player in Aston Villa's League championship and European Cup-winning teams of 1980 and 1981. Born at Castle Bromwich in 1961, Shaw formed a great striking partnership with Peter Withe and starred in the side until hit by a series of injuries in the early 1980s. Most of his 80 goals and 212 senior appearances for Villa came between 1979 and 1983. In 1987-88 he went on loan to Blackpool before being given a free transfer at the end of the season. Shaw later played in Denmark, Austria and Hong Kong as well as for Walsall, Sheffield Wednesday (on loan) and Shrewsbury Town.

v. Southampton

Season	League	Home Date	Home Result	Home Villa	Home South'ton	Away Date	Away Result	Away Villa	Away South'ton	Final Positions Villa	Final Positions South'ton
1936-37	Division 2	5 September	Won	4	0	2 January	Drew	2	2	9th	19th
1937-38	Division 2	15 January	Won	3	0	4 September	Drew	0	0	1stP	15th
1966-67	Division 1	5 September	Lost	0	1	13 May	Lost	2	6	21stR	19th
1974-75	Division 2	15 March	Won	3	0	28 September	Drew	0	0	2ndP	13th
1978-79	Division 1	2 September	Drew	1	1	21 November	Lost	0	2	8th	14th
1979-80	Division 1	6 October	Won	3	0	15 March	Lost	0	2	7th	8th
1980-81	Division 1	28 March	Won	2	1	25 October	Won	2	1	1st	6th
1981-82	Division 1	10 February	Drew	1	1	10 April	Won	3	0	11th	7th
1982-83	Division 1	3 January	Won	2	0	4 September	Lost	0	1	6th	12th
1983-84	Division 1	24 September	Won	1	0	2 January	Drew	2	2	10th	2nd
1984-85	Division 1	17 November	Drew	2	2	20 April	Lost	0	2	10th	5th
1985-86	Division 1	1 February	Drew	0	0	27 August	Drew	0	0	16th	14th
1986-87	Division 1	11 October	Won	3	1	21 March	Lost	0	5	22ndR	12th
1988-89	Division 1	2 May	Lost	1	2	12 November	Lost	1	3	17th	13th
1989-90	Division 1	20 January	Won	2	1	29 August	Lost	1	2	2nd	7th
1990-91	Division 1	25 August	Drew	1	1	15 December	Drew	1	1	17th	14th
1991-92	Division 1	28 December	Won	2	1	31 August	Drew	1	1	7th	16th
1992-93	Premiership	22 August	Drew	1	1	30 January	Lost	0	2	2nd	18th
1993-94	Premiership	24 November	Lost	0	2	30 April	Lost	1	4	10th	18th
1994-95	Premiership	24 August	Drew	1	1	19 December	Lost	1	2	18th	10th
1995-96	Premiership	8 April	Won	3	0	20 November	Won	1	0	4th	17th
1996-97	Premiership	11 May	Won	1	0	7 December	Won	1	0	5th	16th
1997-98	Premiership	20 December	Drew	1	1	18 April	Won	2	1	7th	12th
1998-99	Premiership	10 April	Won	3	0	14 November	Won	4	1	6th	17th
1999-00	Premiership	6 November	Lost	0	1	18 March	Lost	0	2	6th	15th
2000-01	Premiership	21 April	Drew	0	0	18 November	Lost	0	2	8th	10th
2001-02	Premiership	27 April	Won	2	1	24 September	Won	3	1	8th	11th
2002-03	Premiership	21 October	Lost	0	1	22 March	Drew	2	2	16th	8th
2003-04	Premiership	29 November	Won	1	0	8 May	Drew	1	1	6th	12th

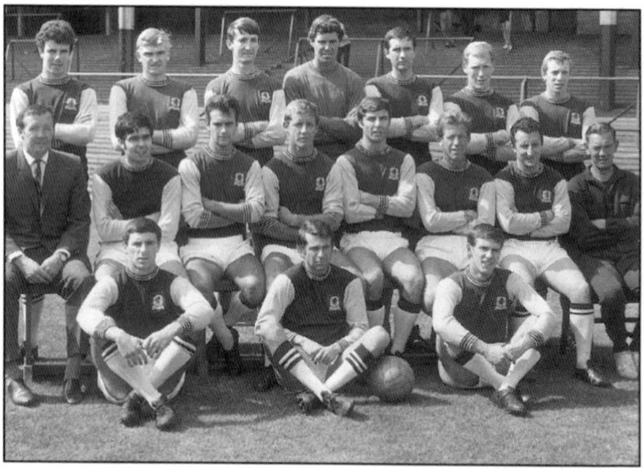

Aston Villa on the eve of the 1967-68 season, with Lew Chatterley who played 164 games for Villa before moving to Southampton and later to become senior coach for the Saints. Standing (left to right): Charlie Aitken, John Sleeuwenhoek, John Woodward, Colin Withers, Lew Chatterley, David Pountney, Alan Deakin. Seated: Tommy Cummings (manager), Willie Anderson, Graham Parker, Barry Stobart, Mike Tindall, Peter Broadbent, John MacLeod, Willie Baxter (trainer). On ground: Keith Bradley, Tony Scott, Michael Wright.

FA Cup		Home Date	Result	Villa	South'ton	Away Date	Result	Villa	South'ton	Final Positions Villa	South'ton
1968-69	Round 4	29 January	Won	**2**	**1**	25 January	Drew	**2**	**2**	Div 2	Div 1
1975-76	Round 3	7 January	Lost*	**1**	**2**	3 January	Drew	**1**	**1**	Div 1	Div 2
1999-00	Round 4	8 January	Won	**1**	**0**					Prem	Prem

League Cup		Home Date	Result	Villa	South'ton	Away Date	Result	Villa	South'ton	Final Positions Villa	South'ton
1986-87	Round 4					18 November	Lost	**1**	**2**	Div 1	Div 1
1999-00	Round 4	1 December	Won	**4**	**0**					Prem	Prem

Summary	P	W	D	L	F	A
Villa's home league record:	29	15	9	5	44	20
Villa's away league record:	29	7	9	13	31	48
Villa's cup record:	7	3	2	2	12	8
TOTAL:	**65**	**25**	**20**	**20**	**87**	**76**

FACT FILE

- **Villa were unbeaten in 10 home league games from 1975 to 1986.**
- **Villa failed to win in 13 visits to Southampton between 1982 and 1994.**
- **In 1999-2000, Villa lost both league matches to the Saints, yet knocked them out of both cups.**
- **The 6-2 defeat in 1967 sealed Villa's relegation to Division Two.**

Villa's top scorers vs Southampton

Dion Dublin 7
Allan Evans, Peter Withe 4
Ronnie Dix, Tony Morley, Darius Vassell, Dwight Yorke 3

Villa hat-tricks vs Southampton

14 Nov 1998 Dion Dublin

Played for both clubs

George Harkus	Villa 1921-23	Southampton 1923-30/31-32
Fred Tully	Villa 1927-29	Southampton 1933-37
Billy Kingdon	Villa 1926-36	Southampton 1936-38
Lew Chatterley	Villa 1962-71	Southampton 1973-75
Chris Nicholl	Villa 1971-77	Southampton 1977-83
John Burridge	Villa 1975-77	Southampton 1987-89
Mark Walters	Villa 1981-88	Southampton 1995-96
Paul Rideout	Villa 1983-85	Southampton 1988-92
Stuart Gray	Villa 1987-91	Southampton 1991-92
Kevin Richardson	Villa 1991-95	Southampton 1997-98
Andy Townsend	Southampton 1984-88	Villa 1993-98
Mark Draper	Villa 1995-2000	Southampton 2000-02
Hassan Kachloul	Southampton 1998-2001	Villa 2001-02

v. Southend United

FA Cup		Home Date	Result	Villa	Southend	Away Date	Result	Villa	Southend	Division Villa	Southend
1971-72	Round 1					20 November	Lost	**0**	**1**	Div 3	Div 4

Summary	P	W	D	L	F	A
Villa's cup record:	1	0	0	1	0	1
TOTAL:	**1**	**0**	**0**	**1**	**0**	**1**

FACT FILE

- **Of Villa's 115 domestic opponents, Southend are the only ones against whom they have never scored.**

Played for both clubs

Joe Walters	Villa 1905-12	Southend 1920-21
Norman Mackay	Villa 1923-24	Southend 1934-35
Albert Surtees	Villa 1923-25	Southend 1926-27
Herbert Smith	Villa 1949-54	Southend 1954-55
John Neal	Villa 1959-63	Southend 1962-66
John Chambers	Villa 1968-69	Southend 1969-70
Ian Hamilton	Southend 1968-69	Villa 1969-76
Alan Little	Villa 1974-75	Southend 1974-77
John Burridge	Villa 1975-77	Southend 1977-78
Martin Carruthers	Villa 1991-93	Southend 1999-2001
Stan Collymore	Southend 1992-93	Villa 1997-99

There weren't a lot of clubs that John Burridge didn't play for during his career, either on loan or after a transfer. Said to be modelled on Peter Shilton, he left Villa to join Southend in 1977.

v. South Shore

FA Cup		Date	Result	Away Villa	Away South Shore	Division Villa
1889-90	Round 1	18 January	Won	**4**	**2**	Div 1

Summary	*P*	*W*	*D*	*L*	*F*	*A*
Villa's cup record:	1	1	0	0	4	2
TOTAL:	**1**	**1**	**0**	**0**	**4**	**2**

Villa's top scorers vs South Shore

Denny Hodgetts 2

FACT FILE

- **South Shore merged with Blackpool in 1899.**

v. Stafford Road

FA Cup		Home Date	Result	Villa	Stafford	Away Date	Result	Villa	Stafford
1879-80	Round 2	24 January	Won	**3**	**1**	13 December	Drew	**1**	**1**
1880-81	Round 4	19 February	Lost	**2**	**3**				
1883-84	Round 2					1 December	Won	**5**	**1**

Summary	P	W	D	L	F	A
Villa's cup record:	4	2	1	1	11	6
TOTAL:	**4**	**2**	**1**	**1**	**11**	**6**

FACT FILE

- **Aston Villa's first-ever FA Cup match was against Wolverhampton-based outfit Stafford Road in 1879 (they had received a bye in Round 1). Andy Hunter scored Villa's goal. In Round 3, Villa were due to play Oxford University but withdrew. Therefore, their first ever FA Cup defeat came the following season... against Stafford Road.**

Villa's top scorers vs Stafford Road

Arthur Brown, Archie Hunter, W.B. Mason, O.H. Vaughton 2

Aston Villa's 1879-80 team and officials with the Birmingham Senior Cup, the first honour won by the club. Standing (left to right): J. Hughes (umpire), William McGregor (vice-president), W.B. Mason, T. Lee, H. Simmonds, Tom Pank, Eli Davis, F. Johnstone (vice-president), H. Jefferies (honorary secretary). Seated: Andy Hunter, G.B. Ramsay (captain), W.M. Ellis (president), Archie Hunter, C.S. Johnstone. On ground: S. Law, H. Ball.

v. Stockport County

		Home				Away				Final Positions	
Season	League	Date	Result	Villa	Stockport	Date	Result	Villa	Stockport	Villa	Stockport
1937-38	Division 2	11 December	Won	**7**	**1**	23 April	Won	**3**	**1**	1stP	22ndR

FA Cup

						Division	
1907-08	Round 1	11 January	Won	**3**	**0**	Div 1	Div 2

League Cup

1995-96	Round 3	25 October	Won	**2**	**0**	Prem	Div 2

Summary	*P*	*W*	*D*	*L*	*F*	*A*
Villa's home league record:	1	1	0	0	7	1
Villa's away league record:	1	1	0	0	3	1
Villa's cup record:	2	2	0	0	5	0
TOTAL:	**4**	**4**	**0**	**0**	**15**	**2**

Villa's top scorers vs Stockport

Frank Broome 4
Frank Shell 3
Freddie Haycock 2

Villa hat-tricks vs Stockport

11 Dec 1937 Frank Shell

Played for both clubs

Baldy Reynolds	Villa 1893-97	Stockport 1903-04
Rowland Codling	Stockport 1903-04	Villa 1905-09
Arthur Layton	Villa 1908-11	Stockport 1920-23
Harold Edgley	Villa 1911-20	Stockport 1923-24
Oliver Tidman	Villa 1932-33	Stockport 1935-36
Trevor Birch	Villa 1954-60	Stockport 1960-62
Kevin Keelan	Villa 1959-60	Stockport 1960-61
Bobby Thomson	Villa 1959-64	Stockport 1967-68
Peter Broadbent	Villa 1966-69	Stockport 1969-70
John Griffiths	Villa 1968-70	Stockport 1970-75
Frank Pimblett	Villa 1974-76	Stockport 1976-77
Gordon Cowans	Villa 1975-85/88-92/93-94	Stockport 1996-97
Mark Lillis	Villa 1987-89	Stockport 1991-92
Simon Grayson	Villa 1997-99	Stockport 2000-01

v. Stoke City

		Home					Away				Final Positions	
Season	League	Date	Result	Villa	Stoke	Date	Result	Villa	Stoke		Villa	Stoke
1888-89	Division 1	15 September	Won	5	1	3 November	Drew	1	1		2nd	12th
1889-90	Division 1	7 December	Won	6	1	17 March	Drew	1	1		8th	12thF
1891-92	Division 1	21 November	Won	2	1	24 October	Won	3	2		4th	13th
1892-93	Division 1	10 October	Won	3	2	12 September	Won	1	0		4th	7th
1893-94	Division 1	11 September	Won	5	1	16 October	Drew	3	3		1st	11th
1894-95	Division 1	26 December	Won	6	0	29 September	Lost	1	4		3rd	14th
1895-96	Division 1	12 February	Won	5	2	4 January	Won	2	1		1st	6th
1896-97	Division 1	2 September	Won	2	1	31 October	Won	2	0		1st	13th
1897-98	Division 1	2 April	Drew	1	1	18 December	Drew	0	0		6th	16th
1898-99	Division 1	3 September	Won	3	1	31 December	Lost	0	3		1st	12th
1899-00	Division 1	23 December	Won	4	1	13 November	Won	2	0		1st	9th
1900-01	Division 1	1 September	Won	2	0	29 December	Drew	0	0		15th	16th
1901-02	Division 1	18 January	Drew	0	0	21 September	Lost	0	1		8th	16th
1902-03	Division 1	13 April	Won	2	0	11 October	Lost	0	1		2nd	6th
1903-04	Division 1	30 January	Won	3	1	3 October	Lost	0	2		5th	16th
1904-05	Division 1	3 September	Won	3	0	31 December	Won	4	1		4th	12th
1905-06	Division 1	23 December	Won	3	0	13 November	Won	1	0		8th	10th
1906-07	Division 1	10 September	Won	1	0	3 September	Won	2	0		5th	20thR
1922-23	Division 1	17 February	Won	6	0	24 February	Drew	1	1		6th	21stR
1933-34	Division 1	24 February	Lost	1	2	14 October	Drew	1	1		13th	12th
1934-35	Division 1	2 March	Won	4	1	20 October	Lost	1	4		13th	10th
1935-36	Division 1	30 November	Won	4	0	7 March	Won	3	2		21stR	4th
1938-39	Division 1	18 March	Won	3	0	12 November	Lost	1	3		12th	7th
1946-47	Division 1	26 May	Lost	0	1	9 November	Drew	0	0		8th	4th
1947-48	Division 1	10 April	Won	1	0	22 November	Won	2	1		6th	15th
1948-49	Division 1	23 April	Won	2	1	30 October	Lost	2	4		10th	11th
1949-50	Division 1	29 October	Drew	1	1	15 April	Lost	0	1		12th	19th
1950-51	Division 1	5 May	Won	6	2	9 December	Lost	0	1		15th	13th
1951-52	Division 1	16 February	Lost	2	3	6 October	Lost	1	4		6th	20th
1952-53	Division 1	25 March	Drew	1	1	1 November	Won	4	1		11th	21stR
1959-60	Division 2	18 April	Won	2	1	30 September	Drew	3	3		1stP	17th
1963-64	Division 1	26 August	Lost	1	3	4 September	Drew	2	2		19th	17th
1964-65	Division 1	14 November	Won	3	0	27 March	Lost	1	2		16th	11th
1965-66	Division 1	13 November	Lost	0	1	9 April	Lost	0	2		16th	10th
1966-67	Division 1	25 March	Won	2	1	10 December	Lost	1	6		21stR	12th
1975-76	Division 1	27 March	Drew	0	0	6 December	Drew	1	1		16th	12th
1976-77	Division 1	16 May	Won	1	0	2 October	Lost	0	1		4th	21stR
1979-80	Division 1	17 November	Won	2	1	29 March	Lost	0	2		7th	18th
1980-81	Division 1	26 December	Won	1	0	20 April	Drew	1	1		1st	11th
1981-82	Division 1	23 September	Drew	2	2	5 May	Lost	0	1		11th	18th
1982-83	Division 1	30 April	Won	4	0	27 November	Won	3	0		6th	13th
1983-84	Division 1	12 November	Drew	1	1	10 March	Lost	0	1		10th	18th
1984-85	Division 1	27 March	Won	2	0	27 August	Won	3	1		10th	22ndR
1987-88	Division 2	26 March	Lost	0	1	24 October	Drew	0	0		2ndP	11th

FA Cup		Home Date	Result	Villa	Stoke	Away Date	Result	Villa	Stoke	Division Villa	Stoke
1890-91	Round 2					31 January	Lost	**0**	**3**	Div 1	Non L
1901-02	Round 1	29 January	Lost*	**1**	**2**	25 January	Drew	**2**	**2**	Div 1	Div 1
1903-04	Round 1					6 February	Won	**3**	**2**	Div 1	Div 1
1913-14	Round 1	10 January	Won	**4**	**0**					Div 1	Non L
1921-22	Round 3	22 February	Won	**4**	**0**	18 February	Drew	**0**	**0**	Div 1	Div 2
1957-58	Round 3	8 January	Drew*	**3**	**3**	4 January	Drew	**1**	**1**	Div 1	Div 2
		13 January		Molineux (2nd replay)			Lost	**0**	**2**		

League Cup		Date	Result	Villa	Stoke					Villa	Stoke
1962-63	Round 3	17 October	Won	**3**	**1**					Div 1	Div 2

Summary	*P*	*W*	*D*	*L*	*F*	*A*
Villa's home league record:	44	31	7	6	108	36
Villa's away league record:	44	13	13	18	54	66
Villa's cup record:	11	4	4	3	21	16
TOTAL:	**99**	**48**	**24**	**27**	**183**	**118**

FACT FILE

- **Villa were unbeaten in their first 19 home league matches against Stoke.**
- **From 1958 to 1982, Stoke were unbeaten in 11 home games against Villa.**
- **Villa were unbeaten in nine home games between 1967 and 1985.**

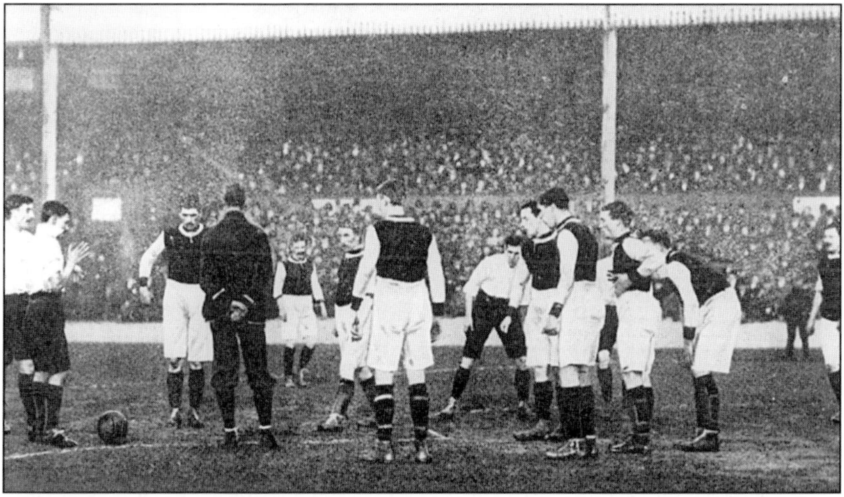

There is quite a crowd in front of the Villa goal as Stoke get ready to take a free-kick during the FA Cup first-round replay at Villa Park in January 1902. A crowd of 22,000 saw Villa go down 2-1. Note that goalkeeper Billy George, crouching on the goal-line, is wearing the same colours as his teammates. George made 398 League and Cup appearances for Villa.

Villa's top scorers vs Stoke

Harry Hampton 8
Jack Devey, Johnny Dixon, Billy Garraty 7
Charlie Athersmith, Ian Dickson, Peter Withe 6

Villa hat-tricks vs Stoke

7 Dec 1889 Batty Garvey
26 Dec 1894 Charlie Athersmith
22 Feb 1896 Johnny Campbell
22 Feb 1922 Ian Dickson (cup)
17 Feb 1923 Ian Dickson
2 Mar 1935 Dai Astley
1 Nov 1952 Johnny Dixon

Played for both clubs

Billy Dickson	Villa 1888-92	Stoke 1892-97
Peter Dowds	Villa 1892-93	Stoke 1893-94
Tom Wilkes	Villa 1894-99	Stoke 1897-98/99-1903
Alf Wood	Stoke 1895-1901	Villa 1900-05
Arthur Cartlidge	Stoke 1899-1901	Villa 1908-11
Jack Whitley	Villa 1900-02	Stoke 1904-06
Arthur Lockett	Stoke 1900-03	Villa 1902-05
Martin Watkins	Stoke 1900-04/07-08	Villa 1903-05
Dick Roose	Stoke 1901-04/05-08	Villa 1911-12
Jimmy Lee	Villa 1919-21	Stoke 1921-22
Tommy Weston	Villa 1911-22	Stoke 1922-23
John Roxburgh	Villa 1922-23	Stoke 1923-24
Alex McClure	Villa 1923-25	Stoke 1924-26
Jackie Palethorpe	Stoke 1932-34	Villa 1935-36
Tommy Thompson	Villa 1950-55	Stoke 1961-63
Jimmy Adam	Villa 1959-61	Stoke 1961-62
Harry Burrows	Villa 1959-65	Stoke 1964-73
John Woodward	Stoke 1964-67	Villa 1966-69
John Gidman	Villa 1972-80	Stoke 1988-89
Mike Pejic	Stoke 1968-77	Villa 1979-80
Noel Blake	Villa 1979-82	Stoke 1989-92
Mark Walters	Villa 1981-88	Stoke 1993-94
Tony Dorigo	Villa 1983-87	Stoke 2000-01
Simon Stainrod	Villa 1985-88	Stoke 1987-89
Phil Robinson	Villa 1986-87	Stoke 1998-2000
Adrian Heath	Stoke 1978-82/91-92	Villa 1989-90
Martin Carruthers	Villa 1991-93	Stoke 1993-97
Bryan Small	Villa 1991-95	Stoke 1998-2001
Graham Fenton	Villa 1993-96	Stoke 2000-01
Neil Cutler	Villa 1999-2000	Stoke 2001-04

v. Sunderland

		Home						Away		Final Positions	
Season	League	Date	Result	Villa	Sunderland	Date	Result	Villa	Sunderland	Villa	Sunderland
1890-91	Division 1	26 December	Drew	**0**	**0**	10 January	Lost	**1**	**5**	9th	7th
1891-92	Division 1	28 September	Won	**5**	**3**	26 March	Lost	**1**	**2**	4th	1st
1892-93	Division 1	17 September	Lost	**1**	**6**	14 January	Lost	**0**	**6**	4th	1st
1893-94	Division 1	11 November	Won	**2**	**1**	9 September	Drew	**1**	**1**	1st	2nd
1894-95	Division 1	15 September	Lost	**1**	**2**	2 January	Drew	**4**	**4**	3rd	1st
1895-96	Division 1	5 October	Won	**2**	**1**	9 November	Lost	**1**	**2**	1st	5th
1896-97	Division 1	16 January	Won	**2**	**1**	9 January	Lost	**2**	**4**	1st	15th
1897-98	Division 1	27 November	Won	**4**	**3**	23 October	Drew	**0**	**0**	6th	2nd
1898-99	Division 1	3 December	Won	**2**	**0**	1 April	Lost	**2**	**4**	1st	7th
1899-00	Division 1	30 December	Won	**4**	**2**	2 September	Won	**1**	**0**	1st	3rd
1900-01	Division 1	19 January	Drew	**2**	**2**	22 September	Drew	**0**	**0**	15th	2nd
1901-02	Division 1	1 February	Lost	**0**	**1**	5 October	Lost	**0**	**1**	8th	1st
1902-03	Division 1	4 October	Lost	**0**	**1**	31 January	Lost	**0**	**1**	2nd	3rd
1903-04	Division 1	2 January	Won	**2**	**0**	5 September	Lost	**1**	**6**	5th	6th
1904-05	Division 1	1 October	Drew	**2**	**2**	28 January	Won	**3**	**2**	4th	5th
1905-06	Division 1	9 September	Won	**2**	**1**	28 February	Lost	**0**	**2**	8th	14th
1906-07	Division 1	5 January	Drew	**2**	**2**	8 September	Lost	**1**	**2**	5th	10th
1907-08	Division 1	9 September	Won	**1**	**0**	5 October	Lost	**0**	**3**	2nd	16th
1908-09	Division 1	19 September	Won	**2**	**0**	23 January	Lost	**3**	**4**	7th	3rd
1909-10	Division 1	12 February	Won	**3**	**2**	2 October	Drew	**1**	**1**	1st	8th
1910-11	Division 1	7 January	Won	**2**	**1**	10 September	Lost	**2**	**3**	2nd	3rd
1911-12	Division 1	7 October	Lost	**1**	**3**	10 February	Drew	**2**	**2**	6th	8th
1912-13	Division 1	23 April	Drew	**1**	**1**	23 November	Lost	**1**	**3**	2nd	1st
1913-14	Division 1	17 January	Won	**5**	**0**	20 September	Lost	**0**	**2**	2nd	7th
1914-15	Division 1	5 September	Lost	**1**	**3**	2 January	Lost	**0**	**4**	14th	8th
1919-20	Division 1	6 September	Lost	**0**	**3**	30 August	Lost	**1**	**2**	9th	5th
1920-21	Division 1	12 February	Lost	**1**	**5**	23 February	Won	**1**	**0**	10th	12th
1921-22	Division 1	11 February	Won	**2**	**0**	4 February	Won	**4**	**1**	5th	12th
1922-23	Division 1	5 May	Won	**1**	**0**	28 April	Lost	**0**	**2**	6th	2nd
1923-24	Division 1	9 February	Lost	**0**	**1**	13 February	Lost	**0**	**2**	6th	3rd
1924-25	Division 1	4 April	Lost	**1**	**4**	29 November	Drew	**1**	**1**	15th	7th
1925-26	Division 1	5 October	Won	**4**	**2**	19 December	Lost	**2**	**3**	6th	3rd
1926-27	Division 1	5 March	Won	**3**	**1**	16 October	Drew	**1**	**1**	10th	3rd
1927-28	Division 1	15 October	Won	**4**	**2**	25 February	Won	**3**	**2**	8th	15th
1928-29	Division 1	25 March	Won	**3**	**1**	10 November	Won	**3**	**1**	3rd	4th
1929-30	Division 1	28 September	Won	**2**	**1**	1 February	Lost	**1**	**4**	4th	9th
1930-31	Division 1	18 February	Won	**4**	**2**	11 October	Drew	**1**	**1**	2nd	11th
1931-32	Division 1	28 March	Won	**2**	**0**	25 March	Drew	**1**	**1**	5th	13th
1932-33	Division 1	29 August	Won	**1**	**0**	7 September	Drew	**1**	**1**	2nd	12th
1933-34	Division 1	23 September	Won	**2**	**1**	3 February	Lost	**1**	**5**	13th	6th
1934-35	Division 1	15 September	Drew	**1**	**1**	6 February	Drew	**3**	**3**	13th	2nd
1935-36	Division 1	16 September	Drew	**2**	**2**	1 January	Won	**3**	**1**	21stR	1st
1938-39	Division 1	27 December	Drew	**1**	**1**	26 December	Won	**5**	**1**	12th	16th
1946-47	Division 1	8 April	Won	**4**	**0**	4 April	Lost	**1**	**4**	8th	9th

				Home				Away		*Final Positions*	
Season	*League*	*Date*	*Result*	Villa	Sunderland	*Date*	*Result*	Villa	Sunderland	Villa	Sunderland
1947-48	Division 1	1 September	Won	**2**	**0**	27 August	Drew	**0**	**0**	6th	20th
1948-49	Division 1	19 April	Drew	**1**	**1**	15 April	Drew	**0**	**0**	10th	8th
1949-50	Division 1	12 November	Won	**2**	**0**	1 April	Lost	**1**	**2**	12th	3rd
1950-51	Division 1	21 August	Won	**3**	**1**	30 August	Drew	**3**	**3**	15th	12th
1951-52	Division 1	27 August	Won	**2**	**1**	5 September	Won	**3**	**1**	6th	12th
1952-53	Division 1	1 September	Won	**3**	**0**	1 January	Drew	**2**	**2**	11th	9th
1953-54	Division 1	14 September	Won	**3**	**1**	1 January	Lost	**0**	**2**	13th	18th
1954-55	Division 1	23 August	Drew	**2**	**2**	1 September	Drew	**0**	**0**	6th	4th
1955-56	Division 1	29 August	Lost	**1**	**4**	24 August	Lost	**1**	**5**	20th	9th
1956-57	Division 1	8 April	Drew	**2**	**2**	25 December	Lost	**0**	**1**	10th	20th
1957-58	Division 1	11 January	Won	**5**	**2**	7 September	Drew	**1**	**1**	14th	21stR
1959-60	Division 2	31 August	Won	**3**	**0**	26 August	Lost	**0**	**1**	1stP	16th
1964-65	Division 1	14 September	Won	**2**	**1**	9 September	Drew	**2**	**2**	16th	15th
1965-66	Division 1	6 September	Won	**3**	**1**	15 September	Lost	**0**	**2**	16th	19th
1966-67	Division 1	27 December	Won	**2**	**1**	26 December	Lost	**1**	**2**	21stR	17th
1972-73	Division 2	27 September	Won	**2**	**0**	4 November	Drew	**2**	**2**	3rd	6th
1973-74	Division 2	20 April	Lost	**1**	**2**	8 December	Lost	**0**	**2**	14th	6th
1974-75	Division 2	26 April	Won	**2**	**0**	19 October	Drew	**0**	**0**	2ndP	4th
1976-77	Division 1	23 March	Won	**4**	**1**	16 October	Won	**1**	**0**	4th	20thR
1980-81	Division 1	4 October	Won	**4**	**0**	7 March	Won	**2**	**1**	1st	17th
1981-82	Division 1	2 February	Won	**1**	**0**	2 September	Lost	**1**	**2**	11th	19th
1982-83	Division 1	28 August	Lost	**1**	**3**	15 January	Lost	**0**	**2**	6th	16th
1983-84	Division 1	29 August	Won	**1**	**0**	24 March	Won	**1**	**0**	10th	13th
1984-85	Division 1	1 December	Won	**1**	**0**	4 May	Won	**4**	**0**	10th	21stR
1990-91	Division 1	6 October	Won	**3**	**0**	23 March	Won	**3**	**1**	17th	19thR
1996-97	Premiership	1 February	Won	**1**	**0**	26 October	Lost	**0**	**1**	5th	18thR
1999-00	Premiership	29 April	Drew	**1**	**1**	18 October	Lost	**1**	**2**	6th	7th
2000-01	Premiership	22 October	Drew	**0**	**0**	5 March	Drew	**1**	**1**	8th	7th
2001-02	Premiership	16 September	Drew	**0**	**0**	1 January	Drew	**1**	**1**	8th	17th
2002-03	Premiership	3 May	Won	**1**	**0**	28 September	Lost	**0**	**1**	16th	20thR

FA Cup

										Division	
1891-92	Semi-Final	27 February				Bramall Lane, Sheffield	Won	**4**	**1**	Div 1	Div 1
1893-94	Round 2	21 February	Won	**3**	**1**	10 February	Drew*	**2**	**2**	Div 1	Div 1
1894-95	Semi-Final	16 March				Ewood Park, Blackburn	Won	**2**	**1**	Div 1	Div 1
1902-03	Round 1	7 February	Won	**4**	**1**					Div 1	Div 1
1912-13	Final	19 April				Crystal Palace	Won	**1**	**0**	Div 1	Div 1
1919-20	Round 3	21 February	Won	**1**	**0**					Div 1	Div 1
1932-33	Round 4	28 January	Lost	**0**	**3**					Div 1	Div 1
1933-34	Round 4	27 January	Won	**7**	**2**					Div 1	Div 1

League Cup

1962-63	Semi-Final	22 April	Drew	**0**	**0**	12 January	Won	**3**	**1**	Div 1	Div 2
1965-66	Round 3					13 October	Won	**2**	**1**	Div 1	Div 1
1993-94	Round 3					26 October	Won	**4**	**1**	Prem	Div 1

Summary	*P*	*W*	*D*	*L*	*F*	*A*
Villa's home league record:	74	47	14	13	146	89
Villa's away league record:	74	14	23	37	91	140
Villa's cup record:	13	10	2	1	33	14
TOTAL:	**161**	**71**	**39**	**51**	**270**	**243**

FACT FILE

- **The 1913 FA Cup final, which Villa won with a goal from Tommy Barber, is noteworthy for two reasons. Firstly, the attendance exceeded 120,000 at the Crystal Palace, a record at the time, and secondly because it is one of only two domestic cup finals that have ever been contested between the teams finishing first and second in the league. Villa went into the cup final four points behind Sunderland. However, a 1-1 draw at Villa Park against the same opposition just four days after the final more or less decided the title race, and Sunderland wrapped it up with victory over Bolton three days later. Incidentally, the other such cup final was between Liverpool and Everton in 1986.**
- **Villa have conceded only one goal in their last eight home games against Sunderland.**
- **In 2000, Villa failed to score against Sunderland in a home league game for the first time since 1924.**
- **From 1925 to 1954, Villa were unbeaten in 21 home league games.**
- **Villa won only two of their first 27 away games against Sunderland.**

Villa's top scorers vs Sunderland

Joe Bache, Billy Walker 11
Jack Devey, Johnny Dixon 10
Dai Astley, Denny Hodgetts, Pongo Waring 8
Billy Garraty, Eric Houghton 7

Villa hat-tricks vs Sunderland

30 Dec 1899 Billy Garraty
18 Feb 1931 Pongo Waring (4)
27 Jan 1934 Eric Houghton (cup)
27 Jan 1934 Dai Astley (4) (cup)
11 Jan 1958 Stan Lynn

Played for both clubs

James Logan	Sunderland 1891-92	Villa 1892-94
Martin Watkins	Villa 1903-05	Sunderland 1904-05
Dick Roose	Sunderland 1907-11	Villa 1911-12
Jimmy Stephenson	Villa 1914-21	Sunderland 1921-22
Trevor Ford	Villa 1946-51	Sunderland 1950-54
Alan O'Neill	Sunderland 1956-61	Villa 1960-63
Tommy Mitchinson	Sunderland 1962-66	Villa 1967-69
Dariusz Kubicki	Villa 1991-94	Sunderland 1993-97
Darren Byfield	Villa 1997-98	Sunderland 2003-04
Gavin McCann	Sunderland 1998-2003	Villa 2003-04
Thomas Sorensen	Sunderland 1998-2003	Villa 2003-04

v. Swansea City

		Home					Away			Final Positions	
Season	League	Date	Result	Villa	Swansea	Date	Result	Villa	Swansea	Villa	Swansea
1936-37	Division 2	26 December	Won	**4**	**0**	29 August	Won	**2**	**1**	9th	16th
1937-38	Division 2	19 April	Won	**4**	**0**	18 April	Lost	**1**	**2**	1stP	18th
1959-60	Division 2	29 August	Won	**1**	**0**	2 January	Won	**3**	**1**	1stP	12th
1970-71	Division 3	3 April	Won	**3**	**0**	29 August	Won	**2**	**1**	4th	11th
1971-72	Division 3	1 April	Won	**2**	**0**	27 December	Won	**2**	**1**	1stP	14th
1981-82	Division 1	21 May	Won	**3**	**0**	15 December	Lost	**1**	**2**	11th	6th
1982-83	Division 1	25 September	Won	**2**	**0**	2 May	Lost	**1**	**2**	6th	21stR

FA Cup

						Division	
1923-24	Round 2	2 February	Won	**2**	**0**	Div 1	Div 3S
1924-25	Round 2	31 January	Won	**3**	**1**	Div 1	Div 3S

League Cup

1965-66	Round 2	21 September	Won	**3**	**2**	Div 1	Div 3

Summary	*P*	*W*	*D*	*L*	*F*	*A*
Villa's home league record:	7	7	0	0	19	0
Villa's away league record:	7	4	0	3	12	10
Villa's cup record:	3	3	0	0	8	3
TOTAL:	**17**	**14**	**0**	**3**	**39**	**13**

FACT FILE

- **It would be hard to improve on Villa's home record against Swansea. Their away record isn't bad either.**

Jimmy Rimmer kept goal for Aston Villa in 285 domestic and European games between 1977-78 and 1982-83. He began with Manchester United and went on loan to Swansea before Arsenal paid £40,000 for him in March 1974. Two years later he was capped by England and in the 1977 close season Villa paid £65,000 for him to take over from John Burridge. Rimmer was first-choice for Villa for six years before returning to Swansea. He was substitute goalkeeper for Manchester United in the 1968 European Cup Final and was himself subbed after only 10 minutes of the 1982 European Final when he was injured and Nigel Spink took over.

Villa's top scorers vs Swansea

Ronnie Dix 3

Villa hat-tricks vs Swansea

26 Dec 1936 Ronnie Dix

Played for both clubs

Joe Beresford	Villa 1927-36	Swansea 1937-38
Thomas Moore	Villa 1931-32	Swansea 1936-37
Thomas Dodds	Villa 1946-47	Swansea 1946-48
Trevor Ford	Swansea 1946-47	Villa 1946-51
Sydney Howarth	Villa 1948-50	Swansea 1950-52
Norman Lockhart	Swansea 1946-48	Villa 1952-56
Michael Pinner	Villa 1954-57	Swansea 1961-62
Jimmy McMorran	Villa 1960-62	Swansea 1968-69
Dave Roberts	Villa 1965-68	Swansea 1974-75
Barry Hole	Villa 1968-70	Swansea 1970-72
Geoff Crudgington	Villa 1970-72	Swansea 1978-80
Leighton Phillips	Villa 1974-79	Swansea 1978-81
Tommy Craig	Villa 1977-79	Swansea 1979-81
Jimmy Rimmer	Swansea 1973-74/83-86	Villa 1977-83
Warren Aspinall	Villa 1986-88	Swansea 1993-94
Dean Saunders	Swansea 1983-85	Villa 1992-95
Neil Cutler	Villa 1999-2000	Swansea 2002-03

Welshman Leighton Phillips left to join Swansea in 1978. He had joined Villa from Cardiff City for £100,000 in September 1974.

v. Swindon Town

		Home					Away			Final Positions	
Season	League	Date	Result	Villa	Swindon	Date	Result	Villa	Swindon	Villa	Swindon
1969-70	Division 2	23 August	Lost	**0**	**2**	26 December	Drew	**1**	**1**	21stR	5th
1972-73	Division 2	16 September	Won	**2**	**1**	10 February	Won	**3**	**1**	3rd	16th
1973-74	Division 2	6 April	Drew	**1**	**1**	24 November	Lost	**0**	**1**	14th	22ndR
1987-88	Division 2	5 December	Won	**2**	**1**	7 May	Drew	**0**	**0**	2ndP	12th
1993-94	Premiership	12 February	Won	**5**	**0**	30 October	Won	**2**	**1**	10th	22ndR

FA Cup						Division	
1991-92	Round 5	16 February	Won	**2**	**1**	Div 1	Div 2

Summary	P	W	D	L	F	A
Villa's home league record:	5	3	1	1	10	5
Villa's away league record:	5	2	2	1	6	4
Villa's cup record:	1	1	0	0	2	1
TOTAL:	**11**	**6**	**3**	**2**	**18**	**10**

FACT FILE

- **Villa are unbeaten in their last six games against Swindon.**

Villa's top scorers vs Swindon

Dean Saunders 3

Villa hat-tricks vs Swindon

12 Feb 1994 Dean Saunders

Played for both clubs

Len Stiller	Villa 1908-09	Swindon 1920-22
Fred Butcher	Villa 1934-35	Swindon 1938-39
John Neal	Swindon 1957-79	Villa 1959-63
Jake Findlay	Villa 1973-77	Swindon 1985-86
David Geddis	Villa 1979-83	Swindon 1988-89
Mark Walters	Villa 1981-88	Swindon 1996-2000
Paul Rideout	Swindon 1980-83/90-91	Villa 1983-85
Steve McMahon	Villa 1983-86	Swindon 1994-98
Andy Gray	Villa 1987-89	Swindon 1992-93
Frank McAvennie	Villa 1992-93	Swindon 1993-94
Phil King	Swindon 1986-90/96-97	Villa 1994-95
Carl Tiler	Swindon 1994-95	Villa 1995-97
Colin Calderwood	Swindon 1985-93	Villa 1998-2000

v. Torquay United

		Home					Away			Final Positions	
Season	League	Date	Result	Villa	Torquay	Date	Result	Villa	Torquay	Villa	Torquay
1970-71	Division 3	7 November	Lost	**0**	**1**	20 March	Drew	**1**	**1**	4th	10th
1971-72	Division 3	29 April	Won	**5**	**1**	12 April	Lost	**1**	**2**	1stP	23rdR

FA Cup						Division	
1970-71	Round 1	21 November	Lost	**1**	**3**	Div 3	Div 3

Summary	*P*	*W*	*D*	*L*	*F*	*A*
Villa's home league record:	2	1	0	1	5	2
Villa's away league record:	2	0	1	1	2	3
Villa's cup record:	1	0	0	1	1	3
TOTAL:	**5**	**1**	**1**	**3**	**8**	**8**

FACT FILE

- **Villa's five matches against Torquay all came in the space of 18 months, and Villa won only the last of them.**

Villa's top scorers vs Torquay

Geoff Vowden 4

Played for both clubs

Ginger Phoenix	Villa 1924-25	Torquay 1930-31
Percy Maggs	Villa 1930-31	Torquay 1932-39
Nobby Clarke	Villa 1954-55	Torquay 1956-59
Brian Handley	Villa 1959-60	Torquay 1960-64
John Sleeuwenhoek	Villa 1960-68	Torquay 1970-71
Lew Chatterley	Villa 1962-71	Torquay 1974-77
Graham Parker	Villa 1963-68	Torquay 1974-76
Tony Scott	Villa 1965-68	Torquay 1967-70
David Rudge	Villa 1966-70	Torquay 1975-78
Brian Greenhalgh	Villa 1967-69	Torquay 1974-75
Tommy Mitchinson	Villa 1967-69	Torquay 1968-72
Dick Edwards	Villa 1967-70	Torquay 1970-73
John Dunn	Torquay 1966-68	Villa 1967-71
Barrie Lynch	Villa 1968-70	Torquay 1975-77
Bruce Rioch	Villa 1969-74	Torquay 1980-84
Alan Little	Villa 1974-75	Torquay 1982-84
Willie Young	Villa 1978-79	Torquay 1981-83
Phil King	Torquay 1986-87	Villa 1994-95

v. Tottenham Hotspur

		Home					Away			Final Positions	
Season	League	Date	Result	Villa	Tottenham	Date	Result	Villa	Tottenham	Villa	Tottenham
1909-10	Division 1	20 November	Won	3	2	2 April	Drew	1	1	1st	15th
1910-11	Division 1	25 February	Won	4	0	19 November	Won	2	1	2nd	15th
1911-12	Division 1	18 November	Drew	2	2	23 March	Lost	1	2	6th	12th
1912-13	Division 1	1 March	Won	1	0	26 October	Drew	3	3	2nd	17th
1913-14	Division 1	13 December	Drew	3	3	18 April	Won	2	0	2nd	17th
1914-15	Division 1	27 February	Won	3	1	24 October	Won	2	0	14th	20thR
1920-21	Division 1	11 September	Won	4	2	18 September	Won	2	1	10th	6th
1921-22	Division 1	1 October	Won	2	1	24 September	Lost	1	3	5th	2nd
1922-23	Division 1	7 October	Won	2	0	14 October	Won	2	1	6th	12th
1923-24	Division 1	15 March	Drew	0	0	22 March	Won	3	2	6th	15th
1924-25	Division 1	7 March	Lost	0	1	1 November	Won	3	1	15th	12th
1925-26	Division 1	17 April	Won	3	0	5 December	Drew	2	2	6th	15th
1926-27	Division 1	6 November	Lost	2	3	26 March	Won	1	0	10th	13th
1927-28	Division 1	12 November	Lost	1	2	24 March	Lost	1	2	8th	21stR
1933-34	Division 1	6 January	Lost	1	5	2 September	Lost	2	3	13th	3rd
1934-35	Division 1	2 February	Won	1	0	22 September	Won	2	0	13th	22ndR
1936-37	Division 2	7 November	Drew	1	1	13 March	Drew	2	2	9th	10th
1937-38	Division 2	16 April	Won	2	0	4 December	Lost	1	2	1stP	5th
1950-51	Division 1	30 September	Lost	2	3	17 February	Lost	2	3	15th	1st
1951-52	Division 1	8 March	Lost	0	3	20 October	Lost	0	2	6th	2nd
1952-53	Division 1	22 November	Lost	0	3	11 April	Drew	1	1	11th	10th
1953-54	Division 1	12 December	Lost	1	2	15 August	Lost	0	1	13th	16th
1954-55	Division 1	21 August	Lost	2	4	18 December	Drew	1	1	6th	16th
1955-56	Division 1	26 November	Lost	0	2	7 April	Lost	3	4	20th	18th
1956-57	Division 1	15 September	Lost	2	4	19 January	Lost	0	3	10th	2nd
1957-58	Division 1	16 November	Drew	1	1	29 March	Lost	2	6	14th	3rd
1958-59	Division 1	30 March	Drew	1	1	27 March	Lost	2	3	21stR	18th
1960-61	Division 1	11 February	Lost	1	2	24 September	Lost	2	6	9th	1st
1961-62	Division 1	21 February	Drew	0	0	30 September	Lost	0	1	7th	3rd
1962-63	Division 1	20 August	Won	2	1	29 August	Lost	2	4	15th	2nd
1963-64	Division 1	16 September	Lost	2	4	25 January	Lost	1	3	19th	4th
1964-65	Division 1	3 April	Won	1	0	21 November	Lost	0	4	16th	6th
1965-66	Division 1	25 September	Won	3	2	19 March	Drew	5	5	16th	8th
1966-67	Division 1	4 March	Drew	3	3	29 October	Won	1	0	21stR	3rd
1975-76	Division 1	11 October	Drew	1	1	13 March	Lost	2	5	16th	9th
1976-77	Division 1	20 April	Won	2	1	30 April	Lost	1	3	4th	22ndR
1978-79	Division 1	24 March	Lost	2	3	23 August	Won	4	1	8th	11th
1979-80	Division 1	26 April	Won	1	0	15 December	Won	2	1	7th	14th
1980-81	Division 1	18 October	Won	3	0	21 March	Lost	0	2	1st	10th
1981-82	Division 1	17 February	Drew	1	1	5 September	Won	3	1	11th	4th
1982-83	Division 1	30 October	Won	4	0	23 March	Lost	0	2	6th	4th
1983-84	Division 1	27 December	Drew	0	0	18 April	Lost	1	2	10th	8th
1984-85	Division 1	22 September	Lost	0	1	30 March	Won	2	0	10th	3rd
1985-86	Division 1	30 November	Lost	1	2	3 May	Lost	2	4	16th	10th

Season	League	Home Date	Home Result	Home Villa	Home Tottenham	Away Date	Away Result	Away Villa	Away Tottenham	Final Positions Villa	Final Positions Tottenham
1986-87	Division 1	23 August	Lost	**0**	**3**	24 January	Lost	**0**	**3**	22ndR	3rd
1988-89	Division 1	29 October	Won	**2**	**1**	1 March	Lost	**0**	**2**	17th	6th
1989-90	Division 1	9 September	Won	**2**	**0**	21 February	Won	**2**	**0**	2nd	3rd
1990-91	Division 1	16 March	Won	**3**	**2**	29 September	Lost	**1**	**2**	17th	10th
1991-92	Division 1	7 September	Drew	**0**	**0**	4 April	Won	**5**	**2**	7th	15th
1992-93	Premiership	10 March	Drew	**0**	**0**	21 November	Drew	**0**	**0**	2nd	8th
1993-94	Premiership	28 August	Won	**1**	**0**	2 March	Drew	**1**	**1**	10th	15th
1994-95	Premiership	25 January	Won	**1**	**0**	19 November	Won	**4**	**3**	18th	7th
1995-96	Premiership	21 January	Won	**2**	**1**	23 August	Won	**1**	**0**	4th	8th
1996-97	Premiership	19 April	Drew	**1**	**1**	12 October	Lost	**0**	**1**	5th	10th
1997-98	Premiership	26 December	Won	**4**	**1**	27 August	Lost	**2**	**3**	7th	14th
1998-99	Premiership	7 November	Won	**3**	**2**	13 March	Lost	**0**	**1**	6th	11th
1999-00	Premiership	29 December	Drew	**1**	**1**	15 April	Won	**4**	**2**	6th	10th
2000-01	Premiership	11 November	Won	**2**	**0**	28 April	Drew	**0**	**0**	8th	12th
2001-02	Premiership	29 December	Drew	**1**	**1**	18 August	Drew	**0**	**0**	8th	9th
2002-03	Premiership	18 January	Lost	**0**	**1**	24 August	Lost	**0**	**1**	16th	10th
2003-04	Premiership	2 May	Won	**1**	**0**	23 November	Lost	**1**	**2**	6th	14th

FA Cup										Division	
1902-03	Q'ter Final					7 March	Won	**3**	**2**	Div 1	Non L
1903-04	Round 2	25 February	Lost	**0**	**1**					Div 1	Non L
1919-20	Q'ter Final					6 March	Won	**1**	**0**	Div 1	Div 2
1920-21	Q'ter Final					5 March	Lost	**0**	**1**	Div 1	Div 1
1933-34	Round 5					17 February	Won	**1**	**0**	Div 1	Div 1
1960-61	Round 5	18 February	Lost	**0**	**2**					Div 1	Div 1
1961-62	Q'ter Final					10 March	Lost	**0**	**2**	Div 1	Div 1
1968-69	Round 5					12 February	Lost	**2**	**3**	Div 2	Div 1
1981-82	Round 5					13 February	Lost	**0**	**1**	Div 1	Div 1
1991-92	Round 3	5 January	Drew	**0**	**0**	14 January	Won	**1**	**0**	Div 1	Div 1

Villa goalkeeper Harry Morton, seen here grabbing the ball from Spurs forward George Hunt, made his senior debut in unusual circumstances, being called from the stand when Fred Biddletone was injured in the pre-match warm up at Maine Road in November 1931. By the time he moved to Everton in March 1937 he had made 207 first-team appearances for Villa.

League Cup		Home Date	Result	Villa	Tottenham	Away Date	Result	Villa	Tottenham	Final Positions Villa	Tottenham
1968-69	Round 2	4 September	Lost	1	4					Div 2	Div 1
1970-71	Final	27 February		Wembley			Lost	0	2	Div 3	Div 1
1987-88	Round 3	28 October	Won	2	1					Div 2	Div 1
1993-94	Q'ter Final					12 January	Won	2	1	Prem	Prem

Summary	P	W	D	L	F	A
Villa's home league record:	61	27	16	18	91	81
Villa's away league record:	61	19	11	31	93	117
Villa's cup record:	15	6	1	8	13	20
TOTAL:	**137**	**52**	**28**	**57**	**201**	**218**

FACT FILE

- **From 1988 to 2001, Villa were undefeated in 16 home games.**
- **Spurs went 14 games without a win between 1991 and 1996.**
- **Villa failed to win at White Hart Lane for 18 games from 1937 to 1966.**
- **This run included 10 defeats in a row. It came to an end in 1966 when Villa recovered from 5-1 down to draw 5-5, and would have won but for some hesitation in front of an empty net! The run also included seven home defeats in a row.**
- **Villa were the last third division team to reach a major domestic cup final, losing to Spurs in 1971.**
- **The 1904 cup tie was originally played five days earlier. However, the match was abandoned following a pitch invasion after 38 minutes with Villa leading 1-0.**

Villa's top scorers vs Spurs

Harry Hampton 9
Len Capewell 7
Peter McParland, David Platt, Dwight Yorke 5
Stan Collymore, Gordon Cowans, Arthur Dorrell, Dion Dublin, Tony Hateley, Clem Stephenson, Billy Walker 4

Villa hat-tricks vs Spurs

22 Mar 1924 Len Capewell
19 Mar 1966 Tony Hateley (4)
16 Mar 1991 David Platt

Played for both clubs

Jimmy Cantrell	Villa 1904-08	Spurs 1912-23
Cyril Spiers	Villa 1920-27	Spurs 1927-32
Billy Cook	Villa 1926-29	Spurs 1929-31
Ronnie Dix	Villa 1932-37	Spurs 1939-48
Danny Blanchflower	Villa 1950-55	Spurs 1954-64
Gordon Smith	Villa 1976-79	Spurs 1978-82
Steve Hodge	Villa 1985-87	Spurs 1986-88
Andy Gray	Villa 1987-89	Spurs 1991-94
Colin Calderwood	Spurs 1993-99	Villa 1998-2000
David Ginola	Spurs 1997-2000	Villa 2000-02
Oyvind Leonhardsen	Spurs 1999-2002	Villa 2002-03

v. Tranmere Rovers

Season	League	Date	Result	Home Villa	Home Tranmere	Date	Result	Away Villa	Away Tranmere	Final Positions Villa	Final Positions Tranmere
1970-71	Division 3	24 October	Won	**1**	**0**	5 March	Drew	**1**	**1**	4th	18th
1971-72	Division 3	20 October	Won	**2**	**0**	28 January	Won	**1**	**0**	1stP	20th

League Cup

										Division	
1993-94	Semi-Final	27 February	Won* (won 5-4 pens)	**3**	**1**	16 February	Lost	**1**	**3**	Prem	Div 1

Summary	*P*	*W*	*D*	*L*	*F*	*A*	
Villa's home league record:	2	2	0	0	3	0	
Villa's away league record:	2	1	1	0	2	1	
Villa's cup record:	2	1	0	1	4	4	
TOTAL:	**6**	**4**	**1**	**1**	**9**	**5**	(+one penalty shoot-out victory)

Villa's top scorers vs Tranmere

Ian Hamilton,
Dalian Atkinson 2

Played for both clubs

Pongo Waring	Tranmere 1927-28/36-39	Villa 1927-36
David Hickson	Villa 1955-56	Tranmere 1962-64
Jim Cumbes	Tranmere 1966-70	Villa 1971-76
Paul Rideout	Villa 1983-85	Tranmere 2000-02
Derek Mountfield	Tranmere 1980-82	Villa 1988-92
Dariusz Kubicki	Villa 1991-94	Tranmere 1997-98
Shaun Teale	Villa 1991-95	Tranmere 1995-97

Having previously played for Tranmere, goalkeeper Jim Cumbes joined Villa from West Brom for £36,000 in November 1971. Six months later he collected a Third Division championship medal and three years after that played in a winning League Cup side and also helped Villa back to the top flight. In March 1976, after 182 senior appearances, he went to play in the North American Soccer League. As a fast bowler he also played for Surrey, Lancashire, Worcestershire and Warwickshire and gained County Championship and Gillette Cup winners' medals with Worcestershire.

v. Walsall

Season	League	Date	Result	Home Villa	Home Walsall	Date	Result	Away Villa	Away Walsall	Final Positions Villa	Final Positions Walsall
1970-71	Division 3	17 March	Drew	**0**	**0**	2 January	Lost	**0**	**3**	4th	20th
1971-72	Division 3	18 March	Drew	**0**	**0**	21 August	Drew	**1**	**1**	1stP	9th

FA Cup						Division Villa	Division Walsall
1911-12	Round 1	13 January	Won	**6**	**0**	Div 1	Non L
1929-30	Round 4	25 January	Won	**3**	**1**	Div 1	Div 3S

Summary	P	W	D	L	F	A
Villa's home league record:	2	0	2	0	0	0
Villa's away league record:	2	0	1	1	1	4
Villa's cup record:	2	2	0	0	9	1
TOTAL:	**6**	**2**	**3**	**1**	**10**	**5**

FACT FILE

- **Villa have won both cup ties, but none of the four league matches against Walsall.**
- **Walsall were formed in 1888 by a merger between Walsall Swifts and Walsall Town. Aston Villa are the only side to play matches in the FA Cup proper against all three.**

Villa's top scorers vs Walsall

Harry Hampton, Horace Henshall, Billy Walker 2

Played for both clubs

Harry Yates	Villa 1888-90	Walsall 1898-99
Frank Gray	Villa 1889-90	Walsall 1892-93
Jimmy Warner	Villa 1888-92	Walsall 1893-94
Will Devey	Villa 1892-94	Walsall 1894-95/97-98
Charlie Aston	Walsall 1896-98	Villa 1897-1901
George Johnson	Walsall 1896-98	Villa 1897-1905
Albert Wilkes	Walsall 1896-98	Villa 1898-1907
Fred Marshall	Villa 1890-91	Walsall 1892-93
Arthur Stokes	Villa 1892-93	Walsall 1894-95
Len Benwell	Villa 1893-94	Walsall 1894-95
Willie Macaulay	Walsall 1899-1900	Villa 1900-01
Tommy Lyons	Villa 1907-15	Walsall 1922-23
Tommy Barber	Villa 1912-15	Walsall 1921-22
Jack Pendleton	Villa 1919-20	Walsall 1924-25
Alex McClure	Villa 1923-25	Walsall 1927-28
Tommy Muldoon	Villa 1924-27	Walsall 1929-31
Len Capewell	Villa 1921-29	Walsall 1929-30

Ben Olney	Villa 1927-30	Walsall 1931-32
Fred Biddlestone	Walsall 1929-30	Villa 1929-39
Ken Tewkesbury	Villa 1932-33	Walsall 1936-39
Billy Simpson	Villa 1931-35	Walsall 1937-39
George Beeson	Villa 1934-37	Walsall 1938-40
Jack Maund	Villa 1935-38	Walsall 1946-48
Arthur Haynes	Villa 1946-47	Walsall 1948-49
William Goffin	Villa 1946-54	Walsall 1954-55
Albert Vinall	Villa 1947-54	Walsall 1954-56
Sydney Howarth	Villa1948-50	Walsall 1952-53
Ronald Jeffries	Villa 1950-51	Walsall 1953-54
David Walsh	Villa 1950-55	Walsall 1955-56
Derek Pace	Villa 1950-58	Walsall 1966-67
William Myerscough	Walsall 1954-55	Villa 1956-59
John Sharples	Villa 1958-59	Walsall 1959-64
Jimmy MacEwan	Villa 1959-66	Walsall 1966-67
Mike Tindall	Villa 1959-68	Walsall 1968-69
Alan Deakin	Villa 1959-70	Walsall 1969-72
Jimmy McMorran	Villa 1960-62	Walsall 1964-69
Alan Baker	Villa 1960-66	Walsall 1966-71
John Woodward	Villa 1966-69	Walsall 1969-73
Dave Simmons	Villa 1968-71	Walsall 1970-71
Alun Evans	Villa 1972-74	Walsall 1975-78
Graham Moseley	Villa 1974-75	Walsall 1977-78
Gary Shelton	Walsall 1975-78	Villa 1978-82
Colin Gibson	Villa 1978-86	Walsall 1994-95
Gary Williams	Villa 1978-87	Walsall 1979-81
Gary Shaw	Villa 1978-88	Walsall 1989-90
Des Bremner	Villa 1979-85	Walsall 1989-90
Darren Bradley	Villa 1984-86	Walsall 1995-97
Tony Daley	Villa 1984-94	Walsall 1999-2000
Derek Mountfield	Villa 1988-92	Walsall 1995-98
Mark Blake	Villa 1989-93	Walsall 1996-98
Graham Fenton	Villa 1993-96	Walsall 1999-2000
Neil Davis	Villa 1995-96	Walsall 1998-99
Darren Byfield	Villa 1997-98	Walsall 2000-02
Paul Merson	Villa 1998-2002	Walsall 2003-04

Eric Houghton scored 170 goals in 392 games for Villa between 1929-30 and 1946-47. Goodness knows what his tally would have been but for World War Two. And as if that was not enough, he returned to Villa Park as manager in September 1953 and was in charge when they won the FA Cup in 1957. Lincolnshire-born, Houghton missed a penalty on his debut – ironic since he became one of the best penalty takers in the history of the game – and won a Second Division championship medal with Villa in 1938 and was also in the side which won the War Cup in 1944. He was capped seven times for England, served on the boards of both Villa and Walsall, and played county cricket for Warwickshire.

v. Walsall Swifts

FA Cup		Home Date	Home Result	Villa	Walsall Sw	Away Date	Away Result	Villa	Walsall Sw
1882-83	Round 1	21 October	Won	**4**	**1**				
1883-84	Round 1					10 November	Won	**5**	**1**

Summary	*P*	*W*	*D*	*L*	*F*	*A*
Villa's cup record:	2	2	0	0	9	2
TOTAL:	**2**	**2**	**0**	**0**	**9**	**2**

Villa's top scorers vs Swifts

Arthur Brown, Archie Hunter, Howard Vaughton 2

v. Walsall Town

FA Cup		Home Date	Home Result	Villa	Walsall T	Away Date	Away Result	Villa	Walsall T
1882-83	Round 4	27 January	Won	**2**	**1**				
1884-85	Round 2					6 December	Won	**2**	**0**
1885-86	Round 1					17 October	Won	**5**	**0**

Summary	*P*	*W*	*D*	*L*	*F*	*A*
Villa's cup record:	3	3	0	0	9	1
TOTAL:	**3**	**3**	**0**	**0**	**9**	**1**

Villa's top scorers vs Walsall Town

Arthur Brown, Archie Hunter, Howard Vaughton 2

v. Watford

		Home					Away			Final Positions	
Season	League	Date	Result	Villa	Watford	Date	Result	Villa	Watford	Villa	Watford
1969-70	Division 2	13 December	Lost	**0**	**2**	13 September	Lost	**0**	**3**	21stR	19th
1982-83	Division 1	16 October	Won	**3**	**0**	26 February	Lost	**1**	**2**	6th	2nd
1983-84	Division 1	21 April	Won	**2**	**1**	26 December	Lost	**2**	**3**	10th	11th
1984-85	Division 1	24 April	Drew	**1**	**1**	15 September	Drew	**3**	**3**	10th	11th
1985-86	Division 1	12 April	Won	**4**	**1**	9 November	Drew	**1**	**1**	16th	12th
1986-87	Division 1	25 March	Drew	**1**	**1**	18 October	Lost	**2**	**4**	22ndR	9th
1999-00	Premiership	5 February	Won	**4**	**0**	24 August	Won	**1**	**0**	6th	20thR

FA Cup						Division	
1982-83	Round 5	19 February	Won	**4**	**1**	Div 1	Div 1

Summary	P	W	D	L	F	A
Villa's home league record:	7	4	2	1	15	6
Villa's away league record:	7	1	2	4	10	16
Villa's cup record:	1	1	0	0	4	1
TOTAL:	**15**	**6**	**4**	**5**	**29**	**23**

FACT FILE

- **The series has produced only two away wins in 15 matches.**

Villa's top scorers vs Watford

Mark Walters 4

Tony Morley 3

Played for both clubs

Jimmy Stephenson	Villa 1914-21	Watford 1922-27
Frank Barson	Villa 1919-22	Watford 1928-29
Charlie Drinkwater	Villa 1935-36	Watford 1945-47
Mike Kenning	Villa 1960-61	Watford 1971-73
Brian Greenhalgh	Villa 1967-69	Watford 1974-76
Brian Rowan	Villa 1969-70	Watford 1971-72
Gary Williams	Villa 1978-87	Watford 1989-91
Tony Daley	Villa 1984-94	Watford 1998-99
Steve Hodge	Villa 1985-87	Watford 1995-96
Garry Thompson	Villa 1986-89	Watford 1988-90
Malcolm Allen	Watford 1985-88	Villa 1987-88
Steve Sims	Watford 1978-84/86-87	Villa 1987-89
Nigel Callaghan	Watford 1980-87/90-91	Villa 1988-91
Gary Penrice	Watford 1989-91/95-97	Villa 1990-92
Neil Cox	Villa 1991-94	Watford 1999-2004
Kevin Richardson	Watford 1986-87	Villa 1991-95
Guy Whittingham	Villa 1993-95	Watford 1998-99
David James	Watford 1990-92	Villa 1999-2001

v. Wednesbury Old Athletic

FA Cup		Home Date	Result	Villa	Wed'bury OA	Away Date	Result	Villa	Wed'bury OA
1881-82	Round 4					21 January	Lost	**2**	**4**
1882-83	Round 2	18 November	Won	**4**	**1**				
1883-84	Round 3					29 December	Won	**7**	**4**
1886-87	Round 1	30 October	Won	**13**	**0**				

Summary	*P*	*W*	*D*	*L*	*F*	*A*
Villa's cup record:	4	3	0	1	26	9
TOTAL:	**4**	**3**	**0**	**1**	**26**	**9**

FACT FILE

- **The 13-0 win in 1886-87 is Villa's biggest ever FA Cup win. The 35 goals scored in four games between the sides surely constitutes some sort of record.**

Villa's top scorers vs Wednesbury OA

Archie Hunter 6

O.H. Vaughton 5

Albert Brown, Denny Hodgetts 3

Villa hat-tricks vs Wednesbury OA

29 Dec 1883 OH Vaughton (cup)

30 Oct 1886 Denny Hodgetts (cup)

30 Oct 1886 Archie Hunter (cup)

30 Oct 1886 Albert Brown (cup)

v. Wednesbury Strollers

FA Cup		Date	Result	Home Villa	Home Wed'bury St
1880-81	Round 1	30 October	Won	**5**	**3**

Summary	P	W	D	L	F	A
Villa's cup record:	1	1	0	0	5	3
TOTAL:	**1**	**1**	**0**	**0**	**5**	**3**

v. Wednesbury Town

FA Cup		Date	Result	Home Villa	Wed'bury T
1884-85	Round 1	3 November	Won	**4**	**1**

Summary	P	W	D	L	F	A
Villa's cup record:	1	1	0	0	4	1
TOTAL:	**1**	**1**	**0**	**0**	**4**	**1**

FACT FILE

- **Three teams from Wednesbury have played in the FA Cup proper. Only Aston Villa have played against all three.**

Villa's top scorers vs Wednesbury Town
Arthur Brown 2

v. West Bromwich Albion

		Home				Away				Final Positions	
Season	League	Date	Result	Villa	WBA	Date	Result	Villa	WBA	Villa	WBA
1888-89	Division 1	19 January	Won	**2**	**0**	26 January	Drew	**3**	**3**	2nd	6th
1889-90	Division 1	26 October	Won	**1**	**0**	28 September	Lost	**0**	**3**	8th	5th
1890-91	Division 1	27 September	Lost	**0**	**4**	1 November	Won	**3**	**0**	9th	12th
1891-92	Division 1	12 September	Won	**5**	**1**	14 November	Won	**3**	**0**	4th	12th
1892-93	Division 1	5 November	Won	**5**	**2**	19 September	Lost	**2**	**3**	4th	8th
1893-94	Division 1	2 September	Won	**3**	**2**	21 October	Won	**6**	**3**	1st	8th
1894-95	Division 1	13 October	Won	**3**	**1**	17 November	Lost	**2**	**3**	3rd	13th
1895-96	Division 1	2 September	Won	**1**	**0**	12 October	Drew	**1**	**1**	1st	16th
1896-97	Division 1	10 October	Won	**2**	**0**	5 September	Lost	**1**	**3**	1st	12th
1897-98	Division 1	4 September	Won	**4**	**3**	9 October	Drew	**1**	**1**	6th	7th
1898-99	Division 1	24 April	Won	**7**	**1**	12 November	Won	**1**	**0**	1st	14th
1899-00	Division 1	9 September	Lost	**0**	**2**	6 January	Won	**2**	**0**	1st	13th
1900-01	Division 1	5 January	Lost	**0**	**1**	8 September	Won	**1**	**0**	15th	18thR
1902-03	Division 1	1 November	Lost	**0**	**3**	28 February	Won	**2**	**1**	2nd	7th
1903-04	Division 1	12 September	Won	**3**	**1**	9 January	Won	**3**	**1**	5th	18thR
1911-12	Division 1	4 September	Lost	**0**	**3**	30 September	Drew	**2**	**2**	6th	9th
1912-13	Division 1	21 September	Lost	**2**	**4**	18 January	Drew	**2**	**2**	2nd	10th
1913-14	Division 1	7 February	Won	**2**	**0**	4 October	Lost	**0**	**1**	2nd	5th
1914-15	Division 1	19 September	Won	**2**	**1**	23 January	Lost	**0**	**2**	14th	10th
1919-20	Division 1	15 November	Lost	**2**	**4**	10 November	Won	**2**	**1**	9th	1st
1920-21	Division 1	6 November	Drew	**0**	**0**	13 November	Lost	**1**	**2**	10th	14th
1921-22	Division 1	15 October	Lost	**0**	**1**	8 October	Won	**1**	**0**	5th	13th
1922-23	Division 1	9 September	Won	**2**	**0**	16 September	Lost	**0**	**3**	6th	7th
1923-24	Division 1	27 October	Won	**4**	**0**	20 October	Lost	**0**	**1**	6th	16th
1924-25	Division 1	25 October	Won	**1**	**0**	28 February	Lost	**1**	**4**	15th	2nd
1925-26	Division 1	13 February	Won	**2**	**1**	3 October	Drew	**1**	**1**	6th	13th
1926-27	Division 1	23 October	Won	**2**	**0**	12 March	Lost	**2**	**6**	10th	22ndR
1931-32	Division 1	26 March	Won	**2**	**0**	14 November	Lost	**0**	**3**	5th	6th
1932-33	Division 1	11 March	Won	**3**	**2**	29 October	Lost	**1**	**3**	2nd	4th
1933-34	Division 1	28 April	Drew	**4**	**4**	16 December	Lost	**1**	**2**	13th	7th
1934-35	Division 1	3 April	Lost	**2**	**3**	3 November	Drew	**2**	**2**	13th	9th
1935-36	Division 1	19 October	Lost	**0**	**7**	1 April	Won	**3**	**0**	21stR	18th
1949-50	Division 1	25 February	Won	**1**	**0**	8 October	Drew	**1**	**1**	12th	14th
1950-51	Division 1	19 August	Won	**2**	**0**	16 December	Lost	**0**	**2**	15th	16th
1951-52	Division 1	19 April	Won	**2**	**0**	1 December	Won	**2**	**1**	6th	13th
1952-53	Division 1	7 April	Drew	**1**	**1**	6 April	Lost	**2**	**3**	11th	4th
1953-54	Division 1	20 April	Won	**6**	**1**	19 April	Drew	**1**	**1**	13th	2nd
1954-55	Division 1	19 March	Won	**3**	**0**	30 October	Won	**3**	**2**	6th	17th
1955-56	Division 1	28 April	Won	**3**	**0**	8 October	Lost	**0**	**1**	20th	13th
1956-57	Division 1	27 August	Drew	**0**	**0**	22 August	Lost	**0**	**2**	10th	11th
1957-58	Division 1	5 April	Won	**2**	**1**	9 November	Lost	**2**	**3**	14th	4th
1958-59	Division 1	11 October	Lost	**1**	**4**	29 April	Drew	**1**	**1**	21stR	5th
1960-61	Division 1	28 March	Lost	**0**	**1**	29 October	Won	**2**	**0**	9th	10th
1961-62	Division 1	14 March	Won	**1**	**0**	21 October	Drew	**1**	**1**	7th	9th

Season	League	Home Date	Home Result	Villa	WBA	Away Date	Away Result	Villa	WBA	Final Positions Villa	Final Positions WBA
1962-63	Division 1	6 October	Won	**2**	**0**	11 May	Lost	**0**	**1**	15th	14th
1963-64	Division 1	22 February	Won	**1**	**0**	12 October	Lost	**3**	**4**	19th	10th
1964-65	Division 1	17 October	Lost	**0**	**1**	27 February	Lost	**1**	**3**	16th	14th
1965-66	Division 1	16 October	Drew	**1**	**1**	11 February	Drew	**2**	**2**	16th	6th
1966-67	Division 1	5 November	Won	**3**	**2**	15 October	Lost	**1**	**2**	21stR	13th
1973-74	Division 2	2 March	Lost	**1**	**3**	26 December	Lost	**0**	**2**	14th	8th
1974-75	Division 2	29 March	Won	**3**	**1**	21 December	Lost	**0**	**2**	2ndP	6th
1976-77	Division 1	23 May	Won	**4**	**0**	10 November	Drew	**1**	**1**	4th	7th
1977-78	Division 1	10 December	Won	**3**	**0**	22 April	Won	**3**	**0**	8th	6th
1978-79	Division 1	11 May	Lost	**0**	**1**	25 November	Drew	**1**	**1**	8th	3rd
1979-80	Division 1	13 October	Drew	**0**	**0**	23 February	Won	**2**	**1**	7th	10th
1980-81	Division 1	8 April	Won	**1**	**0**	8 November	Drew	**0**	**0**	1st	4th
1981-82	Division 1	30 March	Won	**2**	**1**	8 May	Won	**1**	**0**	11th	17th
1982-83	Division 1	19 April	Won	**1**	**0**	2 October	Lost	**0**	**1**	6th	11th
1983-84	Division 1	27 August	Won	**4**	**3**	14 February	Lost	**1**	**3**	10th	17th
1984-85	Division 1	1 January	Won	**3**	**1**	8 April	Lost	**0**	**1**	10th	12th
1985-86	Division 1	28 December	Drew	**1**	**1**	4 September	Won	**3**	**0**	16th	22ndR
1987-88	Division 2	18 December	Drew	**0**	**0**	16 September	Won	**2**	**0**	2ndP	20th
2002-03	Premiership	14 December	Won	**2**	**1**	16 November	Drew	**0**	**0**	16th	19thR

FA Cup

Season	Round	Home Date	Home Result	Villa	WBA	Away Date / Venue	Away Result	Villa	WBA	Division Villa	Division WBA
1884-85	Round 3	3 January	Drew	**0**	**0**	10 January	Lost	**0**	**3**		
1886-87	Final	2 April				Kennington Oval	Won	**2**	**0**		
1891-92	Final	19 March				Kennington Oval	Lost	**0**	**3**	Div 1	Div 1
1894-95	Final	20 April				Crystal Palace	Won	**1**	**0**	Div 1	Div 1
1913-14	Round 3	21 February	Won	**2**	**1**					Div 1	Div 1
1923-24	Q'ter Final					8 March	Won	**2**	**0**	Div 1	Div 1
1924-25	Round 3	25 February	Lost	**1**	**2**	21 February	Drew	**1**	**1**	Div 1	Div 1
1925-26	Round 4					29 January	Won	**2**	**1**	Div 1	Div 1
1931-32	Round 3					9 January	Won	**2**	**1**	Div 1	Div 1
1956-57	Semi-Final	23 March				Molineux, Wolverhampton	Drew	**2**	**2**	Div 1	Div 1
		28 March				St Andrew's, Birmingham (replay)	Won	**1**	**0**		
1989-90	Round 5					17 February	Won	**2**	**0**	Div 1	Div 2
1997-98	Round 4	24 January	Won	**4**	**0**					Prem	Div 1

League Cup

Season	Round	Home Date	Home Result	Villa	WBA	Away Date	Away Result	Villa	WBA	Division Villa	Division WBA
1965-66	Q'ter Final					17 November	Lost	**1**	**3**	Div 1	Div 1
1966-67	Round 2					14 September	Lost	**1**	**6**	Div 1	Div 1
1969-70	Round 2	3 September	Lost	**1**	**2**					Div 2	Div 1
1981-82	Q'ter Final	20 January	Lost	**0**	**1**					Div 1	Div 1
1983-84	Round 4					30 November	Won	**2**	**1**	Div 1	Div 1
1985-86	Round 4	20 November	Drew	**2**	**2**	27 November	Won	**2**	**1**	Div 1	Div 1

Summary	*P*	*W*	*D*	*L*	*F*	*A*
Villa's home league record:	63	40	8	15	120	75
Villa's away league record:	63	19	16	28	86	99
Villa's cup record:	22	11	4	7	31	30
TOTAL:	**148**	**70**	**28**	**50**	**237**	**204**

FACT FILE

- **Villa have played more cup matches against West Brom than any other club.**
- **Three of these were FA Cup finals, which were Villa's first three cup finals. They were the only clubs to meet in three different FA Cup finals until Arsenal and Newcastle's third such meeting in 1998.**
- **Their first cup final meeting, in 1887, was the first all-Midlands FA Cup final. West Brom dominated the match early on, but when Dennis Hodgetts went through on goal, the West Brom goalkeeper Bob Roberts thought he was offside, and didn't save the shot. He was wrong.**
- **After winning the cup in 1895, Villa displayed it in a shop window, from where it was later stolen and never recovered. Aston Villa are therefore the answer to the popular quiz question 'Which club won the FA Cup and lost it in the same year?'**
- **Villa's heaviest ever home defeat in the league came at the hands of West Brom in 1935.**
- **Between 1899 and 1903, the series produced six successive away wins.**
- **Villa are unbeaten in their last nine home league games against West Brom.**
- **Villa won 10 of their first 11 home league games in the series.**

Villa's top scorers vs West Brom

Jack Devey 10
Billy Walker 7
Dai Astley, Billy Garraty, Eric Houghton, Fred Wheldon 6
Albert Brown, Johnny Dixon, Peter McParland, Tony Hateley 5

Villa hat-tricks vs West Brom

4 Sep 1897 Fred Wheldon
24 Apr 1899 Billy Garraty
27 Oct 1923 Billy Walker
23 May 1977 Andy Gray

Played for both clubs

Bob Roberts	West Brom 1888-90/91-92	Villa 1892-93
Baldy Reynolds	West Brom 1891-93	Villa 1893-97
Fred Wheldon	Villa 1896-1900	West Brom 1900-01
Tom Perry	West Brom 1890-1901	Villa 1901-03
Willie Groves	West Brom 1890-03	Villa 1893-94
Harry Hadley	West Brom 1897-1905	Villa 1905-06
Albert Evans	Villa 1896-1906	West Brom 1907-09
George Garratt	Villa 1905-06	West Brom 1907-08
Billy Garraty	Villa 1897-1908	West Brom 1908-10
George Harris	Villa 1901-08	West Brom 1908-10
David Walsh	West Brom 1946-51	Villa1950-55

Jimmy Dugdale	West Brom 1952-56	Villa 1955-62
Jim Cumbes	West Brom 1969-72	Villa 1971-76
Steve Hunt	Villa 1974-77/85-88	West Brom 1983-86
Andy Gray	Villa 1975-79/85-87	West Brom 1987-89
John Deehan	Villa 1975-80	West Brom 1979-82
Ken McNaught	Villa 1977-83	West Brom 1983-84
Kenny Swain	Villa 1978-83	West Brom 1987-88
Robert Hopkins	Villa 1979-83	West Brom 1986-89
Tony Morley	Villa 1979-84	West Brom 1983-85/87-88
Nigel Spink	Villa 1979-96	West Brom 1995-97
Darren Bradley	Villa 1984-86	West Brom 1985-95
Garry Thompson	West Brom 1982-85	Villa 1986-89
Andy Comyn	Villa 1989-91	West Brom 1995-96
Ugo Ehiogu	West Brom 1990-91	Villa 1991-2001
Cyrille Regis	West Brom 1977-85	Villa 1991-93
Graham Fenton	West Brom 1993-94	Villa 1993-96
Andy Townsend	Villa 1993-98	West Brom 1999-2000
Phil King	Villa 1994-95	West Brom 1995-96
Franz Carr	Villa 1994-96	West Brom 1997-98
Mark Kinsella	Villa 2002-04	West Brom 2003-04

A general view of the 1895 FA Cup Final between Aston Villa and West Brom at the Crystal Palace. Bob Chatt's goal, the only one of the game, gave Villa victory over their West Midlands rivals.

West Ham United

		Home					Away				Final Positions	
Season	*League*	*Date*	*Result*	Villa	WHU	*Date*	*Result*	Villa	WHU	Villa	WHU
1923-24	Division 1	25 December	Drew	**1**	**1**	26 December	Lost	**0**	**1**	6th	13th
1924-25	Division 1	20 September	Drew	**1**	**1**	24 January	Lost	**0**	**2**	15th	13th
1925-26	Division 1	26 December	Won	**2**	**0**	25 December	Lost	**2**	**5**	6th	18th
1926-27	Division 1	2 April	Lost	**1**	**5**	13 November	Lost	**1**	**5**	10th	6th
1927-28	Division 1	9 April	Won	**1**	**0**	6 April	Drew	**0**	**0**	8th	17th
1928-29	Division 1	19 January	Won	**5**	**2**	8 September	Lost	**1**	**4**	3rd	17th
1929-30	Division 1	26 April	Lost	**2**	**3**	21 December	Lost	**2**	**5**	4th	7th
1930-31	Division 1	6 September	Won	**6**	**1**	3 January	Drew	**5**	**5**	2nd	18th
1931-32	Division 1	26 September	Won	**5**	**2**	6 February	Lost	**1**	**2**	5th	22ndR
1936-37	Division 2	17 April	Lost	**0**	**2**	26 April	Lost	**1**	**2**	9th	6th
1937-38	Division 2	28 August	Won	**2**	**0**	1 January	Drew	**1**	**1**	1stP	9th
1958-59	Division 1	3 January	Lost	**1**	**2**	30 August	Lost	**2**	**7**	21stR	6th
1960-61	Division 1	29 August	Won	**2**	**1**	22 August	Lost	**2**	**5**	9th	16th
1961-62	Division 1	9 September	Lost	**2**	**4**	20 January	Lost	**0**	**2**	7th	8th
1962-63	Division 1	18 August	Won	**3**	**1**	15 December	Drew	**1**	**1**	15th	12th
1963-64	Division 1	1 February	Drew	**2**	**2**	21 September	Won	**1**	**0**	19th	14th
1964-65	Division 1	31 March	Lost	**2**	**3**	10 October	Lost	**0**	**3**	16th	9th
1965-66	Division 1	7 February	Lost	**1**	**2**	5 March	Lost	**2**	**4**	16th	12th
1966-67	Division 1	28 March	Lost	**0**	**2**	24 March	Lost	**1**	**2**	21stR	16th
1975-76	Division 1	26 December	Won	**4**	**1**	17 April	Drew	**2**	**2**	4th	18th
1976-77	Division 1	21 August	Won	**4**	**0**	22 January	Won	**1**	**0**	8th	17th
1977-78	Division 1	18 March	Won	**4**	**1**	22 October	Drew	**2**	**2**	8th	20thR
1981-82	Division 1	17 October	Won	**3**	**2**	6 March	Drew	**2**	**2**	11th	9th
1982-83	Division 1	4 December	Won	**1**	**0**	23 April	Lost	**0**	**2**	6th	8th

Dennis Mortimer heads Villa's third goal past West Ham goalkeeper Bobby Ferguson at Villa Park in March 1978. Villa went on to win 4-1.

		Home					**Away**				*Final Positions*	
Season	*League*	*Date*	*Result*	Villa	WHU	*Date*	*Result*	Villa	WHU		Villa	WHU
1983-84	Division 1	3 December	Won	**1**	**0**	5 May	Won	**1**	**0**		10th	9th
1984-85	Division 1	3 November	Drew	**0**	**0**	23 February	Won	**2**	**1**		10th	16th
1985-86	Division 1	19 March	Won	**2**	**1**	19 October	Lost	**1**	**4**		16th	3rd
1986-87	Division 1	25 April	Won	**4**	**0**	22 November	Drew	**1**	**1**		22ndR	15th
1988-89	Division 1	25 March	Lost	**0**	**1**	17 September	Drew	**2**	**2**		17th	19thR
1991-92	Division 1	26 December	Won	**3**	**1**	28 August	Lost	**1**	**3**		7th	22ndR
1993-94	Premiership	15 January	Won	**3**	**1**	16 October	Drew	**0**	**0**		10th	13th
1994-95	Premiership	18 March	Lost	**0**	**2**	17 September	Lost	**0**	**1**		18th	14th
1995-96	Premiership	17 April	Drew	**1**	**1**	4 November	Won	**4**	**1**		4th	10th
1996-97	Premiership	15 March	Drew	**0**	**0**	4 December	Won	**2**	**0**		5th	14th
1997-98	Premiership	4 April	Won	**2**	**0**	29 November	Lost	**1**	**2**		7th	8th
1998-99	Premiership	2 April	Drew	**0**	**0**	17 October	Drew	**0**	**0**		6th	5th
1999-00	Premiership	16 August	Drew	**2**	**2**	15 January	Drew	**1**	**1**		6th	9th
2000-01	Premiership	7 April	Drew	**2**	**2**	9 December	Drew	**1**	**1**		8th	15th
2001-02	Premiership	2 March	Won	**2**	**1**	5 December	Drew	**1**	**1**		8th	7th
2002-03	Premiership	23 November	Won	**4**	**1**	12 April	Drew	**2**	**2**		16th	18thR

FA Cup										*Division*	
1912-13	Round 2	1 February	Won	**5**	**0**					Div 1	Non L
1976-77	Round 4	29 January	Won	**3**	**0**					Div 1	Div 1
1979-80	Q'ter Final					8 March	Lost	**0**	**1**	Div 1	Div 2

League Cup											
1961-62	Round 2					9 October	Won	**3**	**1**	Div 1	Div 1
1963-64	Round 3	16 October	Lost	**0**	**2**					Div 1	Div 1
1988-89	Q'ter Final					18 January	Lost	**1**	**2**	Div 1	Div 1
1989-90	Round 3	25 October	Drew	**0**	**0**	8 November	Lost	**0**	**1**	Div 1	Div 2
1997-98	Round 3					15 October	Lost	**0**	**3**	Prem	Prem
1999-00	Q'ter Final					11 January	Won*	**3**	**1**	Prem	Prem

Summary	*P*	*W*	*D*	*L*	*F*	*A*
Villa's home league record:	40	21	9	10	81	51
Villa's away league record:	40	6	15	19	50	84
Villa's cup record:	10	4	1	5	15	11
TOTAL:	**90**	**31**	**25**	**34**	**146**	**146**

West Ham's Billy Bonds can't stop Andy Gray at Upton Park in January 1977. Gray scored the only goal of this First Division game. The following week Villa beat the Hammers 3-0 in the FA Cup.

FACT FILE

- **Villa failed to win in their first 13 visits to Upton Park. One of these matches finished 5-5, which along with the 5-5 draw against Spurs in 1966, is Villa's highest scoring draw.**
- **Villa are unbeaten in their last 11 games against West Ham, although eight of these were drawn and one went to extra time.**
- **The League Cup tie of 1999-2000 was originally played on 15 December 1999 at Upton Park. In a dramatic tie, Dion Dublin put Villa 2-1 up in injury time, only for West Ham to equalise immediately from the penalty spot. West Ham went on to win the tie 5-4 on penalties, and Villa thought they were out. It soon became apparent, though, that West Ham had brought on a substitute who was ineligible through being cup-tied, and a replay was ordered. The Hammers were punished in full as Villa went through 3-1.**
- **West Ham were unbeaten in nine matches from 1975 to 1982.**

Villa's top scorers vs West Ham

Pongo Waring 8
John Deehan 6
Andy Gray, Billy Walker 5
Joe Beresford, Dion Dublin, Eric Houghton, Dennis Mortimer, Bobby Thomson, Dwight Yorke 4

Villa hat-tricks vs West Ham

6 Sep 1930 Pongo Waring (4)
26 Sep 1931 Pongo Waring (4)

Played for both clubs

Fred Norris	Villa 1925-27	West Ham 1928-33
Thomas Southren	West Ham 1950-54	Villa 1954-59
Phil Woosnam	West Ham 1958-63	Villa 1962-66
Tony Scott	West Ham 1959-66	Villa 1965-68
Alan Curbishley	West Ham 1974-79	Villa 1982-85
Mervyn Day	West Ham 1973-79	Villa 1983-85
Les Sealey	Villa 1991-92	West Ham 1995-97
Frank McAvennie	West Ham 1985-92	Villa 1992-93
Ray Houghton	West Ham 1981-82	Villa 1992-95
Franz Carr	West Ham 1990-91	Villa 1994-96
Gary Charles	Villa 1994-99	West Ham 1999-2001
David James	Villa 1999-2001	West Ham 2001-04

v. Wigan Athletic

League Cup		Home Date	Home Result	Villa	Wigan	Away Date	Away Result	Villa	Wigan	Division Villa	Division Wigan
1981-82	Round 4					1 December	Won	**2**	**1**	Div 1	Div 4
1994-95	Round 2	21 September	Won	**5**	**0**	5 October	Won	**3**	**0**	Prem	Div 3

Summary	*P*	*W*	*D*	*L*	*F*	*A*
Villa's cup record:	3	3	0	0	10	1
TOTAL:	**3**	**3**	**0**	**0**	**10**	**1**

Villa's top scorers vs Wigan

Nii Lamptey 3
Dalian Atkinson 2

Played for both clubs

Bobby Campbell	Villa 1973-75	Wigan 1986-88
Brendan Ormsby	Villa 1978-86	Wigan 1994-95
Warren Aspinall	Wigan 1984-86	Villa 1986-88
Lee Butler	Villa 1988-91	Wigan 1996-98
Gareth Farrelly	Villa 1995-97	Wigan 2003-04

Later to play for Wigan, defender Brendan Ormsby played for Leeds, Doncaster and Shrewsbury after leaving Villa Park.

v. Wimbledon

Season	League	Date	Result	Home Villa	Home Wimbledon	Date	Result	Away Villa	Away Wimbledon	Final Positions Villa	Final Positions Wimbledon
1986-87	Division 1	4 March	Drew	**0**	**0**	26 August	Lost	**2**	**3**	22ndR	6th
1988-89	Division 1	8 October	Lost	**0**	**1**	11 February	Lost	**0**	**1**	17th	12th
1989-90	Division 1	24 February	Lost	**0**	**3**	25 November	Won	**2**	**0**	2nd	8th
1990-91	Division 1	20 April	Lost	**1**	**2**	20 October	Drew	**0**	**0**	17th	7th
1991-92	Division 1	26 October	Won	**2**	**1**	8 February	Lost	**0**	**2**	7th	13th
1992-93	Premiership	27 February	Won	**1**	**0**	3 October	Won	**3**	**2**	2nd	12th
1993-94	Premiership	11 December	Lost	**0**	**1**	21 August	Drew	**2**	**2**	10th	6th
1994-95	Premiership	11 February	Won	**7**	**1**	9 November	Lost	**3**	**4**	18th	9th
1995-96	Premiership	16 September	Won	**2**	**0**	24 February	Drew	**3**	**3**	4th	14th
1996-97	Premiership	22 December	Won	**5**	**0**	9 April	Won	**2**	**0**	5th	8th
1997-98	Premiership	18 October	Lost	**1**	**2**	21 February	Lost	**1**	**2**	7th	15th
1998-99	Premiership	12 September	Won	**2**	**0**	21 February	Drew	**0**	**0**	6th	16th
1999-00	Premiership	23 October	Drew	**1**	**1**	6 May	Drew	**2**	**2**	6th	18thR

FA Cup										Division	
1988-89	Round 4	28 January	Lost	**0**	**1**					Div 1	Div 1
1990-91	Round 3	5 January	Drew	**1**	**1**	9 January	Lost*	**0**	**1**	Div 1	Div 1
1992-93	Round 4	23 January	Drew	**1**	**1**	3 February	Drew*	**0**	**0**	Prem	Prem
							(lost 5-6 pens)				

League Cup											
1996-97	Round 4					26 November	Lost	**0**	**1**	Prem	Prem

Summary	*P*	*W*	*D*	*L*	*F*	*A*	
Villa's home league record:	13	6	2	5	22	12	
Villa's away league record:	13	3	5	5	20	21	
Villa's cup record:	6	0	3	3	2	5	
TOTAL:	**32**	**9**	**10**	**13**	**44**	**38**	(+one penalty shoot-out defeat)

FACT FILE

- **The 7-1 win in February 1995 is Villa's record Premiership victory.**
- **Wimbledon are the only team to knock Villa out of the FA Cup on penalties.**
- **The six cup matches between the sides have produced only seven goals.**
- **Villa failed to win in their first six home games with Wimbledon.**

Villa's top scorers vs Wimbledon

Dwight Yorke 7

Dean Saunders 6

Savo Milosevic, Ian Taylor 4

Tommy Johnson 3

Villa hat-tricks vs Wimbledon

11 Feb 1995 Tommy Johnson

Played for both clubs

Kevin Gage	Wimbledon 1980-87	Villa 1987-91
John Fashanu	Wimbledon 1985-94	Villa 1994-95
Oyvind Leonhardsen	Wimbledon 1994-97	Villa 2002-03

Peter Withe had already won League Championship and League Cup honours with Brian Clough's Nottingham Forest when he joined Villa in May 1980, from Newcastle for a club record £500,000. At Villa Park he carried on where he had left off at Forest, scoring 20 goals as Villa won the League championship in 1980-81 and hitting the only goal of the 1982 European Cup Final as Villa beat Bayern Munich. By the time he left Villa on a free transfer for Sheffield United in the summer of 1986, he had scored 90 goals in 232 starts for the club. Liverpool-born, Withe had a host of clubs starting with Southport and then, in turn, Barrow, Port Elizabeth City and Arcadia Shepherds (South Africa), Wolves, Birmingham, Forest, Newcastle, Villa, Sheffield United, Birmingham again and as player-coach at Huddersfield. He also played in the NASL for Portland Timbers. Briefly assistant to Josef Venglos at Villa Park, he also managed Wimbledon.

v. Witton

FA Cup		Date	Result	Home Villa	Home Witton	Division Villa	Division Witton
1888-89	Round 1	2 February	Won	**3**	**2**	Div 1	Non L

Summary	*P*	*W*	*D*	*L*	*F*	*A*
Villa's cup record:	1	1	0	0	3	2
TOTAL:	**1**	**1**	**0**	**0**	**3**	**2**

v. Wolverhampton Wanderers

		Home				Away				Final Positions	
Season	*League*	*Date*	*Result*	Villa	Wolves	*Date*	*Result*	Villa	Wolves	Villa	Wolves
1888-89	Division 1	24 November	Won	**2**	**1**	8 September	Drew	**1**	**1**	2nd	3rd
1889-90	Division 1	2 November	Won	**2**	**1**	21 December	Drew	**1**	**1**	8th	4th
1890-91	Division 1	14 March	Won	**6**	**2**	6 September	Lost	**1**	**2**	9th	4th
1891-92	Division 1	18 April	Lost	**3**	**6**	19 December	Lost	**0**	**2**	4th	6th
1892-93	Division 1	3 April	Won	**5**	**0**	8 October	Lost	**1**	**2**	4th	11th
1893-94	Division 1	26 March	Drew	**1**	**1**	23 December	Lost	**0**	**3**	1st	9th
1894-95	Division 1	15 April	Drew	**2**	**2**	22 December	Won	**4**	**0**	3rd	11th
1895-96	Division 1	6 April	Won	**4**	**1**	26 December	Won	**2**	**1**	1st	14th
1896-97	Division 1	19 April	Won	**5**	**0**	26 December	Won	**2**	**1**	1st	10th
1897-98	Division 1	11 April	Lost	**1**	**2**	27 December	Drew	**1**	**1**	6th	3rd
1898-99	Division 1	10 December	Drew	**1**	**1**	3 April	Lost	**0**	**4**	1st	8th
1899-00	Division 1	11 November	Drew	**0**	**0**	16 April	Won	**1**	**0**	1st	4th
1900-01	Division 1	27 October	Drew	**0**	**0**	8 April	Drew	**0**	**0**	15th	13th
1901-02	Division 1	23 November	Won	**2**	**1**	22 March	Won	**2**	**0**	8th	14th
1902-03	Division 1	4 April	Won	**3**	**1**	6 December	Lost	**1**	**2**	2nd	11th
1903-04	Division 1	14 November	Won	**2**	**0**	12 March	Lost	**2**	**3**	5th	8th
1904-05	Division 1	27 April	Won	**3**	**0**	17 December	Drew	**1**	**1**	4th	14th
1905-06	Division 1	25 November	Won	**6**	**0**	31 March	Lost	**1**	**4**	8th	20thR
1932-33	Division 1	26 December	Lost	**1**	**3**	27 December	Won	**4**	**2**	2nd	20th
1933-34	Division 1	25 December	Won	**6**	**2**	26 December	Lost	**3**	**4**	13th	15th
1934-35	Division 1	27 August	Won	**2**	**1**	3 September	Lost	**2**	**5**	13th	17th
1935-36	Division 1	10 April	Won	**4**	**2**	13 April	Drew	**2**	**2**	21stR	15th
1938-39	Division 1	11 April	Drew	**2**	**2**	10 April	Lost	**1**	**2**	12th	2nd
1946-47	Division 1	16 September	Won	**3**	**0**	11 September	Won	**2**	**1**	8th	3rd
1947-48	Division 1	26 December	Lost	**1**	**2**	27 December	Lost	**1**	**4**	6th	5th
1948-49	Division 1	27 December	Won	**5**	**1**	25 December	Lost	**0**	**4**	10th	6th
1949-50	Division 1	27 December	Lost	**1**	**4**	26 December	Won	**3**	**2**	12th	2nd
1950-51	Division 1	27 March	Won	**1**	**0**	26 March	Won	**3**	**2**	15th	14th
1951-52	Division 1	25 December	Drew	**3**	**3**	26 December	Won	**2**	**1**	6th	16th
1952-53	Division 1	15 September	Lost	**0**	**1**	8 September	Lost	**1**	**2**	11th	3rd
1953-54	Division 1	26 December	Lost	**1**	**2**	24 December	Won	**2**	**1**	13th	1st
1954-55	Division 1	12 April	Won	**4**	**2**	11 April	Lost	**0**	**1**	6th	2nd
1955-56	Division 1	3 April	Drew	**0**	**0**	2 April	Drew	**0**	**0**	20th	3rd
1956-57	Division 1	22 April	Won	**4**	**0**	23 April	Lost	**0**	**3**	10th	6th
1957-58	Division 1	23 September	Lost	**2**	**3**	16 September	Lost	**1**	**2**	14th	1st
1958-59	Division 1	8 September	Lost	**1**	**3**	17 September	Lost	**0**	**4**	21stR	1st
1960-61	Division 1	24 December	Lost	**0**	**2**	26 December	Lost	**2**	**3**	9th	3rd
1961-62	Division 1	2 October	Won	**1**	**0**	28 August	Drew	**2**	**2**	7th	18th
1962-63	Division 1	16 April	Lost	**0**	**2**	15 April	Lost	**1**	**3**	15th	5th
1963-64	Division 1	28 December	Drew	**2**	**2**	26 December	Drew	**3**	**3**	19th	16th
1964-65	Division 1	22 March	Won	**3**	**2**	26 December	Won	**1**	**0**	16th	21stR
1975-76	Division 1	24 February	Drew	**1**	**1**	23 September	Drew	**0**	**0**	16th	20thR
1977-78	Division 1	23 September	Won	**2**	**0**	2 May	Lost	**1**	**3**	8th	15th
1978-79	Division 1	19 August	Won	**1**	**0**	11 November	Won	**4**	**0**	8th	18th

		Home				Away				Final Positions	
Season	League	Date	Result	Villa	Wolves	Date	Result	Villa	Wolves	Villa	Wolves
1979-80	Division 1	10 March	Lost	**1**	**3**	27 October	Drew	**1**	**1**	7th	6th
1980-81	Division 1	20 September	Won	**2**	**1**	28 February	Won	**1**	**0**	1st	18th
1981-82	Division 1	13 March	Won	**3**	**1**	24 October	Won	**3**	**0**	11th	21stR
1983-84	Division 1	25 February	Won	**4**	**0**	23 October	Drew	**1**	**1**	10th	22ndR
2003-04	Premiership	14 December	Won	**3**	**2**	14 March	Won	**4**	**0**	6th	20thR

FA Cup

										Division	
1886-87	Round 3	11 December	Drew	**2**	**2**	15 January	Drew*	**1**	**1**		
			(2nd replay)			22 January	Drew*	**3**	**3**		
		29 January	Won	**2**	**0**	(3rd replay)					
1891-92	Q'ter Final					13 February	Won	**3**	**1**	Div 1	Div 1
1893-94	Round 1	27 January	Won	**4**	**2**					Div 1	Div 1
1950-51	Round 4					27 January	Lost	**1**	**3**	Div 1	Div 1
1959-60	Semi-Final	26 March				The Hawthorns	Lost	**0**	**1**	Div 2	Div 1
1964-65	Round 5	20 February	Drew	**1**	**1**	24 February	Drew*	**0**	**0**	Div 1	Div 1
		1 March				The Hawthorns (2nd replay)	Lost	**1**	**3**		
1982-83	Round 4	29 January	Won	**1**	**0**					Div 1	Div 2

League Cup

1981-82	Round 2	7 October	Won	**3**	**2**	27 October	Won	**2**	**1**	Div 1	Div 1
1989-90	Round 2	20 September	Won	**2**	**1**	4 October	Drew	**1**	**1**	Div 1	Div 2
1995-96	Q'ter Final	10 January	Won	**1**	**0**					Prem	Div 1

Summary	*P*	*W*	*D*	*L*	*F*	*A*
Villa's home league record:	49	27	10	12	112	66
Villa's away league record:	49	16	12	21	72	86
Villa's cup record:	17	8	6	3	28	22
TOTAL:	**115**	**51**	**28**	**36**	**212**	**174**

FACT FILE

- **8 September 1888 was the very first day of league football in England. Villa drew 1-1 with Wolves, and Tommy Green scored Villa's first league goal.**
- **Villa have lost only one of their last 15 home games in the series.**
- **Villa have won 12 and drawn two of their last 14 games in the series, home and away.**
- **Villa lost eight games in a row from 1957 to 1960.**

Villa's top scorers vs Wolves

Charlie Athersmith 8
Denny Hodgetts 7
Jack Devey, Johnny Dixon, Billy Garraty, Tommy Thompson 6

Villa hat-tricks vs Wolves

14 Mar 1891 Charlie Athersmith
25 Nov 1905 Jimmy Cantrell
27 Dec 1948 Trevor Ford (4)
12 Apr 1955 Tommy Thompson

Played for both clubs

Will Devey	Wolves 1891-93	Villa 1892-94
George Kinsey	Wolves 1891-94	Villa 1894-95
Herbert Smart	Villa 1913-14	Wolves 1919-20
Cyril Spiers	Villa 1920-27	Wolves 1933-35
Pongo Waring	Villa 1927-36	Wolves 1936-37
Charlie Phillips	Wolves 1929-36	Villa 1935-38
Bob Iverson	Wolves 1934-37	Villa 1936-48
James Clayton	Wolves 1933-38	Villa 1937-39
Dickie Dorsett	Wolves 1937-47	Villa 1946-53
Dennis Parsons	Wolves 1948-52	Villa 1952-55
Peter McParland	Villa 1952-62	Wolves 1961-63
William Baxter	Wolves 1948-54	Villa 1953-57
Roy Pritchard	Wolves 1946-55	Villa 1955-58
Leslie Smith	Wolves 1947-56	Villa 1955-58
Nigel Sims	Wolves 1948-56	Villa 1955-64
Bobby Thomson	Wolves 1956-57	Villa 1959-64
Mike Kenning	Villa 1960-61	Wolves 1967-69
Geoff Sidebottom	Wolves 1958-61	Villa 1960-65
Derek Dougan	Villa 1961-63	Wolves 1966-75
Barry Stobart	Wolves 1959-64	Villa 1964-68
Peter Broadbent	Wolves 1950-65	Villa 1966-69
Evan Williams	Wolves 1967-68	Villa 1969-70
Alun Evans	Wolves 1967-69	Villa 1972-74
Bobby McDonald	Villa 1972-76	Wolves 1987-88
John Burridge	Villa 1975-77	Wolves 1982-84
Andy Gray	Villa 1975-79/85-87	Wolves 1979-84
Gordon Cowans	Villa 1975-85/88-92/93-94	Wolves 1994-96
Gordon Smith	Villa 1976-79	Wolves 1982-84
Peter Withe	Wolves 1973-75	Villa 1980-85
Andy Blair	Villa 1981-84/85-88	Wolves 1983-84
Mark Walters	Villa 1981-88	Wolves 1994-95
Paul Birch	Villa 1983-91	Wolves 1990-96
Tony Daley	Villa 1984-94	Wolves 1994-98
Phil Robinson	Villa 1986-87	Wolves 1987-89
Mark Burke	Villa 1986-88	Wolves 1990-92
Derek Mountfield	Villa 1988-92	Wolves 1991-94
Mark Blake	Villa 1989-93	Wolves 1990-91
Cyrille Regis	Villa 1991-93	Wolves 1993-94
Steve Froggatt	Villa 1991-94	Wolves 1994-99
Dariusz Kubicki	Villa 1991-94	Wolves 1997-98
Guy Whittingham	Wolves 1993-94/98-99	Villa 1993-95
Michael Oakes	Villa 1996-99	Wolves 1999-2004
Hassan Kachloul	Villa 2001-02	Wolves 2003-04
Joey Gudjonsson	Villa 2002-03	Wolves 2003-04

v. Wrexham

Season	League	Date	Result	Home Villa	Home Wrexham	Date	Result	Away Villa	Away Wrexham	Final Positions Villa	Final Positions Wrexham
1970-71	Division 3	1 May	Lost	**3**	**4**	26 September	Won	**3**	**2**	4th	9th
1971-72	Division 3	25 September	Won	**2**	**0**	31 March	Won	**2**	**0**	1stP	16th

League Cup										Division	
1960-61	Q'ter Final	22 February	Won	**3**	**0**					Div 1	Div 4
1971-72	Round 1	18 August	Drew	**2**	**2**	23 August	Drew*	**1**	**1**	Div 3	Div 3
		31 August		The Hawthorns (replay)			Won	**4**	**3**		
1976-77	Round 4	27 October	Won	**5**	**1**					Div 1	Div 3

Summary	*P*	*W*	*D*	*L*	*F*	*A*
Villa's home league record:	2	1	0	1	5	4
Villa's away league record:	2	2	0	0	5	2
Villa's cup record:	5	3	2	0	15	7
TOTAL:	**9**	**6**	**2**	**1**	**25**	**13**

Villa's top scorers vs Wrexham

Willie Anderson 5

Andy Lochhead 4

Played for both clubs

Bert Goode	Villa 1911-12	Wrexham 1921-26
Tom Griffiths	Wrexham 1922-27/38-39	Villa 1935-37
Jackie Williams	Villa 1935-36	Wrexham 1938-40
Frederick Goss	Villa 1936-37	Wrexham 1938-39
Tommy Gardner	Villa 1933-38	Wrexham 1945-47
Freddie Haycock	Villa 1936-40	Wrexham 1945-47
John Graham	Villa 1946-49	Wrexham 1949-52
Kenneth Roberts	Wrexham 1951-52	Villa 1953-58
William Myerscough	Villa 1956-59	Wrexham 1963-64
Kevin Keelan	Villa 1959-60	Wrexham 1961-63
Terry Morrall	Villa 1959-61	Wrexham 1963-65
Bobby Park	Villa 1964-69	Wrexham 1969-72
Frank Carrodus	Villa 1974-79	Wrexham 1979-82

v. Wycombe Wanderers

League Cup		Date	Result	Away Villa	Away Wycombe	Division Villa	Division Wycombe
2003-04	Round 2	23 September	Won	**5**	**0**	Prem	Div 2

Summary	*P*	*W*	*D*	*L*	*F*	*A*
Villa's cup record:	1	1	0	0	5	0
TOTAL:	**1**	**1**	**0**	**0**	**5**	**0**

Villa's top scorers vs Wycombe

Juan Pablo Angel 3

Villa hat-tricks vs Wycombe

23 Sep 2003 Juan Pablo Angel (cup)

Played for both clubs

Paul Kerr	Villa 1983-87	Wycombe 1994-95
Cyrille Regis	Villa 1991-93	Wycombe 1994-95
Dave Farrell	Villa 1992-94	Wycombe 1995-97
Guy Whittingham	Villa 1993-95	Wycombe 2000-01
Neil Davis	Villa 1995-96	Wycombe 1996-97
Richard Walker	Villa 1997-2000	Wycombe 2001-02
Luke Moore	Villa 2003-04	Wycombe 2003-04

v. York City

		Home					Away			Final Positions	
Season	League	Date	Result	Villa	York	Date	Result	Villa	York	Villa	York
1971-72	Division 3	5 February	Won	**1**	**0**	8 April	Won	**1**	**0**	1stP	19th
1974-75	Division 2	14 December	Won	**4**	**0**	17 August	Drew	**1**	**1**	2ndP	15th

League Cup

						Division	
1973-74	Round 2	9 October	Lost	**0**	**1**	Div 2	Div 3

Summary	*P*	*W*	*D*	*L*	*F*	*A*
Villa's home league record:	2	2	0	0	5	0
Villa's away league record:	2	1	1	0	1	0
Villa's cup record:	1	0	0	1	0	1
TOTAL:	**5**	**3**	**1**	**1**	**7**	**2**

Villa's top scorers vs York

Ray Graydon 2

Played for both clubs

Neil Rioch	Villa 1969-75	York 1971-72
Martin Carruthers	Villa 1991-93	York 1998-99

Villa in Europe

Villa in Europe vs Belgian clubs

Year	Competition	versus	Date	Home	Villa		Date	Away	Villa		Aggregate		
1975-76	UEFA Cup R1	Royal Antwerp	1 October	Lost	**0**	**1**	17 September	Lost	**1**	**4**	Lost	**1**	**5**
1981-82	European Cup SF	Anderlecht	7 April	Won	**1**	**0**	21 April	Drew	**0**	**0**	Won	**1**	**0**

	P	W	D	L	F	A
TOTAL:	4	1	1	2	2	5

Villa in Europe vs Croatian clubs

Year	Competition	versus	Date	Home	Villa		Date	Away	Villa		Aggregate		
2001-02	UEFA Cup R1	Varteks Varazdin	20 September	Lost	**2**	**3**	27 September	Won	**1**	**0**	Lost (away goals)	**3**	**3**

	P	W	D	L	F	A
TOTAL:	2	1	0	1	3	3

Villa in Europe vs Czech clubs

Year	Competition	versus	Date	Home	Villa		Date	Away	Villa		Aggregate		
1990-91	UEFA Cup R1	Banik Ostrava	19 September	Won	**3**	**1**	3 October	Won	**2**	**1**	Won	**5**	**2**

	P	W	D	L	F	A
TOTAL:	2	2	0	0	5	2

Villa in Europe vs East German clubs

Year	Competition	versus	Date	Home	Villa		Date	Away	Villa		Aggregate		
1981-82	European Cup R2	Dynamo Berlin	4 November	Lost	**0**	**1**	21 October	Won	**2**	**1**	Won (away goals)	**2**	**2**

	P	W	D	L	F	A
TOTAL:	2	1	0	1	2	2

Villa in Europe vs French clubs

Year	Competition	versus	Date	Home	Villa		Date	Away	Villa		Aggregate		
1997-98	UEFA Cup R1	Bordeaux	30 September	Won*	**1**	**0**	16 September	Drew	**0**	**0**	Won*	**1**	**0**

	P	W	D	L	F	A
TOTAL:	2	1	1	0	1	0

Villa in Europe vs Icelandic clubs

			Home				Away						
Year	*Competition*	*versus*	*Date*		Villa		*Date*		Villa		*Aggregate*		
1981-82	European Cup R1	Valur Reykjavik	16 September	Won	**5**	**0**	30 September	Won	**2**	**0**	Won	**7**	**0**

	P	*W*	*D*	*L*	*F*	*A*
TOTAL:	2	2	0	0	7	0

Villa in Europe vs Italian clubs

			Home				Away						
Year	*Competition*	*versus*	*Date*		Villa		*Date*		Villa		*Aggregate*		
1982-83	European Cup QF	Juventus	2 March	Lost	**1**	**2**	16 March	Lost	**1**	**3**	Lost	**2**	**5**
1990-91	UEFA Cup R2	Inter Milan	24 October	Won	**2**	**0**	7 November	Lost	**0**	**3**	Lost	**2**	**3**
1994-95	UEFA Cup R1	Inter Milan	29 September	Won*	**1**	**0**	15 September	Lost	**0**	**1**	Won*	**1**	**1**
											penalties (4-3)		

	P	*W*	*D*	*L*	*F*	*A*	
TOTAL:	6	2	0	4	5	9	(+one penalty shoot-out victory)

Villa in Europe vs Norwegian clubs

			Home				Away						
Year	*Competition*	*versus*	*Date*		Villa		*Date*		Villa		*Aggregate*		
1998-99	UEFA Cup R1	Stromsgodset	15 September	Won	**3**	**2**	29 September	Won	**3**	**0**	Won	**6**	**2**

	P	*W*	*D*	*L*	*F*	*A*
TOTAL:	2	2	0	0	6	2

Aston Villa in the 1982 European Cup Final against Bayern Munich in Rotterdam. Nigel Spink, with only one League game behind him, takes over from the injured Jimmy Rimmer.

Villa in Europe vs Polish clubs

					Home				Away				
Year	*Competition*	*versus*	*Date*		Villa		*Date*		Villa		*Aggregate*		
1977-78	UEFA Cup R2	Gornik Zabrze	19 October	Won	**2**	**0**	2 November	Drew	**1**	**1**	Won	**3**	**1**

	P	*W*	*D*	*L*	*F*	*A*
TOTAL:	2	1	1	0	3	1

Villa in Europe vs Portuguese clubs

					Home				Away				
Year	*Competition*	*versus*	*Date*		Villa		*Date*		Villa		*Aggregate*		
1983-84	UEFA Cup R1	Vitoria Guimaraes	28 September	Won	**5**	**0**	14 September	Lost	**0**	**1**	Won	**5**	**1**

	P	*W*	*D*	*L*	*F*	*A*
TOTAL:	2	1	0	1	5	1

Villa in Europe vs Romanian clubs

					Home				Away				
Year	*Competition*	*versus*	*Date*		Villa		*Date*		Villa		*Aggregate*		
1982-83	European Cup R2	Dinamo Bucharest	3 November	Won	**4**	**2**	20 October	Won	**2**	**0**	Won	**6**	**2**
1997-98	UEFA Cup R3	Steaua Bucharest	9 December	Won	**2**	**0**	25 November	Lost	**1**	**2**	Won	**3**	**2**

	P	*W*	*D*	*L*	*F*	*A*
TOTAL:	4	3	0	1	9	4

Villa in Europe vs Slovakian clubs

					Home				Away				
Year	*Competition*	*versus*	*Date*		Villa		*Date*		Villa		*Aggregate*		
1993-94	UEFA Cup R1	Slovan Bratislava	29 September	Won	**2**	**1**	15 September	Drew	**0**	**0**	Won	**2**	**1**

	P	*W*	*D*	*L*	*F*	*A*
TOTAL:	2	1	1	0	2	1

Villa in Europe vs Spanish clubs

					Home				Away				
Year	*Competition*	*versus*	*Date*		Villa		*Date*		Villa		*Aggregate*		
1977-78	UEFA Cup R3	Athletic Bilbao	23 November	Won	**2**	**0**	7 December	Drew	**1**	**1**	Won	**3**	**1**
1977-78	UEFA Cup QF	Barcelona	1 March	Drew	**2**	**2**	15 March	Lost	**1**	**2**	Lost	**3**	**4**
1993-94	UEFA Cup R2	Deportivo La Coruna	3 November	Lost	**0**	**1**	19 October	Drew	**1**	**1**	Lost	**1**	**2**
1997-98	UEFA Cup R2	Athletic Bilbao	4 November	Won	**2**	**1**	21 October	Drew	**0**	**0**	Won	**2**	**1**
1997-98	UEFA Cup QF	Atletico Madrid	17 March	Won	**2**	**1**	3 March	Lost	**0**	**1**	Lost	**2**	**2**
											(away goals)		
1998-99	UEFA Cup R2	Celta Vigo	3 November	Lost	**1**	**3**	20 October	Won	**1**	**0**	Lost	**2**	**3**

	P	*W*	*D*	*L*	*F*	*A*
TOTAL:	12	4	4	4	13	13

Villa in Europe vs Swedish clubs

				Home				Away				
Year	*Competition*	*versus*	*Date*		Villa		*Date*		Villa		*Aggregate*		
1996-97	UEFA Cup R1	Helsingborgs	10 September	Drew	**1**	**1**	24 September	Drew	**0**	**0**	Lost **1** **1** (away goals)

	P	*W*	*D*	*L*	*F*	*A*
TOTAL:	2	0	2	0	1	1

Villa in Europe vs Turkish clubs

				Home				Away			
Year	*Competition*	*versus*	*Date*		Villa		*Date*		Villa		*Aggregate*
1977-78	UEFA Cup R1	Fenerbahce	14 September	Won	**4**	**0**	28 September	Won	**2**	**0**	Won **6** **0**
1982-83	European Cup R1	Besiktas	15 September	Won	**3**	**1**	29 September	Drew	**0**	**0**	Won **3** **1**
1994-95	UEFA Cup R2	Trabzonspor	1 November	Won	**2**	**1**	18 October	Lost	**0**	**1**	Lost **2** **2** (away goals)

	P	*W*	*D*	*L*	*F*	*A*
TOTAL:	6	4	1	1	11	3

Villa in Europe vs Soviet clubs

				Home				Away			
Year	*Competition*	*versus*	*Date*		Villa		*Date*		Villa		*Aggregate*
1981-82	European Cup QF	Dinamo Kiev	17 March	Won	**2**	**0**	3 March	Drew	**0**	**0**	Won **2** **0**
1983-84	UEFA Cup R2	Spartak Moscow	2 November	Lost	**1**	**2**	19 October	Drew	**2**	**2**	Lost **3** **4**

	P	*W*	*D*	*L*	*F*	*A*
TOTAL:	4	1	2	1	5	4

Villa in Europe vs West German clubs

				Home				Away			
Year	*Competition*	*versus*	*Date*		Villa		*Date*		Villa		*Aggregate*
1981-82	European Cup F	Bayern Munich	26 May	Rotterdam				Won	**1**	**0**	Won **1** **0**

	P	*W*	*D*	*L*	*F*	*A*
TOTAL:	1	1	0	0	1	0

Aston Villa in the 1982 European Cup Final against Bayern Munich in Rotterdam. Villa players celebrate Withe's goal.

FACT FILE

- Surely the greatest night of Villa's history came in Rotterdam against the mighty Bayern Munich on 26 May 1982. A close-range goal from Peter Withe after 67 minutes secured European glory for a club who only a year earlier had won their first league title for 71 years. Tony Barton had been manager for only seven weeks, so it was an incredible start for him. It also meant that the cup stayed in England for the sixth year in a row. Will those days ever return?
- That victory gave Villa the right to compete in both the European Super Cup and the World Club Championship. On 12 December 1982, goals from Jair and Charrua gave Uruguayan side Peñarol a 2-0 victory in Tokyo to dash Villa's hopes of becoming Britain's first ever unofficial world champion club.
- The following month, however, Villa overcame Barcelona for the European Super Cup. On 19 January they lost 1-0 in the Nou Camp, but seven days later, a late goal from Gary Shaw forced extra time, and the tie was sealed with extra-time goals from Cowans and McNaught.
- Villa have had a great record of qualifying for Europe in recent years. In 10 seasons from 1993 to 2003, Villa competed in the UEFA Cup six times, and the Intertoto Cup on a further two occasions.
- Four of Villa's last five UEFA Cup campaigns have ended, agonisingly enough, being decided on away goals.
- Only Inter Milan and Athletic Bilbao have been drawn against Villa twice in European competition. The two ties against Inter Milan were particularly memorable. Villa put in a brilliant performance to beat them 2-0 at home in 1990, only for Inter to turn the tie round in devastating fashion two weeks later. Four years later a goal from Ray Houghton took the sides to a penalty shoot-out in which Phil King became Villa's unlikely hero with the winning penalty.

Villa's top scorers in Europe

Peter Withe 9

Gary Shaw 8

Stan Collymore, John Deehan, Tony Morley 5

Ken McNaught 4

Villa hat-tricks in Europe

3 Nov 1982 Gary Shaw (vs Dinamo Bucharest)

28 Sep 1983 Peter Withe (vs Vit. Guimaraes)

29 Sep 1998 Stan Collymore (vs Stromsgodset)

Roll of Honour

Aston Villa Football Club
Aston Villa Football Club
Aston Villa Football Club
Arthur Bent
Jasken Bolland
Richard Parry
John (Villa) Power
Mark Homer
Alan & Gerald Pritchard
William Stevens
Adrian Rogers
Darren Lee Smith
Alison Horton
Malcolm Cooper
Kevin Larkin
Paul Eccles (Burntwood)
Michael 'Max' Wall
Dave Bell
Jim Bell
Steve (Rennie) Renshaw
Dan The Villaman Renshaw
Rob Vincent
Rick Vincent
Matthew Young
Arthur Rowley (RIP)
Ralph Willis, Middlesbrough
Alex Ashford
A.C.E. Ashford
Keith Morris
Eric Roe
Ashley Richardson
Simon Corry
Mark Goodwin
Andy Campkin
Christopher Teasdale
Miles Thomas
Guy Thomas
Francis Cooney
Michael Sheldon
Steven Sheldon
John Foster
Stephen Miceli
Wendy Jordan
John Holder
Frank MacDonald
Michael Morgan
Philip Gray
Andrew Webb
Tony Starbuck
Lynsey Holloway
Guinness
Adrian O'Donnell
Daniel Stanley
Matthew Ruston
Gary & Natalie
Nathan Hargrave
Dennis Hirons
Michael Hirons
Marie Hirons
Curtis Newby
Bill Willcox
Michael D Butler
James. C. Lillis (DIM)
Malcolm Taylor
Andrew Brown
Lucien Goddard
Colin Fisher
Stephen & Tamsin
Graham & Marlene
Darren Cunningham
Ian Cunningham
Paul Young
Bob Young
Donald James Jones
Ronald Jones
Scott G Wright
Martin J Pember
Robert Edward Garratt
Adrian O'Brien
Gary. R. James
Mr. Fumitsugu Enokida
Mrs. Lian Enokida
Mark Flatley
Tim Smith
Paul Houghton
Darren Felsenstein
Paul Simpson
Simon & Jake Aston Foxall
Pete Abrahams
Luke Marson
Carol Goodman
Nicholas David Clarke
Robert Clarke
Robert Bartlett
Robert Gough
Joseph Venencia
Nick Hawkes
Roger Levicki
Tim Levicki
Andrew Levicki
Warren H. McDivitt
Harry W. McDivitt
Peter Howard
Richard Burton
Oliver Sudborough
Don Taylor
David Hodges, Southam
Gillian Anne Leedam
Paul Badger (Berlin)